Brand Management

"Without question, branding is a complex management area that deserves study from a variety of different perspectives and academic traditions. By providing a multi-disciplinary approach, this textbook provides a welcome and invaluable resource for thoughtful students, scholars, and practitioners who want to fully understand branding and brand management."
Kevin Lane Keller, Tuck School of Business at Dartmouth

"At last a book that cuts through the clutter about understanding brand and so clearly clarifies the brand concept. A book that superbly bridges the academic domain and enables practitioners use it to build brand equity."
Leslie de Chernatony, Birmingham University Business School

"We think this is an excellent treatment of our topic. Thorough and complete, yet concise and very readable. We love the design and structure, both with regards to the seven approaches, as well as to the four layers within each approach."
Albert M. Muniz, Jr., DePaul University and Thomas C. O'Guinn, University of Wisconsin

For over two decades it has been argued that the brand is an important value creator and should therefore be a top management priority. However, the definition of what a brand is remains elusive.

This comprehensive book presents the reader with an exhaustive analysis of the scientific and paradigmatic approaches to the nature of brand as it has developed over the last twenty years. Taking a multidisciplinary approach and offering an exhaustive analysis of brand research literature, it delivers a thorough understanding of the managerial implications of these different approaches to the management of the brand.

Brand Management: Research, theory and practice fills a gap in the market, providing an understanding of how the nature of brand and the idea of the consumer differ in these approaches, and offers in-depth insight into the opening question of almost every brand management course: 'What is a brand?'

Tilde Heding and **Charlotte F. Knudtzen** both lecture in strategic brand management at Copenhagen Business School. Tilde and Charlotte have published widely, while also running their own brand management consultancy, Heding & Knudtzen. **Mogens Bjerre** is associate professor of Marketing at Copenhagen Business School. He has published extensively in the fields of franchising, key accounts management, strategic relationship marketing and retailing.

Brand Management
Research, theory and practice

**Tilde Heding, Charlotte F. Knudtzen
and Mogens Bjerre**

Routledge
Taylor & Francis Group

LONDON AND NEW YORK

First published 2009 by Routledge
2 Park Square, Milton Park, Abingdon, Oxon OX14 4RN

Simultaneously published in the USA and Canada
by Routledge
711 Third Avenue, New York, NY 10017

Routledge is an imprint of the Taylor & Francis Group, an informa business

Typeset in Times New Roman by Saxon Graphics Ltd, Derby

British Library Cataloguing in Publication Data
A catalogue record for this book is available from the British Library

Library of Congress Cataloguing in Publication Data
Library of Congress Cataloging-in-Publication Data
Heding, Tilde.
Brand management : research, theory and practice / Tilde Heding,
Charlotte F. Knudtzen and Mogens Bjerre.
p. cm.
ISBN 978–0–415–44326–5 (hbk.) – ISBN 978–0–415–44327–2 (pbk.) –
ISBN 978–0–203–99617–1 (ebook) 1. Brand name products–Management.
2. Branding (Marketing) I. Knudtzen, Charlotte F. II. Bjerre, Mogens,
1959- III. Title.
HD69.B7H43 2008
658.8'27–dc22
2008021896

ISBN10: 0–415–44326–1 (hbk)
ISBN10: 0–415–44327-X (pbk)
ISBN10: 0–203–99617–8 (ebk)

ISBN13: 978–0–415–44326–5 (hbk)
ISBN13: 978–0–415–44327–2 (pbk)
ISBN13: 978–0–203–99617–1 (ebk)

Contents

List of illustrations

List of tables

List of boxes

Foreword

Leslie de Chernatony

Given the research I have undertaken over the years helping managers understand the nature of their brand and the opportunities for strategically growing brands, I am delighted to write the foreword for this insightful and most timely book. The authors have done an extremely thorough job, diligently working through the brand research literature to devise seven perspectives from diverse schools of thought about perceptions of brands. From this typology, among other things, they consider how the all-important brand equity is created and managed. The authors are to be congratulated on grounding this text so expertly in the literature yet still enabling management implications to be wisely crystallized.

Seeking to elucidate the nature of a brand is a daunting task, since brands are like amoeba, constantly changing. At the most basic, brands start life in brand planning documents, evolving as pan-company teams revise their ideas. Ultimately, after being finessed by stakeholders in the value chain, brands reside in the minds and hearts of consumers – hopefully in a form not too dissimilar from that desired by the firm. The research neatly synthesized in this text coherently brings more understanding to the challenge of understanding a corporation's brand and managing its growth trajectory. It is clear from the authors' work why diverse interpretations exist about the nature of brands.

From this well argued text it can be appreciated that one of the challenges managers face is finding a suitable metaphor to ensure common understanding of the firm's brand. Without this, supporting brand resources may not be coherently integrated. Furthermore, under the service dominant logic paradigm, it is more widely recognized that brands are co-created through stakeholder interactions. Managers not only have to understand each other's understanding and inputs to brand building, but also to recognize the way brand communities want to shape the brand. Again, the authors helpfully elucidate the importance of brand communities.

There is much in this book that makes it an inspirational read.

Leslie de Chernatony
Professor of Brand Marketing
Birmingham University Business School

Preface

There are numerous strengths of this book. Firstly the authors have been very brave to take a recent time period, to divide it up into phases and to then identify management types that have been employed to build brand. There are those who will question this particularly typology, however unless someone makes a start at putting forward such a typology, we will not see advancement in terms of the topic of brand management.

We received this comment from one of the 'blind' reviewers contributing to the lengthy process of turning a lot of our thoughts, knowledge, and words into a real, tangible book. The overall approach of this book is quite different compared to how other brand management books communicate the scope of brand management and we sure hope that the typology will be a subject of discussion. We, however, also hope that it is a step in the right direction when it comes to creating a solid and serious foundation for the evolution of brand management, both academically and in practice. Our motivation for writing this book has from day one been to provide clarity and equip students and practitioners with insights and tools to deal with brand management in a valid and insightful way.

The book offers its readers a new chest of drawers. The seven drawers are filled with the assumptions, theories, and concepts that are presented higgledy-piggledy in many other brand management books. Some will probably disagree with the content of the individual drawers, while many hopefully will enthuse in the structure and clarity they provide. The three authors have tested the material at lectures at Copenhagen Business School and concluded that by far the majority of students belong to the latter category. The seven approaches seem to provide clarity and answer many of the questions left unanswered in other brand management books; meanwhile they also spur great discussions of what a brand is and how it can be managed. The communication of brand management as seven ideal types of different brand approaches – with the necessary chopping of toes and squeezing of heels – hopefully will also lead to independent and critical thinking!

Keeping our ears to the ground, we sense that typology and scientific clarity are sought more and more in brand management and it seems to us that brand management is about to enter a new era where a deeper understanding of the many aspects of the brand is needed. Since the mid-1980s it has been argued over and over again that corporations should make brand management a top priority in order to sharpen their competitive edge. That message has sunk in and things are now cooking when it comes to understanding the nature of the brand better and turning brand management into a management discipline as scientifically valid as comparable disciplines.

We hope that the book will be of value to students, academics, and practitioners alike. Not too long ago, Charlotte and Tilde were still students faced with the insufficiencies of existing brand management books on a daily basis. Today, both Charlotte and Tilde as well as Mogens advise companies on brand matters and teach brand management at Copenhagen Business School. We believe that the book has both valuable pedagogical potential and can be of great help to practitioners who demand validity and thorough analysis as a foundation for brand strategy in practice.

T.H.
C.F.K.
M.B.

Acknowledgements

First, we would like to thank Francesca Heslop and Simon Alexander, Commissioning Editors for Business and Management, and Sharon Golan, Editorial Assistant for Business and Management, at Routledge for their faith in the project and help along the way.

We are truly honoured that some of the most inspirational people in brand management research have agreed to contribute to the book with their valuable thoughts and insights. We gratefully acknowledge Professor Leslie de Chernatony (Birmingham University) for writing the foreword and Professor Majken Schultz (Copenhagen Business School), Professor Emerita Mary Jo Hatch (University of Virginia), Adjunct Professor Joseph Plummer (Columbia Business School), Professor Kevin Lane Keller (Tuck School of Business, Dartmouth College), Associate Professor Susan Fournier (Boston University), Associate Professor Albert M. Muniz, Jr. (DePaul University), Professor Thomas C. O'Guinn (University of Wisconsin), and Professor Douglas B. Holt (Saïd Business School, Oxford) for writing comments for the approach chapters.

We deeply thank the Columbus Foundation, Copenhagen, and the Thomas B. Thrige's Foundation, Copenhagen, for financial support for this project.

We are grateful for the permissions granted by the American Marketing Association, California Management Review, Copenhagen Business School Press, Harvard Business School Publishing, Indiana University Press, University of Chicago Press, Westburn Publishers, and World Advertising Research Centre.

On a personal note, Tilde would like to thank Charlotte and Mogens for the long and inspiring collaboration on this project. Among *so* many things, I thank my parents Mette and Troels Heding for once a week taking me to the library bus as a child. My most heartfelt thanks go to my husband Flemming Pedersen for his admirable patience, love and support. For my part, I dedicate this book to the lights of my life – our daughters Iris and Marie.

Personally, Charlotte wishes to thank Tilde for giving me inspiration to overcome this long and at times exhausting writing process. Your spirit, supportive and caring friendship has kept me going. I also thank Mogens for never doubting the project, and for his invaluable input and encouragement. I would also like to thank my parents Jytte and Børge Knudtzen for always supporting my not always straight path to my goals and dreams. Fulfilling this dream would never have been possible for me without the support, love and constructive criticism from my darling husband Michael K. Fagernæs.

T.H.
C.F.K.
M.B.

Part I

Setting the scene

1 Introduction

Branding is the talk of the town. Corporations spend millions planning and implementing brand activities. New research is published and frameworks are developed on a daily basis in the attempt to find the holy grail of brand management. Since the mid-80s, in particular, researchers and practitioners alike have explored the domain, scope and potential of the brand. Many different concepts, theoretical frameworks and ideas have seen the light of day and, as a result, a wide spectrum of different perspectives on how a brand ought to be conceptualized and managed is in play today. Therefore, to obtain an overview of the field of brand management is an overwhelming task.

This book provides a complete overview of brand management by taking you through seven brand approaches. These seven 'schools of thought' represent fundamentally different perceptions of the brand, the nature of the brand–consumer exchange, and how brand equity is created and managed. Understanding the seven brand approaches separately provides a deep insight into the strengths and weaknesses of each approach and hence the potential of brand management as a whole. This comprehensive understanding will enable the reader to create customized brand strategies matching the unique challenges and possibilities facing a brand at any time.

The seven approaches are:

- *The economic approach:* the brand as part of the traditional marketing mix.
- *The identity approach:* the brand as linked to corporate identity.
- *The consumer-based approach:* the brand as linked to consumer associations.
- *The personality approach:* the brand as a human-like character.
- *The relational approach:* the brand as a viable relationship partner.
- *The community approach:* the brand as the pivotal point of social interaction.
- *The cultural approach:* the brand as part of the broader cultural fabric.

The identification of the seven approaches is based on an extensive analysis of the most influential brand research articles published between 1985 and 2006 (300+ articles from *Journal of Marketing, Journal of Marketing Research, Journal of Consumer Research, Harvard Business Review* and *European Journal of Marketing*). This body of literature is supplemented with key non-research literature that has shaped the field of brand management since the mid-1980s. The analysis has been conducted using a methodology uncovering the development of scientific knowledge. The methodology is based on theory developed by American philosopher of science Thomas Kuhn (Bjerre, Heding and Knudtzen 2008). Since (scientific) knowledge is in constant development, it is important to stress new brand approaches most likely will emerge in the future.

Traditionally, brand management textbooks offer an introduction to main concepts and the wide array of theories, but often fail to discriminate between how different approaches result in very different outcomes and why. Brand management draws on many different scientific traditions such as economics, strategic management, organizational behaviour, consumer research, psychology and anthropology just to mention a few. A complete overview of brand management hence requires multidimensional thinking. Most textbooks take on this multidimensionality through integration of several perspectives in all-encompassing frameworks. If you look at the list of brand approaches, you will most likely recognize many of the brand elements (e.g. personality, relation, and consumer) that are encompassed in the classical textbook models (e.g. see Aaker's brand identity model, Kapferer's brand prism, and Keller's customer-based brand equity pyramid). The integrated frameworks are, however, not necessarily ideal when it comes to understanding and getting an overview of the field of brand management. Integration tends to blur the differences and similarities between different approaches in brand management and leave the reader rather confused. Still, the integrated frameworks have the advantage that a strategist can take into consideration all relevant aspects without losing oneself in details.

This book can be read in two ways: either as a stand-alone textbook or as a supplement to the textbooks by the above-mentioned authors. Read as a supplement, the book offers the inquiring reader the opportunity to understand the components of the traditional models in depth. Read alone, the book offers the opportunity to evaluate the most important schools of thought in brand management and create his or her brand management model featuring the components that are most relevant for the challenge at hand.

Resting on a comprehensive analysis of brand management as a scientific discipline, *Brand Management: Research, Theory and Practice* offers the reader a scientifically grounded overview of the main schools/approaches in brand management, – and of their managerial implications. *Brand Management: Research, Theory and Practice* presents each approach separately and as an 'ideal type' based on the conviction that understanding the exact content of each approach and its origin will better equip the reader to combine different approaches, being in an educational or a managerial setting.

The four layers of an approach

The seven 'schools of thought' are 'clusters' of literature sharing distinct brand perceptions. In each cluster, there is coherence between assumptions, theories and

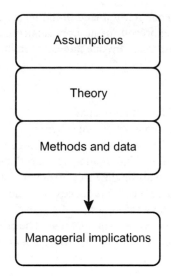

Figure 1.1 The logic of the approach chapters

methods/data. The three 'scientific layers' (assumptions, theories and methods/data) add up to managerial implications. The structure of the seven approach chapters is guided by this coherence between assumptions, theories, methods/data and managerial implications.

Assumptions are not to be understood in a high-flung sense of the word. Each approach holds its own implicit view of the nature of the brand and the premises of the brand–consumer exchange. Clarifying these assumptions facilitates the understanding of the theories, methods and managerial implications of each approach. Assumptions also illuminate the intangibles inherent in the nature of the brand.

The 'theory' layer represents the concepts, models and figures that are key to the understanding of each brand approach. The third layer of 'methods and data' provides insight into what data to look for and how to collect them when researching the content of a specific brand strategy. These three scientific layers add up to managerial implications guiding how the assumptions, theories and methods of each approach can be converted into a brand management strategy. The four layers comprising an approach are thus closely interconnected. The scientific clarification and the practical implications of the approaches will enable the reader to reflect on the compatibility of different elements of brand management strategies and ensure the creation of more accurate brand management.

True to its objective, *Brand Management: Research, Theory and Practice* does not provide one 'how to' solution meaning that we sustain from being normative when it comes to the overall management of a brand. Still, we are normative *within* each approach and leave it to the reader to reflect upon how different situations and circumstances require different means of action. It is our hope that this book will equip readers with an overview and a deeper understanding that will enable them to create splendid customized brand management strategies and that this somewhat different approach to the communication of brand management will provide a sound platform for anyone interested in the field.

A reader's guide

The chapters of this book fall into three parts.

Part I 'Setting the scene', consists of three chapters: *1 Introduction, 2 'Key words in brand management'* and *3 'Overview: brand management 1985–2006'*.

Chapter 1: Introduction. The reader is introduced to the seven brand approaches, the literature analysis they stem from, and arguments supporting the importance of understanding these approaches separately before combining them in real-life brand management strategies.

Chapter 2: Keywords in brand management. The reader is provided with an introduction to key elements in brand management and brand management

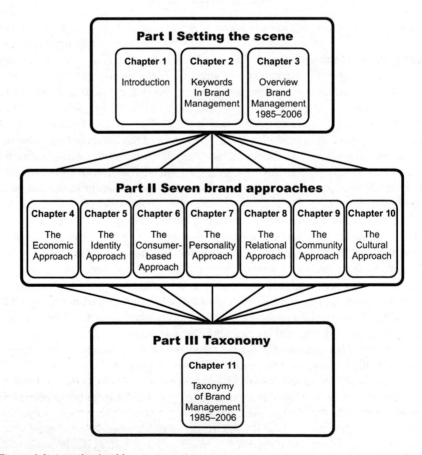

Figure 1.2 A readers' guide

strategy. Being familiar with these elements is essential when reading the seven approach chapters, since each approach implies a distinct take on these elements.

Chapter 3: Overview brand management 1985–2006. This chapter provides an overview of the chronological development brand management has undergone since it became a management priority in the mid-1980s and until 2006. The seven brand approaches are presented in a contextual and chronological setting. This overview facilitates the further reading of the seven brand approach chapters.

Part II, 'Seven brand approaches', consists of seven chapters, one for each brand approach. Each chapter from 4 to 10 follows the structure presented below:

- A short introduction, followed by the assumptions of the approach.
- The theoretical building blocks of the approach are presented. This presentation is divided into supporting themes and core theme. *Supporting* themes clarify the concepts that brand management 'borrows' from other disciplines, making up the core theme. The *core* theme clarifies the theoretical building blocks in a brand management context.
- Methods and data are reviewed. The approaches stem from different scientific traditions, which are all associated with specific methods and perceptions of validity. Understanding the methods associated with each approach enables the reader to request the best data possible.
- The managerial implications associated with the assumptions, theories, methods and data of each approach will round off the approach chapters. The assumed role of the marketer is explained as well as the managerial 'do's' and 'don'ts'.
- The key elements of each approach are illustrated by best-practice case examples of international well known brands. The core theme of each approach is highlighted by student questions.
- Each chapter also features a text box overview focusing on present scope and future directions of the approach by one or two of its academic 'founding fathers'.

Part III, 'Key takeouts'. Chapter 11, 'Taxonomy of brand management 1985–2006' rounds off the book. It is an overview as well as a checklist. The chapter will through comparison give a clear picture of the differences and similarities of the seven approaches. Furthermore, the concluding chapter provides a comparison between the proposed taxonomy and other brand categorizations.

References and further reading

Aaker, D. A. and Joachimsthaler, E. (2002), *Brand Leadership*, Sydney: Free Press Business

Berthon P., Nairn A. and Money A. (2003), 'Through the paradigm funnel: conceptual tool for literature analysis', *Marketing Education Review*, Vol. 13, No. 2: 55–66

Bjerre, M., Heding, T. and Knudtzen, C. F. (2008), 'Using the dynamic paradigm funnel to analyze brand management', in K. Tollin and A. Caru (eds) *Strategic Market Creation: A New Perspective on Marketing and Innovation Management,* Chichester: Wiley

Kapferer, J-N. (1997), *Strategic Brand Management: Creating and Sustaining Brand Equity Long Term*, London: Kogan Page

Keller, K. L. (2003), *Strategic Brand Management: Building, Measuring, and Managing Brand Equity*, Upper Saddle River NJ: Prentice Hall

Kuhn, T. S. (1996), *The Structure of Scientific Revolutions*, Chicago: University of Chicago Press

2   Key words in brand management

This chapter introduces the reader to key words often used in brand management; it does not offer an extensive step-by-step description of the reasoning behind branding as such. Where the seven chapters about different approaches to brand management focus on how the field of brand management has evolved over time and aim at facilitating a thorough understanding of the different approaches, rather, the idea in this chapter is to give the reader an overview of key terms to be familiar with when understanding what brand management is all about on a daily managerial basis.

This chapter hence provides a list of key words that readers will often stumble upon when reading brand management texts in general. Some of the key words will be elaborated on in the approach chapters while some of them will not be elaborated further in this book. These key words are provided with references to recommended supplementary reading.

Brand

The brand is and has been defined in many different ways over the years, depending on the perspective from which the brand is perceived. Often that depends on the academic background of the author/originator of the different definitions. In the classical definition, the brand is linked to the identification of a product and the differentiation from its competitors, through the use of a certain name, logo, design or other visual signs and symbols. The American Marketing Association (AMA) defined the brand in 1960 as:

> A name, term, sign, symbol, or design, or a combination of them which is intended to identify the goods or services of one seller or a group of sellers and to differentiate them from those of competitors.

Other more recent definitions of branding also include internal and organizational processes. Many brand management books today feature extremely broad definitions, because they aim at covering all the different aspects and facets of the brand and how it has developed over time.

This book is all about understanding the core of different brand perspectives and their implications. The seven approaches offer seven quite different understandings of the brand and would hence result in seven different definitions. We will therefore not give any definite brand definitions, but will provide the reader with different perspectives on the nature of the brand. It is up to the reader to create their own definitions after having read the seven brand approach chapters.

Brand architecture

Brand architecture is the structure that organizes the brand portfolio. It defines brand roles and relationships among a company's brands, e.g. the role between a car brand and the model brand (as in Volkswagen Golf). Some corporations choose to communicate the corporate brand to the market while others choose to market product brands to specific segments and keep the corporate brand in the background. According to Olins (1990) a brand architecture can be structured in three main ways. Monolithic brand structure equals a structure where the company relies solely on a corporate brand, at the other end of the spectrum there are the individually branded products and finally the brand architecture can consist of endorsed brands, which are a hybrid, where a corporate brand is used to endorse the corporate brands in the portfolio. If interested in more information about brand architecture, Aaker and Joachimsthaler (2002), part III and Kapferer (1997), chapter 7 offer very good treatments of this subject. The main differences between product and corporate branding are explained in figure 5.2 of this book.

Brand audit

A brand audit assesses the health of a brand. Typically, it consists of a brand inventory and a brand exploratory. The brand inventory is a detailed internal description of exactly how the brand has been marketed. The brand exploratory is an external investigation of what the brand means to consumers (through focus groups and other marketing research techniques). Brand audits are most useful when conducted on a regular basis (source: Keller 2000). The seven brand approaches do not go into depth with how to conduct a brand audit in practice, but inspiration for how to conduct a brand exploratory in the seven different brand perspectives can be found in the methods and data sections of the seven approach chapters.

Brand community

A brand community is a social entity where consumers interact socially with a brand as the pivotal point of their interaction. Brand communities take place in Internet-based settings, in geographically bound clubs, and at so-called brandfests (social gatherings arranged by the marketer). The emergence of brand communities implies a shift in negotiation power between marketer and consumer as consumers claim more power when acting in groups. The topic will be reviewed in detail in the community approach, chapter 9, this book.

Brand culture

Brand culture is a term that has been increasingly used over the last few years. It sometimes refers to the organizational culture of the brand and sometimes to the brand as part of the broader cultural landscape. For insight into the organizational perspective of brand culture the reader can turn to the identity approach of brand management in chapter 5. How brands affect macro-level culture and how they can benefit from playing an active role in mainstream culture are the topics of the cultural approach in chapter 10. For further insight into the different meanings of brand culture we can recommend the anthology *Brand Culture* (Schroeder and Salzer-Morling 2006).

Brand equity

Fundamentally, the goal for any brand manager is to endow products and/or services with brand equity (Park and Srinivasan 1994; Farquhar 1989). Brand equity defines the value of the brand and can refer to two understandings of brand value, namely a strategic, subjective understanding or brand equity as a financial, objective expression of the value of the brand.

In the financial understanding of brand equity, the concept is a way to account for how much value a brand holds. Brand equity is one of the intangible entries on the balance sheet (like *goodwill* and *know-how*). Being able to account for how much the brand holds is extremely important, both in relation to financial statements, mergers, acquisitions, and as a tool for brand managers to argue their case.

The subjective understanding of brand equity refers to the consumers' perception of the brand and is strategically valuable for brand management. Consumers are the ones who experience the brand, and their perception of brand equity can be defined as: 'A consumer perceives a brand's equity as the value added to the functional product or service by associating it with the brand name' (Aaker and Biel 1993 p. 2).

A good introduction to the concept of brand equity can be found in Kapferer (1997), chapter 1. For more information about the financial approach to brand equity Simon and Sullivan (1993) and Lindemann (2004) offer good explanations. More literature about strategic approaches to brand equity can be found in Aaker (1991) and Keller (1993). Creation of brand equity is at the heart of brand management and the seven brand approaches feature seven varied perspectives on how to work strategically with brand equity optimization.

Brand essence

Most academic brand management authors agree that every brand has an identity and that every brand identity contains an essence (DNA or kernel) that is the very core of the brand. The brand essence is most often an abstract idea or sentence summarizing what is the heart and soul of the brand. In order for the brand not to become compromized, the brand essence should stay the same over the course of time and no marketing actions that will compromise the brand essence should be allowed. We believe that finding the right brand essence requires insight into as many facets of the brand as the seven approaches provide. For an introduction to brand essence turn to the brand identity system in Aaker and Joachimsthaler (2002) and Kapferer (1997, where the same notion is called brand kernel), and in Keller (2003, where it is called brand mantra).

Brand extensions

A brand can be extended into new product categories. Brand extensions are often necessary when adapting to changes in the environment or in order to reap the full benefits of a strong brand. Extensions have many benefits. In the beginning, brand extensions were used as a strategic tool mainly to enter new markets (Aaker and Keller 1990). Today, brand extensions are also used to underpin and develop the brand to meet market changes.

A successful brand extension should respect the brand essence and thereby be based on the core of the brand and be true to the brand vision. If a brand is extended to a product category or to clients in a way that does not at all consider the core of the original brand, both brands risk dilution. We do not address the subject in this book: excellent treatments can be found in Kapferer (1997), chapter 8 and Keller (2003), chapter 12.

Brand genealogy

A genealogist goes back in history, uncovers family histories and constructs family trees. Brand genealogy is a managerial mindset introduced in the cultural branding model (Holt 2004) where the brand manager goes back and uncovers the brand's history. In the cultural approach, it is assumed that brands play important roles in mainstream culture and that the ways they play these roles determine their level of success. An introduction to this managerial mindset is found in chapter 10 (this book), for the full treatment turn to *How Brands become Icons* by Douglas B. Holt (2004).

Brand icon

An exclusive elite of valuable brands can claim icon status, which is considered the holy grail of brand management. An iconic brand holds references that most people agree upon and it obtains that status by playing an active role in contemporary culture. An introduction to brand icons is found in chapter 10 of this book, for the full treatment turn to *How Brands Become Icons* by Douglas B. Holt (2004).

Brand identity

Brand identity refers to the identity of the brand. There are many different perceptions of what the brand identity consists of. But the more common definition of brand identity is that it is; 'a set of associations the brand strategist seek to create or maintain' (Aaker and Joachimsthaler 2002, p. 43). The brand identity is hence something that the marketer 'has' as well as something he tries to create through the right brand strategy. The brand identity must express the particular vision and uniqueness of the brand – what the brand stands for basically, and the brand identity must be of a long-lasting or permanent nature. If the brand identity is both unique, distinct, and a clear expression of what the brand is all about as well as long-lasting, then it can create the basis of a solid, coherent and long-lasting brand and be the driver of all brand-related activities.

Brand image

The image of the brand is the perception of the brand by consumers. The goal of working strategically with brand image is to ensure that consumers hold strong and favourable associations of the brand in their minds. The brand image typically consists of multiple concepts: perception, because the brand is perceived; cognition, because that brand is cognitively evaluated; and finally attitude, because consumers continuously after perceiving and evaluating what they perceive form attitudes about the brand (Aaker and Joachimsthaler 2002, p. 43; Keller 1993, 2003; Grunig 1993). Brand image is the pivotal point of the consumer-based approach (chapter 6, this book).

Brand loyalty

Achieving a high degree of loyalty is an important goal in the branding process. Loyal consumers are valuable consumers because it is much more expensive to recruit new customers than nursing and keeping existing ones. Brands are important vehicles when building consumer loyalty as they provide recognizable fix points in the shopping experience. Read Keller chapter 5 in (2003) about developing loyalty programs. The concept of brand loyalty has been elaborated in the relational approach (chapter 8) that seeks to answer *how* and *why* loyal brand consumers consume the brand of choice.

Brand personality

Consumers display a tendency to endow brands with human-like personalities. Working strategically with brand personalities has been a widespread practice for many years. The Big Five of human personality psychology and Jungian archetypes are frameworks often implied to deepen the symbolic exchange between brands and consumers. Brand personality is part of most identity systems in the traditional brand management books. The topic of brand personality is carefully reviewed in chapter 7 (this book) about the personality approach.

Brand portfolio

A brand portfolio is the range of brands a company has in the market. How the brand portfolio is managed relates to strategic issues of brand architecture, market segmentation and product versus corporate branding. *Brand Management: Research, Theory and Practice* does not touch upon this subject. We recommend Kapferer 1997, chapter 9 and Aaker and Joachimsthaler (2002), part III for book treatments of this topic. New theories suggest that a brand portfolio should be analysed in three-dimensional molecule systems, including those of competitors, Hill and Lederer (2001) and Lederer and Hill (2001).

Brand positioning

The idea of brand positioning is based on the assumption that consumers have limited mind space for commercial messages and that the most successful brands hence are the ones able to position themselves in the minds of consumers by adapting the most congruent and consistent commercial message. The idea is linked to the information-processing theory of consumer choice that is the basis of the consumer-based approach in chapter 6 of this book. Another recommended reading is *Positioning: the Battle for your Mind* by Ries and Trout (2001).

Brand relation

The relationship metaphor has been added to the general vocabulary of brand management after having been associated with business-to-business marketing for a number of years. Consumers can perceive certain brands as viable relationship partners and achieving that position can be an important goal in the brand management process. Brand relation (like brand personality) is also part of the traditional brand identity models. Understanding brand relationships implies a deeper understanding of brand loyalty as the brand relation provides an understanding of *how* and *why* the brand is consumed, where brand loyalty answers *if* the brand is being consumed. The background and implications of brand relationships are described in chapter 8, this book.

Brand revitalization

A brand sometimes ages and declines in strength because as time goes by it loses its relevance and attractiveness for consumers. There can be different reasons for that ageing or decline in brand relevance, e.g. the brand may not have adapted to changes in the environment or to changes in consumer preferences. Sometimes the situation occurs where the brand simply ages along with the ageing of its core consumers.

The solution for an ageing brand or a brand in decline can be revitalization. The key for brand management when revitalizing a brand is always to start the process by identifying or reviving an existing brand vision and finding new and innovative ways of making that brand vision relevant once again for existing or new consumers. This book does not elaborate the topic, but we recommend chapter 11 in Kapferer (1997).

Brand strategy

The majority of brand management books feature generic 'one size fits all' guidelines for building a brand strategy. It is our conviction that the every brand is unique and requires its own unique recipe for success.

The aim of a brand strategy is to enhance the internal and external opportunities of the brand. The brand strategy must be strategic, visionary and proactive rather than tactical and reactive. Each brand must find its own holy grail to success – in the shape of a unique and relevant brand identity and brand vision, which are the first elements that must be in place when developing a brand strategy. The brand vision is brought to life through a customized brand strategy able to release the full potential of the brand. Brand managers must have long-term rather than a short-term focus. If the performance of the brand is based on quarterly sales figures, chances are that the brand strategy will end up being much more tactical than strategic, without enough visionary thinking to drive the growth and the strength of the brand in the future.

A prerequisite for making the brand strategy work is that it is closely linked to the business strategy. This means that the brand and the brand strategy should not be perceived as something other than or as an addition to business strategy developed at late stages in a product launch for example. In an ideal world, business and brand strategy should be developed simultaneously and support each other. The brand vision must also resonate with consumers and differentiate the brand from competitors. Once the brand vision has been established, a customized range of elements that comprise the brand strategy should be prioritized and developed. The brand strategy will typically consist of a customized range of elements from the seven brand approaches. Each of the seven brand approaches has certain strengths and weaknesses, which is why a customized combination of elements from the relevant approaches that matches the specific challenges and opportunities the brand faces will provide a foundation for the right brand strategy.

Great guidelines for the implementation of the brand strategy can be found in the managerial implications of each approach. Here, it is possible to evaluate which managerial steps are in line with the approaches on which the brand identity and brand vision are based.

Brand stretch

It is assumed that all brands have a core that should stay the same over the course of time (see the section about brand essence). When a brand is extended into new product categories, or joins co-branding ventures, its identity is stretched. The trick is to stretch it enough to be able to go in new directions, but never to stretch it to such an extent that the essence is diluted. Since this book does not go into more detail with brand stretch, for a more thorough review of the subject we recommend chapter 8 in Kapferer (1997).

Co-branding

Co-branding occurs when two or more brands are combined in a joint product or brand. This phenomenon is also called brand alliances or brand bundling. The two companies should consider carefully what their strategic alliance means for their respective brand portfolios, as their brands will become more associated in the future through the new product. Keller (2003) chapter 7 describes this phenomenon in more detail.

Corporate brand

When the corporation is branded instead of the individual products, a corporate brand is the case. In most literature on corporate branding it is assumed that the energy and inspiration of the brand stem from within the organization and that a branding strategy, in order to be successful, requires the engagement of the whole corporation. Read more in chapter 5 (this book) about the identity approach.

Employee branding

Employee branding is defined as 'the process by which employees internalize the desired brand image and are motivated to project the image to customers and other organizational constituents' (Miles and Mangold 2004 p. 68). It is a notion resembling the 'living the brand' concept a lot; turn to chapter 5 (this book) about the identity approach, Miles and Mangold (2004) and the references mentioned under 'living the brand' for further insight.

Employer branding

The term 'employer branding' relates to strategies for communicating about a company as an attractive employer to both current and potential employees. It is a hot management topic at the moment with a corresponding number of books and articles. Employer branding will not be elaborated on in this book; relevant literature to turn to is Barrow and Mosley (2005) emphasizing the interrelationship between HR, communication and top management, and Lievens and Highhouse (2003) about the emotive and tangible benefits for both potential and actual employees.

Living the brand

Employees are important bearers of the brand, especially when it comes to service brands. 'Living the brand' is an end-goal in the process of engaging employees in the branding process. Making employees live the brand mean that employees incorporate and live brand values and thereby deliver the brand promise fully to consumers. The concept is briefly reviewed in the identity approach, chapter 5 of this book, other recommended readings are Ind (2001) and Karmark (2005).

Product brand

A product brand is a brand linked to the product and not to the corporation and describes a situation where each individual product has its own brand. Choosing to brand the corporation or the product is a question of brand architecture. Marketing a product brand holds several advantages, such as the liberty to market to different segments, the ability to close unsuccessful brands without harming the mother corporation, etc. Product branding is compared to corporate branding in figure 5.2 in this book.

Service brand

Service brands are brands that sell services instead of products. This means that the brand is experienced in the process of consuming the service and that the employee delivering the service becomes a central communicator of the brand. Service brands can benefit from all the same insights as product brands, but as the service encounter requires dedicated employees and human interaction, service brand managers might benefit more from the identity approach and the relational approach (Vallaster and de Chernatony 2005, de Chernatony and Drury 2004).

Viral branding

The term covers mechanisms where consumers help or in some cases take over the marketing of the brand. A marketer who applies a certain amount of 'coolness' to the brand often initiates viral branding, the coolness starts a process where consumers spread the brand like a virus. Having consumers support the marketing process, and by their autonomy giving the brand a higher level of authenticity, can be beneficial for the marketer. Still, viral branding implies a risk of a contrary marketing effort, where the brand is 'hijacked' and taken in unintended directions through autonomous meaning-making among consumers. Even though a brand community is a narrower concept than viral branding, the mechanisms behind the two concepts are comparable; they are described in the community approach, chapter 9. Another suggested read is *Brand Hijack: Marketing without Marketing* by Wipperfürth (2005).

References and further reading

Aaker, D. A. (1991), *Managing Brand Equity*, New York: Free Press
Aaker, D. A. and Biel, A. L. (1993) *Brand Equity and Advertising: Advertising's Role in Building Strong Brands*, Hillsdale NJ: Lawrence Erlbaum Associates
Aaker, D. A. and Joachimsthaler, E. (2002) *Brand Leadership*, Sydney: Free Press Business
Aaker, D. A. and Keller, K. L. (1990) 'Consumer evaluations of brand extensions', *Journal of Marketing*, 54 (1): 27–41
Abratt, R. (1989) 'A new approach to the corporate image management process', *Journal of Marketing Management*, 5 (1): 63–76

Balmer, J. M. T. and Greyser, S. T. (2003) *Revealing the Corporation: Perspectives on Identity, Image, Reputation, Corporate Branding and Corporate-level Marketing,* London: Routledge

Barrow, S. and Mosley, R. (2005),*The Employer Brand: Bringing the Best of Brand Management to People at Work,* Chichester: Wiley

Chernatony, L. de and Drury, S. (2004) 'Identifying and sustaining services brands' values', *Journal of Marketing Communications,* 10: 73–93

Farquhar, P. H. (1989) 'Managing brand equity', *Marketing Research,* 1 (3): 24–33

Gray, E. R. and Schmeltzer, L. R. (1987) 'Planning a face-lift: implementing a corporate image programme', *Journal of Business Strategy,* 8 (1): 4–10

Grunig, J. (1993) 'Image and substance: from symbolic to behavioural relationships', *Public Relations Review,* 19 (2): 121–39

Hatch, M. J. and Schultz, M. (1997) 'Relations between organizational culture, identity and image', *European Journal of Marketing,* 31 (5–6): 356–65

Hatch, M. J. and Schultz, M. (2003) 'Bringing the corporation into corporate branding', *European Journal of Marketing,* 37 (7–8): 1041–64

Hill, S. and Lederer, C. (2001), *The Infinite Asset,* New York: McGraw-Hill

Holt, D. B. (2004) *How Brands become Icons: The Principles of Cultural Branding,* Boston MA: Harvard Business School Press

Ind, N. (2001) *Living the Brand,* London: Kogan Page

Kapferer, J-N. (1997), *Strategic Brand Management: Creating and Sustaining Brand Equity Long Term,* London: Kogan Page

Karmark, E. (2005) 'Living the brand', in M. Schultz, Y. M. Antorini and F. F. Csaba (eds.) *Corporate Branding: Purpose, People, Process,* Copenhagen: Copenhagen Business School Press

Keller, K. L. (1993) 'Conceptualizing, measuring, and managing customer-based brand equity', *Journal of Marketing,* 57 (1): 1–22

Keller, K. L. (2000) 'The brand report card', *Harvard Business Review,* January/February: 147–57

Keller, K. L. (2003) *Strategic Brand Management: Building, Measuring, and Managing Brand Equity,* 2nd edn, Upper Saddle River NJ: Pearson

Kennedy, S. H. (1977) 'Nurturing corporate images', *European Journal of Marketing,* 11 (3): 119–64

King, S. (1991) 'Brand building in the 1990s', *Journal of Marketing Management,* 7: 3–13

Lederer, C. and Hill, S. (2001) 'See your brand through your customers' eyes', *Harvard Business Review,* June: 125–33

Lievens, F. and Highhouse, S. (2003) 'The relation of instrumental and symbolic attributes to a company's attractiveness as an employer', *Personnel Psychology,* 56 (1): 75–102

Lindemann, J. (2004) 'Brand valuation' in R. Clifton (ed.), *Brands and Branding,* London: *Economist*

Miles, S. J. and Mangold, G. (2004) 'A conceptualization of the employee branding process', *Journal of Relationship Marketing,* 3 (2–3): 65–88

Olins, W. (1990) *The Wolff Olins Guide to Corporate Identity,* London: Design Council

Park, C. S. and Srinivasan, V. (1994), 'A survey-based method for measuring and understanding brand equity and its extendibility', *Journal of Marketing Research,* 31 (May): 271–88

Ries, A. and Trout, J. (1983, 2001) *Positioning: the Battle for your Mind,* New York: McGraw-Hill

Schroeder, J. E. and Salzer-Morling, M. (eds) (2006) *Brand Culture,* London: Routledge

Simon, C. J. and Sullivan, M. W. (1993) 'The measurement and determinants of brand equity: a financial approach', *Marketing Science*, 12 (1): 28–52

Vallaster, C. and de Chernatony, L. (2005), 'Internalisation of services brands: the role of leadership during the internal brand building process', *Journal of Marketing Management*, (21): 181–203

Wipperfürth, A. (2005) *Brand Hijack: Marketing without Marketing*, New York: Portfolio

3   Overview: brand management 1985–2006

Learning objectives

The purpose of this chapter is to:

Provide an overview of brand management
- How brand management as a scientific discipline has evolved between 1985 and 2006

Provide insight into the different paradigms in brand management 1985–2006
- A positivist paradigm ruled brand management in the first period of time
- An interpretive paradigm surfaced over the course of the 1990s

Introduce the seven brand approaches
- The reader is introduced to the seven brand approaches before they are explored more in detail in part II

Understand three distinctly different periods of time
- The overall evolution of brand management can be divided into three periods of time
- Each period displays different approaches in brand management

This chapter provides an overview of how brand management has developed from its first hesitant beginning in 1985 and onwards. As described in the introduction, we have identified seven brand approaches forming the backbone of this book. But before going into detail with the seven approaches in Part II, we will present them briefly and explore the overall evolution that has taken place in brand management between 1985 and 2006. Weaknesses of one approach often lead to the development of a new one and this interconnectedness of the seven brand management approaches is briefly introduced in this chapter. This overview of how brand management has evolved, the seven approaches, and the environmental drivers and changes that have triggered this evolution will facilitate the further reading and enable the reader to understand how the seven brand approaches are interconnected.

The seven approaches can be seen as links in a continuous evolution that slowly but surely has changed the field of brand management, making some approaches more relevant than others in a given time frame. But it is important for us to stress that the birth of one approach does not imply the end of the 'previous' one(s). The brand approaches complement rather than substitute each other if one looks at them one by one. When we claim that an approach becomes important in a given period of time, it does not necessarily mean that it becomes dominant, but rather that it is novel and that the research behind it is strong enough to constitute a new school of thought. Some of the older approaches are easy to criticize because much effort has been put into creating new and more suitable methods to explain consumption phenomena since their day. Still, we believe that valuable things can be learned from all seven approaches.

In this introductory chapter, we will first describe the two brand management paradigms that have been present between 1985 and 2006. Thereafter, the seven brand approaches will be described. It makes sense to break the period of time down into three main periods. The periods are distinctively different and form the backdrop of the seven approaches. Understanding the dynamic movement from one period to another provides insight into the development of the body of research literature constituting the academic discipline of brand management.

Two brand management paradigms

Perhaps due to the elusive nature of the brand, the term 'brand paradigm' is often used at random in the branding discipline. The analysis of brand management that has provided the seven approaches framework or categorization of brand management presented in this book is based on the philosophy of science by Thomas Kuhn, who is one of the most influential contributors to knowledge about 'paradigms'. Without going into too much detail with the paradigm concept, we will touch briefly upon the paradigmatic development of brand management. From 1985 to 2006 two overriding paradigms have been present in the academic world of brand management: one with a positivistic point of departure and one of a constructivist or interpretive nature. The positivistic stance implies a notion of the brand being 'owned' by the marketer, who controls the communication to a passive recipient/consumer. Brand equity is perceived to be created by the marketer and the brand is seen as: 'A manipulable lifeless artefact (product plus that is created by its owners/managers and that can be positioned, segmented and used to create an image)' (Hanby 1999, p. 12). The interpretive paradigm reflects on the nature of the brand and the value of brand equity as something created in the interaction between marketer and an active consumer: 'As holistic entities with many of the characteristics of living beings' (Hanby 1999, p. 10) and 'As a living entity (with a personality with which we can form a relationship and that can change and evolve over time)' (Hanby 1999, p. 12).

A paradigm shift takes place in brand management over the course of the 1990s. It does not happen overnight but is an incremental process changing the discipline. The birth of the relational approach is an important indicator of the shift from a positivist paradigm with the more functionalistic brand perspective to an inter-pretive paradigm with a constructivist perspective on the brand and how it should be managed.

Seven brand approaches

Analyzing more than twenty years of brand management has been a fascinating journey and the seven brand approaches can be described as the mountain peaks we have encountered along the way. An approach is not a paradigm in itself (at least not in the original Kuhnian sense of the word) but a particular 'school of thought' governing the global understanding of the nature of the brand, the consumer perspective and the methods associated with the scientific tradition behind the approach. Under the umbrella of a paradigm, different approaches are able to coexist.

The seven approaches are presented in the chronological order in which they have appeared in the data set of our analysis. Going through the period of time we have studied, it makes sense to divide it into three sections. The first period of time is 1985–92, the second is 1993–99 and the last one begins from 2000 and onwards.

In the first period, brand management focused on the company behind the brand and the actions the company would take to influence the consumer. In the next period of time, the receiver of brand communication is the main point of interest and brand management adopts a human perspective on the nature of the brand. In the last period, it is the contextual and cultural forces behind consumption choices and brand loyalty that are investigated in the ground-breaking articles and new literature.

In this section we will briefly describe the three periods, explain how the seven approaches are anchored in them, and touch upon the dynamic development leading from one period to the next.

1985–1992: company/sender focus

In the infancy of brand management, the research focuses on the company as sender of brand communication. This focus forms the background of the two first approaches in brand management; the economic approach and the identity approach.

The research of the economic approach is centered on the possibilities of the company to manage the brand via the marketing mix elements: product, placement, price and promotion, and how these factors can be manipulated to affect consumer brand choice. Quantitative data are the principal rule in this period. Researchers often use either data from supermarket scanner systems or laboratory experiments as the empirical basis of data. In the identity approach, research focuses on how the identity of the company as whole can shape a coherent brand message that is communicated to all shareholders.

It is assumed that the brand is 'owned' by the company and that the brand is communicated in a linear fashion from the company to the consumer.

The economic approach: the brand as part of the traditional marketing mix

The point of departure for brand management is that it is a breakaway discipline from the broad scope of marketing. Hence, the discipline starts out with a research environment marked by traditional marketing mix theory (the Four Ps). The creation of brand value is investigated as influenced by changes in e.g. distribution channels, price modifications and promotions. A functionalistic brand perspective applies, as does a consumer perspective based on the notion of the 'economic man'. The economic consumer bases consumption decisions on rational consider-ations and the exchange between the brand and the consumer is assumed to be isolated tangible transactions. Laboratory settings and scanner data are illustrative of the methodologies and (always quantitative) data. The marketer is definitely in charge of brand value creation, and hence consumers are believed to 'receive' and understand the messages 'sent' to them from the marketer exactly as intended.

The identity approach: the brand as linked to corporate identity

The economic approach lays the foundation for brand management as an inde-pendent scientific discipline, but one more stream of research is also influential during the first years of this inquiry. This approach behind the notion of corporate branding is the second oldest one in this context, but is still very influential and under constant theoretical development. Especially in the European research envi-ronment the brand as linked with corporate identity is a very influential school of thought. Focusing on corporate identity, the brand is also primarily perceived as an entity 'owned' by the marketer (even though that perception has changed in recent years). Integration of the brand on all organizational levels is key in the management of the brand. The marketer (as corporation) is in charge of brand value creation. Processes of organizational culture and corporate construction of identity are key influences.

1993–1999: human/receiver focus

The shift in attention towards the receiver of brand communication instigates a new period of time entirely different from the period 1985–93. New and ground-breaking research articles investigate the receiver of communication, and knowledge from different veins of human psychology are adapted to brand management theory. The human perspective is two-sided: the consumer is investi-gated closely *and* different human brand perspectives are coming into play. The humanistic and individualistic approaches – namely the consumer-based approach, the personality approach, and the relational approach – see the light of day in these years.

During 1993–99 data collection becomes 'softer'; quantitative, qualitative as well as mixed research designs are applied to the studies of the brand–consumer exchange. The relational approach is the first approach founded on an entirely qualitative study.

The consumer-based approach: the brand as linked with consumer associations

In 1993 Kevin Lane Keller founded a completely new approach to brand management. The brand is perceived as a cognitive construal in the mind of the consumer. It is assumed that a strong brand holds strong, unique and favourable associations in the minds of consumers. In this fashion, attention shifts from the sender towards the receiving end of brand communication. The consumer is the 'owner' of the brand in this approach, but still an assumption of linear communication applies. The consumer perspective of this approach is rooted in cognitive psychology, and in this tradition the computer is the main metaphor for man as a consumer. This consumer perspective implies linear communication because the marketer is perceived to be able to 'program' the consumer into intended action. This school of thought has since become the most dominant one in brand management.

The personality approach: the brand as a human-like character

Another mountain top in brand management was established in 1997 when a research study into brand personality was published. This study shows that consumers have a tendency to endow brands with human-like personalities. It is the 'human' brand perspective and the symbol-consuming consumer that are in the spotlight in this approach. Consumers endow brands with personalities and use these personalities in a dialogue-based exchange of symbolic value for their individual identity construction and expression. The personality approach is rooted in human personality psychology and uses of quantitative scaling techniques in a combination with more explorative methods to identify and measure brand personality. The personality approach is a prerequisite for and very much associated with the relational approach.

The relational approach: the brand as a viable relationship partner

The idea of a dyadic relationship between brand and consumer profoundly changed the academic discipline of brand management. The notion of the brand being a viable relationship partner builds on the same human brand metaphor as the personality approach. The approach extends the dialogue-based approach to brand management as instigated in the personality approach. The relational approach is rooted in the philosophical tradition of existentialism and the methods are of a phenomenological nature. These roots imply that a paradigm shift is taking place because they are so fundamentally different from the roots of research methods used in the first approaches to brand management.

2000–2006: cultural/context focus

Profound theoretical changes emerge both from academic discussions and from significant environmental changes affecting how humans consume brands. Environmental changes often imply a development of our theoretical frameworks because new phenomena arise that cannot be explained by means of the existing theories. A need for new theoretical tools to explain new phenomena is very much the driver behind the two newest approaches. Technological and cultural changes have profoundly changed the rules of the game in brand management in the last period of time.

The new phenomena calling for new theories are phenomena like autonomous consumers, brand icons, anti-branding movements and internet-based brand communities. The most novel and innovative research looks at these new consumption patterns through new lenses trying to explain the context of brand consumption.

Two approaches can be identified in this period of time: the community approach and the cultural approach. The community approach brings influences from anthropological consumption studies, socio-cultural influences and consumer empowerment. The cultural approach explores how brands are an inherent part of our culture and explains how playing an active role in mainstream culture can turn a brand into an icon. Hence, cultural and contextual influences add new perspectives to the discipline of brand management from 2000 to 2006.

The community approach: the brand as the pivotal point of social interaction

The community approach is based on anthropological research into so-called brand communities. Brand value is created in these communities where a brand serves as the pivotal point of social interaction among consumers. This approach thus adds an understanding of the social context of consumption to the overall picture of brand management. This understanding has become a prerequisite for managing many brands, especially after the Internet has profoundly changed the market place. In the community approach, the marketer deals with 'autonomous' groups of consumers who are able to collectively influence marketing actions and potentially 'take over' the brand and take it into a direction not at all intended by the marketer. The field of brand management has come a long way from the assumptions of linear communication behind the earlier approaches to accepting the chaotic autonomous consumer forces in this approach.

The cultural approach: the brand as part of the broader cultural fabric

The last approach in this context is the cultural approach. Just like the community approach, the cultural approach emanates around the millennium. The brand is seen as a cultural artefact in this approach, giving life to both a fierce anti-branding discourse and a theory of how to build an iconic brand. The approach borrows from the scientific tradition of cultural studies and makes use of a wide variety of qualitative methods. The attention has shifted from the transaction between a marketer and a consumer (or groups of consumers) to a macro perspective. The approach both explains what branding does to macro-level culture and how embedding the brand in cultural forces can be used strategically to build an iconic brand.

Summary

In marketing research, seven brand management approaches have been identified during 1985–2006: the economic approach, the identity approach, the consumer-based approach, the personality approach, the relational approach, the community approach and the cultural approach. These approaches reflect a development where the focus has shifted from the sending end of brand communications in the first period of time; have then turned their attention to the receiving end in the second period; and finally have addressed contextual and cultural influences on the brand to the global understanding of brand consumption.

Somewhere around the birth of the relational approach in 1998 a paradigm shift is instigated in brand management, with an implied shift from quantitative to qualitative methods, an acknowledgement of consumers' ownership of the brand, and an embrace of the more chaotic forces in consumer culture.

Box 3. 1 Overview of brand management 1985–2006

Two paradigms	*Three periods of time*	*Seven brand approaches*
Positivistic	Company/sender focus	The economic approach
		The identity approach
	Human/receiver focus	The consumer-based approach
		The personality approach
Constructivist		The relational approach
	Cultural/context focus	The community approach
		The cultural approach

Box 3.1 depicts how the paradigm shift has taken place somewhere around the birth of the relational approach, and how the three periods of time form the background of the seven brand approaches. This is only a brief introduction to a fascinating journey into the world of brand management. The interconnected web of assumptions, brand perspective, consumer perspective, theories and methods of each approach will be explained in Part II of this book.

Reference

Hanby, T. (1999), 'Brands dead or alive', *Journal of Market Research Society*, 41 (1): 7–19

Part II

Seven brand approaches

4 The economic approach

Learning objectives

The purpose of this chapter is to:

Understand the assumptions of the economic approach
- Consumers base consumption decisions on rational parameters and the exchange between brand and consumer is perceived to be linear, functional and transaction-based

Understand the theoretical building blocks of the economic approach
- The supporting themes – transaction theory and marketing mix theory – make up the core theme: the economic brand

Provide insights into the methods of the economic approach
- The economic approach primarily uses quantitative methods to explore how the management of marketing mix variables affects consumer brand choice

Understand the managerial implications
- The Four Ps can help the brand manager plan and execute a brand strategy within the economic approach
- The strengths and weaknesses of the economic approach and the key points of critique to which the economic approach has been subject

The economic approach is the first approach of this book and the approach upon which all the consecutive approaches in brand management rest. Since the economic approach describes the first approach to brand management, and hence the foundation for how brands have been (and are) managed, it is important to understand the line of thought underlying the economic approach. Since the economic approach is more comprehensible and not as complex as some in the consecutive chapters, this chapter is somewhat shorter than the other approach chapters and focuses more on the background and assumptions of the approach. It is important to understand this background in depth because understanding the background will enable the reader to get a good idea of the strengths and weaknesses of the economic approach as well as understand the foundation for the other approaches in brand management.

Fast-moving consumer goods manufacturer Procter & Gamble gave birth to the first management practices of brand management with its product management approach. The theories underlining the way that this big multinational producer of fast-moving consumer goods during the 1930s dealt with brand management were mainly borrowed from neoclassical economics and classical marketing theory. The fast-moving consumer goods industry has since played a major role in the evolution of brand management research and practice.

The economic approach builds on one of the most fundamental concepts in marketing, namely the idea that the right marketing mix will generate optimal sales. Neil Borden first introduced the marketing mix concept when he deducted twelve factors that management should consider when planning and implementing marketing strategy. One can argue that the whole idea of brand management really rests on his initial factor theory of marketing (Borden 1964). The twelve elements reflected internal considerations and relevant market forces in relation to marketing strategy. It was a framework constructed to guide managers through marketing questions and help them structure the planning and implementation of marketing strategy.

E. Jerome McCarthy later narrowed Borden's framework down into the Four Ps framework we know today (McCarthy 1964). The Four Ps (reflecting product, place, price and promotion) have since been immortalized by numerous marketing books and become everyday marketing practice in countless marketing departments around the world and often make up the first introduction students get to marketing and brand management.

Brand management adopted the Four Ps concept from marketing and during the mid and late 1980s, much research focus was directed towards exploring how different factors of the marketing mix affect consumers' brand choice. This chapter will give the reader an overview of key themes and concepts that have shaped the economic approach and its applicability in practice.

The description of the economic approach is divided into four main sections, according to the structure laid out in the introduction. The assumptions describe the implicit view of the nature of the brand and the premises of the brand–consumer exchange. The theoretical building blocks describe the concepts, models and figures key to the economic approach. Methods and data provide insight into what data to look for and how to collect it, when researching the content of a specific brand strategy. These three scientific layers add up to a managerial 'how-to' guide for how the assumptions, theories and methods of the approach can be converted into a brand management strategy in practice.

The economic approach is the first identified approach in brand management and the elements of the economic approach serve as a prerequisite for most planning and execution of brand management still today. The economic approach is therefore of great importance, but since brand management has evolved drastically over the years, the approach has also been subjected to criticism as new perceptions of consumption and new theories have evolved. The chapter will hence be rounded off with a discussion of the key points of critique, which serves as a natural point of departure for understanding the development of the forthcoming approaches in brand management.

Assumptions of the economic approach

In the economic approach, it is assumed that the brand can be controlled and managed by the company. If management gets the marketing mix right, then the brand will be successful and strong. Consumers in this approach to brand management are perceived to be more or less passive receivers of marketing messages, who analyse and evaluate brand messages rationally. This perception of the consumer is associated with how the concept the *economic man* perceives exchanges of goods and consumption.

Microeconomics and the economic man

The assumptions and premises of the economic approach have their origin in the theoretical model of exchange derived from micro-economic theory and marketing. The model of exchange in micro-economics is a purely theoretical model, which means that the assumptions and key models are the result of theorizing rather than empirical research. The basic premises of the economic approach go back to a neoclassical micro-economic perception of market forces in society. In *The Wealth of Nations* Adam Smith argued that if one would let market forces govern the allocation of resources and the exchange of goods, then an 'invisible hand' would allocate resources in a way that optimizes both the individual and societal beneficial use of available resources. In this perception of market forces lies an assumption that individuals pursue self-interest and attempt to maximize revenue or utility function.

The principle of the 'invisible hand' assumes that resources are allocated according to where they will give the highest possible functional outcome or revenue because efficient methods of production will be adopted by manufacturers in order to accommodate the utility-maximizing behaviour displayed by the

Figure 4.1 The brand–consumer exchange of the economic approach

individual. The *economic man* is the concept that is often used about these assumptions of human behaviour. The assumptions of the economic man are:

- Human behaviour is guided by rational parameters.
- Humans will attempt to maximize their own satisfaction and strive for maximum utility in any exchange – self-interest is an important parameter.
- Humans have 'perfect information' about the available alternatives.
- The exchange between two parties is perceived as an isolated event.
- Consumers are constrained by limited income, which forces them to behave in a way that will ensure that they get the most out of their income – they will act to maximize the utility of their income.

The logic is hence applicable both at the market scale and at an individual level, because it is assumed that the individual will always pursue self-interest and make consumption decisions that are based on rational parameters, deliver individual utility maximization and hence make the best rational choice possible. In a consumption and brand management context this means that a consumer will always go for the deal that provides the best functional utility compared with the price of the product. It is hence assumed not only that consumers are able to oversee all available choices, but also that they are able to and will evaluate all these choices and choose the best deal from a rational point of view.

Box 4.1 Economic man: Individual and societal maximization in a supermarket checkout queue

A simple example of how the principle of the 'invisible hand' works in practice is how customers behave in the queue for a supermarket checkout. According to the assumptions of the economic man, each customer will automatically try to maximize her own self-interest – which in a supermarket checkout queue is to check out in the shortest time possible. Most people will hence choose the shortest queue whenever getting in line. In this example customer utility maximizing choice is hence to queue up in the line with fewest people. From a general perspective this has the consequence that customers queue up in lines that all end up having the same length. Therefore without the slightest direction and by following only their own self-interest, customers will automatically have queued up in a manner that is most efficient on an individual level, but also from a societal perspective.

The brand–consumer exchange and transaction cost theory

Transaction cost theory is closely linked with the stream of neoclassical micro-economic logic explained above and describes the relationship companies have to the market; it defines the firm theoretically in relation to the marketplace. The theory of transaction costs builds on the same assumption as the principle of the 'invisible hand' that all actors involved in the exchange of goods will display behaviour of optimization. From a manufacturer point of view, not only is it hence important to supply the best deal, but from a marketing perspective it is equally important to reduce the transaction costs associated with the search, purchase and consumption of a product. It is on these assumptions of behaviour of optimization and minimization of transaction costs that the theories of the economic approach to brand management are based. These assumptions define the relationship a company has with the market focusing on price, demand and supply. The theoretical origin of the marketing mix concept in neoclassical micro-economics and transaction theory is reflected in how the exchange between brands and consumers is perceived.

The transaction costs the *economic consumer* might have when finding the best possible deal can however be a barrier that, from a rational perspective, makes it difficult to choose the right brand or product. If transaction costs are too high – if e.g. it is too difficult to find and buy the product – then the consumer might choose another product even though it might not deliver maximum utility compared with other products or compared with the price. In the economic approach, it is therefore crucial that transaction costs are minimized. The marketer can do this by ensuring that the right product, at the right price, is made known and accessible to consumers through adequate brand management. This will ensure that consumers are always aware of the product whenever they need it and that they have easy access to purchasing the product. Hence it aims at mini mizing the transaction costs consumers might have and facilitates consumers' decision process because it aims at diminishing the barriers to an 'economic man' brand choice behaviour. The exchange between the brand and the consumer is hence perceived to be of a transaction-like nature, where the consumer acts as an 'economic man' who rationally evaluates all available choices and chooses the best available offer. The communication between the brand and the consumer is perceived to be linear and rather functional, because once a certain frame has been set by the marketer it is expected that consumers will respond with a certain brand choice behaviour.

Consumption is hence perceived to be the result of consumers' insatiable desire for goods and services and is not influenced by social interaction, culture or the well-being of others. This is why very rational factors like awareness, price and income are perceived to be key factors in the economic approach when consumers make consumption choices. Brands are regarded as signals that can reduce the uncertainty that will always be present in any transaction, before consumers make a brand choice. Hence the economic approach does not, like the other approaches described in this book, include consumers' hedonic consumption that satisfies more emotional and irrational wants and desires. The brand–consumer exchange is perceived merely as an exchange of goods consisting of one or more transactions, as opposed to the other approaches, where the exchange between brand and consumer is perceived more broadly as a relationship with different characteristics, depending on the specific approach. So what does this difference in the perception of the brand–consumer exchange imply? It implies that every time the primary goal is to achieve a transaction, as opposed to a lasting relationship, the exchange is hence analysed as an isolated event.

In the theoretical models there is little interaction between the brand and the consumer. It is assumed that brand choice is based on a linear communication, where the marketer sends off brand messages in the shape of a product, price, a placement and promotions, and the consumer receives these messages and acts on them (make the purchase) if they are right. That exchange is hence perceived to consist of the mere transaction without interactivity; in fact very few or no external, uncontrollable factors are included in the theoretical apparatus

Summary

The assumptions of the economic approach are based on neoclassical micro-economics of how market forces allocate resources most efficiently through the principle of the 'invisible hand' and classic marketing theory. The consumer is assumed to be able to make rationally based brand consumption choices and to be focused on utility maximization, which is why they will always choose whatever brand delivers the best utility value compared with the price. The theoretical apparatus is based on the basic ideas from transaction marketing, where it is assumed that the exchange between brand and consumer consists of isolated transactions rather than an ongoing relationship. The primary goal of brand communication is hence to ensure that consumers are aware of the fine qualities of the brand at the right time and place through linear communication from the brand to the consumer.

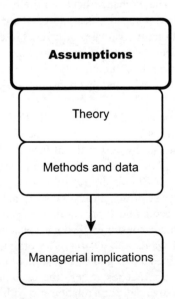

Figure 4.2 Assumptions of the economic approach

Theoretical building blocks of the economic approach

The economic approach builds on traditional economic theory of exchange where the principles of the invisible hand and the economic man guide behaviour and transaction cost theory. This section will account for each of the theoretical building blocks (supporting themes) that make up the core theme – the economic brand. The supporting themes of the economic approach to brand management consist respectively of transaction cost theory describing the transaction-based perspective on exchange between brand and consumer and the concept of the marketing mix describing the marketing mix parameters that are key when building a brand strategy in the economic approach.

Supporting theme: transaction cost theory

The principle of the invisible hand and the perception of the consumer as an economic man imply that any consumption choice is the result of a reasoning process, where the involved partners will choose whatever will maximize their own profit or utility. However, in consumer behaviour there are some exceptions to this rule, because consumer behaviour does not always display a utility-maximizing consumption choice behaviour. Transaction cost theory takes these exceptions into consideration. Consumers, for example, do not have perfect information and accessibility to all choice available, or consumers can have switching costs when shifting from one brand to another. According to the assumptions of the 'invisible hand' and the economic man, these barriers to the perfect exchange are called transaction costs.

Transaction costs are hence barriers to utility maximization. The goal for brand management in the economic approach is to eliminate these transaction costs and facilitate transactions. The next transaction is hence the ultimate goal in the economic approach. A good measurement of whether or not a brand strategy is efficient is hence measuring the number of transactions or, expressed differently, sales figures. Focusing excessively on sales figures alone implies a rather short-term focus as opposed to the focus of the remaining brand approaches in this book that have a more relational perspective on brand-building activities.

Figure 4.3 Supporting themes of the economic approach

Box 4.2 Transactional versus relational perspective on brand management

The transactional perspective has a rather short-term time perspective, because transactions are perceived to be isolated events and the primary focus for the marketer is hence the next transaction rather than relationship building. Price is believed to be an important parameter and consumers are assumed to be focused on the functional, technical quality of the brand or product they purchase. Managerial efforts for companies operating in a transactional momentum are often directed to the rather tactical management and improvement of the marketing mix, to target large numbers of consumers with mass communication, and ensuring product quality, sold in the right place, for the right price.

In a relational perspective, the time perspective is longer and the primary focus is on building long-lasting relationships with consumers. Consumers are in the relational perspective perceived to be less sensitive to price and more concerned with the quality of the interaction or relation they have with the brand. Companies operating in the relational *modus operandi* often focus on the combination of database techniques and direct marketing tools aimed at ensuring a good and stable relation with the individual consumer, rather than the more mass communication-oriented means of communication used in the transactional perspective.

Source Hultman and Shaw (2003)

The barriers to transactions described in the transaction cost theory stand in opposition to the assumption that consumers act rationally because transaction cost theory proposes that in any exchange or prior to any transaction consumers are limited by bounded rationality. This means that transaction cost theory acknowledges that consumers are not able to have a complete overview of options and they are hence not able to make a perfect rationally based consumption decision, because they are not cognitively able to grasp all information about all available brand alternatives. Since consumers are constrained by limited cognitive capabilities which confine their ability to make rational consumption choices, it is crucial that the marketer facilitates transactions by providing the consumer with the right information about the product and about the product utility benefits, and ensures that the product itself is available at all relevant points of contact with the consumer. Insights into these barriers to transactions have spurred the development of the next supporting theme: the concept of marketing mix. It was originally developed as a means for transaction marketing and provided the operational planning and execution tools that can facilitate transaction exchanges between brand and consumer and help consumers make the right rationally based consumption decisions. The second supporting theme of the economic approach is hence the marketing mix also known as the Four Ps.

Supporting theme: marketing mix

Within the economic approach, where the transaction exchange between the brand and consumers is the core, the marketing mix offers a managerial approach to facilitating these exchanges. Expressed by the American Marketing Association in 1985: 'Marketing is the process of planning and executing the conception, pricing, promotion and distribution of ideas, goods and services to create exchanges that satisfy individual and organisational objectives' (Hultman and Shaw 2003, p. 37). The aim with the marketing mix concept is to understand how transactions are created and how these insights can be used to apply a more systematic management of marketing strategy and activities. Furthermore the objective with the marketing mix is, through analysis, to ensure profitable spending of marketing resources adhering not only to marketing, but also to other functions that have an influence on the effectiveness of the relation between the company and its markets. The marketing mix hence describes the function of the marketer as:

> the marketing man as an empiricist seeking in any situation to devise a profitable 'pattern' or 'formula' of marketing operations from among the many procedures and policies were open to him. If he was a 'mixer of ingredients', what he designed was a 'marketing mix'
>
> (Borden 1984, p. 9).

The line of thought is that the right marketing mix can ensure an efficient connection between the company and the market place. The point of departure of the marketing mix is, hence, that attributes related to the Four Ps (product, price, place and promotion) are the main mechanisms behind the creation and management of brand equity. The primary purpose for brand management is, according to these premises, to produce, promote and distribute goods that are attractive to consumers because they deliver the best deal measured by the utility value the goods offer, compared with the utility value competitors offer, related to the price consumers are willing to pay. Brand managers are assumed to be able to control consumers' brand choice behaviour by ensuring an optimum mix between the four main elements of the marketing mix. The marketing mix is hence a key instrument for understanding and facilitating transactions between the company and the market. The logic is that a brand will succeed only if the manufacturer of that brand is able to produce a product that delivers high utility benefits, then sells it at the right price, in the right places, and promotes it to such an extent and in such a way that spurs consumer awareness. The Four Ps – product, place, price and promotion – are hence key denominators of a brand's success.

The marketing mix quickly became an unchallenged basic model of marketing and the Four Ps have gone their course of victory across the world of marketing: 'since its introduction, McCarthy's (1960) description of a marketing mix comprised of product, price, promotion and place has widely become regarded as an 'infallible' guide for the effective planning and implementation of marketing strategy' (Grönroos 1994, p. 4)

Product

The product represents the tangible, physical product itself and the benefits that the consumer can gain from buying the brand. It includes the design, brand name, functionality, quality, safety, packaging, etc. The product encompasses all the tangible aspects of the product a manufacturer offers. The primary aim of the product is to be able to satisfy a functional demand – the functionality of the product, as such, is very important and the first prerequisite in the economic approach.

Price

The price refers to the price that consumer will eventually pay for the product. The price is in the economic approach based on the total cost of manufacturing the product, the distribution and advertising cost. These direct and indirect production costs combined with a competitive analysis, and perhaps uncovering how much consumers are willing to pay for the product, make up the input for the analysis of what the price of the product should be. There are, however, other aspects of price that are important in the economic approach. The price factor of the marketing mix is closely linked with the marketing mix factor of promotion. Since promotions are often used as a way to increase awareness or boost sales in the economic approach – pricing strategies are often planned based on scanner data from supermarket checkouts measuring how promotions affect the overall demand for the brand.

Place

Place in the marketing mix refers to the distribution of the product from the manufacturer to the end consumer. In short it is about making goods available in the right quantities in the right locations. It is essential here to consider which distribution channels will be most effective for the brand and to develop a supply chain strategy that fits with the attributes of the brand and the demands of the consumers. This supply chain strategy implies the identification of the right channel partners, inventory management basically ensuring that all steps from when the brand leaves the production site until it reaches the consumer are geared and optimized.

Promotion

Promotion represents the various elements that a marketing plan can consist of when promoting a brand. In the economic approach, the aspects of promotion that have received most interest are promotion and advertising. Advertising covers all the primary functions involved in ensuring that consumers are aware of the brand at the best possible moment when they are looking to buy a product in the relevant product category. An important part of advertising in recent research in the economic approach is signalling theory. Signalling theory investigates what signals are the most efficient to reveal the unobserved product qualities of a brand. The brand name, packaging or placement can help reveal unobserved product qualities and communicate important marketing messages to the consumer. Promotion is a tool that has been heavily used and researched in the economic approach. The accessibility of scanner panel data has made research into the short- and long-term effect that promotion has on sales a key topic not only in research but also in practice in many sales and marketing departments.

Core theme: the economic brand

The premises of the economic brand is hence that it operates in a market, that the consumer is assumed to make primarily rational consumption decisions, and the interactions with consumers are standalone isolated events rather than an ongoing relationship. These premises make the utility attributes the brand has to offer judged against its price relative to competitors, level of awareness and recognition, and last but not least, the accessibility of the brand essential for whether or not a brand will be successful.

Summary

The theoretical building blocks of the economic approach consist of two supporting themes: transaction cost theory and the concept of the marketing mix. Transaction cost theory describes the barriers that can impede transactions taking place according to the principles of the invisible hand and the economic man. It also describes the economic perspective on exchange between brands and consumers as isolated events, where money and goods are exchanged. The primary aim is to achieve the next transaction by eliminating or breaking down the barriers that inhibit the transaction from taking place. These barriers to transactions must be overcome. The tool used in the economic approach to overcome these barriers is the marketing mix, or the Four Ps. Using the toolbox of the Four Ps can ensure that the right product is available to consumers at the right price, in the right locations, and that it is promoted by using advertising and promotion to make consumers aware of and interested in purchasing the product.

Figure 4.4 Core theme and supporting themes of the economic approach to brand management

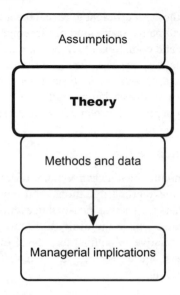

Figure 4.5 Theoretical building blocks of the economic approach

Methods and data of the economic approach

The aim of data collection in the economic approach is to gather data that can deliver insights that can guide the marketer in defining the exact marketing mix that will deliver optimal brand performance – and thereby maximize the number of transactions. The methods used in the economic approach are predominantly quantitative, and data are interpreted using largely analytical techniques from micro-economics, where focus is on the causal effects marketing activities have on demand.

Since the Four Ps are rather operational and tactically focused, the methods used in the economic approach are also very output and managerially oriented, emphasizing the replicability of data and results. It is important that the results can be applied directly and used for decision making and problem solving in relation to the planning and execution of a marketing strategy. Creating mathematical models that can measure and quantify data and thereby explain the phenomenon of exchange between two entities is hence central. The mathematical models are key because the process of measurement is considered the only valid connection between empirical observations and the expression or explanation of how these empirical observations are linked.

The overall objective of research and data collection in the economic approach is to investigate how manipulating one or more factors of the marketing mix will affect consumers' brand choice. It is hence the investigation of the causal effects between two or more variables relating to the marketing mix that is primarily researched. It could for example be researched how sensitive consumers are to promotions, where the research focus could be investigating consumers' response to price reductions by exploring how promotions are reflected in the demand for a product. Or any other quantitative investigation of how different marketing mix variables affect consumers' brand behaviour.

Data and analysis in the economic approach

Because methods are mainly quantitative in the economic approach, large quantities of data are preferred. The big data samples can be used to deduct correlations between variables and are suitable because of the need for data and results to be replicable; it is important to ensure that they are representative. The disadvantage is that it is difficult to gain a sound understanding of why variables are correlated, because the data are sampled broad instead of deep. As opposed to qualitative research methods, where smaller samples deliver rich and descriptive conclusions, the results of quantitative research designs are often expressed in tables or other statistical representations of data.

The economic approach rests upon a positivist research ideal. This line of thought is very much in opposition to the stream of qualitative research methods that have become more and more dominant in marketing research in recent decades. In the quantitative methods, objectiveness is important and phenomena are presumed to be measurable. The objectivity of data is important for validity, and closeness to the subject of research is not essential. Data like scanner panel data from cash registers at supermarkets and laboratory experiments are considered valid. The data are then subjected to different kinds of statistical analysis that often consist of some sort of regression analysis.

Box. 4.3 Regression analysis

Regression analysis is a statistical tool for the investigation of relationships between variables. Any regression study sets out with a hypothesis that the investigator formulates, e.g. when a brand is on promotion (the price is lower than usual) then the demand will increase. After having formulated the hypothesis the researcher assembles data on the variables of interest – data on price levels over time and data of demand levels over time. The data are then subjected to regression analysis that estimates the quantitative effect or correlation between the variables. Hereby it is possible to ascertain the causal effect of one variable upon another; hence how a price cut in the shape of a promotion affects sales. The illustration reflects the correlation between how price promotions affect demand (the x axis reflecting the price and the y axis illustrating the fluctuations in demand). It is clear that whenever the product has been on promotion – sold at a reduced price – the demand for the product is higher.

Once a correlation between two variables has been established the statistical significance of the estimated relationships can be seen. In figure 4.6 the relation between price and demand is reflected: whenever the product or brand is on promotion, it is reflected in the sales figures – the demand for the brand is higher.

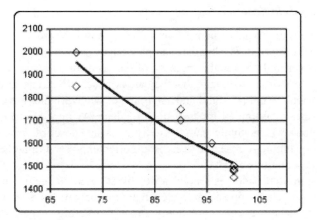

Figure 4.6 Relation between price and demand

To accommodate the need for investigating different marketing mix variables that affect different factors of consumer brand choice behaviour, like brand switching or brand market shares, customized regression models are often developed to fit the exact problem at hand.

Summary

The methods of the economic approach are mainly quantitative and focus on exploring how consumers' brand choice behaviour is affected by changes in one or more factors of the marketing mix. The data used are very factual and measurable in statistical models. Data are often derived from scanner panel data or other factual, statistical data. The method of analysis mostly focuses on the construction of mathematical regression models that can be used to measure the causal effects of how changing a variable in the marketing mix of a brand will affect consumer brand choice behaviour. The replicability of results is important because results are mostly used for decision making and problem solving on a general basis in practice.

Managerial implications: strengths and weaknesses

In the economic approach, the primary focus of the brand manager is to eliminate the barriers to exchange and facilitate the next transaction. The marketing mix is considered to be the best toolkit for this transactional approach to brand management. Brand managers hence in the economic approach have the Four Ps

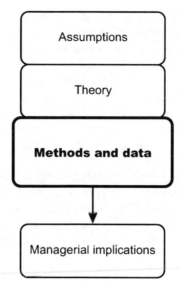

Figure 4.7 Methods and data of the economic approach

at their disposal to create a strong brand and optimize brand performance. Because of the rather operational nature of the theoretical building blocks, this section will not, as is the case in the other approach chapters, elaborate extensively on how to manage the marketing mix variables, since the key issues have already been explained in the theoretical building blocks. Rather it will focus on the strengths and weaknesses of using the economic approach as a basis of brand building. It will also summarize the main points of critique that the approach has been subject to since its foundation and application in the context of brand management.

As already mentioned the marketing mix approach has in many ways dominated the marketing environment and become an indisputable paradigm. The economic approach and the transactional approach to brand management represent a push approach to the marketing of brands, where some of the newer approaches represent a more pull-oriented approach to brand strategy. The economic approach has been subject to some critique since its foundation, but it is important to keep in mind that the economic approach is the foundation of how brand management has evolved until today. Understanding the premises of the approach will enable the reader to critically evaluate how the approach is still relevant for some key problems in brand management while insufficient for others. The managerial branding focus of the economic approach is, as mentioned, individual transactions, and branding is considered to be a management problem that can be solved through managerial tasks of analysing, planning, and implementing marketing activities with the purpose of selling as many products as possible. In the research literature and in management practice the tools of economic approach, e.g. the Four Ps and the marketing mix and how it can affect consumers' brand choice behaviour, are still widely researched. From an operational viewpoint the marketing mix toolbox is still relevant and beneficial for the brand manager to know about – especially if he or she is aware of its strengths and limitations.

In practice, managing a brand according to the theory of the marketing mix means that companies believe that by manipulating a series of interrelated marketing decisions the marketing manager can target and position products within a defined market segment which will respond in a planned and desirable manner – the consumer reacts to the marketing mix and does not engage in any interaction with the company as such. Hence as a planning and execution tool the marketing mix is indeed considered to be appropriate.

> the marketing process consist of analysing market opportunities, researching and selecting target markets, designing marketing programs, and organising, implementing, and controlling the marketing effort … [and] to transform marketing strategy into marketing programs marketing managers must make basic decisions on marketing expenditure, marketing mix, and marketing allocation.
>
> (Kotler 1997 p. 86–7)

The down side is, however, that using the marketing mix as the primary marketing tool to manage brands can result in a rather short-term focus because of the extensive emphasis on the next transaction. The marketer is concerned with 'hooking new clients' and sales figures, and the exchange between the brand and the consumer is reduced to the isolated transaction. The brand-building qualities are, however, difficult to catch sight of, especially from the field of service branding, the critique of this perception of transactions as isolated events has been harsh. In service marketing it is clear that other rules of the game apply – interaction with the consumer is perceived as an ongoing relationship rather than isolated transactions and individual exchanges.

The other main critique stems from the origin of the theoretical models of exchange the approach builds on. The exchange model the marketing mix line of thought draws on has its origin in micro-economics. The model of exchange from micro-economics is a purely theoretical model, which means that the assumptions and key models are the result of theorizing rather than empirical research. Hence, since the models and theories are based on theorizing rather than empirical data, the economic approach has been criticized for not portraying the world of consumption adequately. Especially, how the approach deals with or rather does not deal with the consumer has been the primary focus of critique. In the real world, consumers do not have perfect information on the market place, and their knowledge about different alternatives is fragmented. Furthermore, individual preferences often violate utility theory – different people have different preferences, which cannot be explained by theories of maximization – and these considerations are not incorporated in the theoretical apparatus of the economic approach. Hence, the very nature of the Four Ps as manageable, controllable factors combined with the intrinsic lack of market input in the model is in contrast with the ideals of the principles of market orientation implying that all marketing activities should be based on the identification of consumer needs and wants which are very much in line with the widely accepted brand management theory.

The thoughts behind the economic approach serve as the foundation for brand management and from here the discipline develops into still more complicated theories of consumer behaviour and brand consumption. One can say that the following approaches all accommodate the shortcomings of the economic approach as they each explain a specific brand and consumption perspective not accounted for in the economic approach.

Summary

The value of the tools of the economic approach for the planning and implementation of marketing plans short-term are, however, great and a prerequisite in brand management, but the strategic value and potential for brand building of the marketing mix tools is questionable. The economic approach is hence a suitable planning and execution tool in brand management, but it cannot stand alone, if one wishes to reap the full potential of brands and brand management reflecting how consumers in the new millennium consume brands.

Student questions

1 What theories are the theoretical building blocks based on?
2 How is the consumer perceived to consume brands in the economic approach?
3 Which elements are key for the creation of brand equity in the economic approach?
4 What are the strengths and weaknesses of the marketing mix?
5 What methods are primarily used to explore the brand in the economic approach?
6 Why is the economic approach perceived not to deliver sufficient theoretical tool for the management of brands today?

References and further reading

Key readings are in **bold type**.

Ackerman, F. (1997) 'Consumed in theory: alternative perspectives on economics of consumption', *Journal of Economic Issues*, 31 (3): 651–64

Ailawadi, K. L., Lehman, D. R. and Neslin, S. A., 'Marketing response to major policy change in the marketing mix: learning from Procter & Gamble's value pricing strategy', *Journal of Marketing*, 65 (1): 44–61

Bath, S. and Reddy, S. K. (1998) 'Symbolic and functional positioning of brands', *Journal of Consumer Marketing*, 15 (1): 32–43

Borden, N. (1964) 'The concept of the marketing mix', in G. Schwartz (ed.) *Science in Marketing*, New York: Wiley

Bucklin, R. E., Gupta, S. and Han, S. (1995) 'A brand's eye view of response segmentation in consumer brand choice behavior', *Journal of Marketing Research*, February 66–74

Carpenter, G. and Lehman D. R. (1985) 'A model of marketing mix, brand switching, and competition', *Journal of Marketing Research*, 22: 318–29

Constantinides, E. (2006) 'The marketing mix revisited: towards the twenty-first century marketing', *Journal of Marketing Management*, 22: 407–38

Demirdjian, Z. S. and Turan, S. (2004) 'Perspectives in consumer behavior: paradigm shifts in prospect', *Journal of American Academy of Business*, March: 348–53

Erdem, T., Swait, J. and Valenzuela, A. (2006) 'Brands as signals: a cross-country validation study', *Journal of Marketing*, 70: 34–49

Gardner, B. B. and Levy, S. J. (1955) 'The product and the brand', *Harvard Business Review*, March/April: 33–9

Grönroos, C. (1994a) '*Quo vadis*, marketing? Toward a relationship marketing paradigm', *Journal of Marketing Management*, 10 (5): 347–60

Grönroos, C. (1994b) 'From marketing mix to relationship marketing: towards a paradigm shift in marketing', *Management Decision*, 32 (2): 4–26

Hultman, C. M. and Shaw, E. (2003) 'The interface between transactional and relational orientation in small service firms' marketing behavior: a study of Scottish and Swedish small firms in the service sector', *Journal of Marketing Theory and Practice*, 11 (1): 110–12

Keller, K. L., Heckler, S. E. and Houston, M. J. (1998) 'The effects of brand name suggestiveness on advertising recall', *Journal of Marketing*, 62: 48–57

Kirmani, A. and Rao, A. R. (2000), 'No pain, no gain: a critical review of the literature on signaling unobservable product quality', *Journal of Marketing*, 64 (April): 66–79

Kotler, P. (1965) 'Competitive strategies for new product marketing over the life cycle', *Management Science*, 12 (4): 104–19

Kotler, P. (1997) *Marketing Management: Analyses, Planning, Implementation, and Control*, Upper Saddle River NJ: Prentice-Hall

McCarthy, E. J. (1960) *Basic Marketing: a Managerial Approach*, Homewood IL: Irwin

Mela, C. F., Gupta S. and Lehman D. R. (1997) 'The long-term impact of promotion and advertising on consumer brand choice', *Journal of Marketing Research*, May: 248–61

Nelson, J. A. (1998) 'Abstraction, reality and gender of "economic man"', in J. G. Carrier and D. Miller (eds) *Virtualism: A New Political Economy*, Oxford: Berg

Papatla, P. and Krishnamurthi, L. (1996) 'Measuring the dynamic effects of promotion on brand choice', *Journal of Marketing Research*, February: 20–35

Park, C. W., Jaworski, B. J. and MacInnis, D. J. (1986) 'Strategic brand concept–image management', *Journal of Marketing*, October: 135–45

Shugan, S. M. (1987) 'Estimating brand positioning maps using supermarket scanning data', *Journal of Marketing Research*, February: 1–18

Shultz, D. E. (2001) 'Marketers: bid farewell to strategy based on old Four Ps', *Marketing News: American Marketing Association*, 12 February: 7–8

Vargo, S. L. and Lusch, R. F. (2004) 'Evolving a new dominant logic for marketing', *Journal of Marketing*, January: 1–17

Vilcassim, N. J. and Dipak, C. J. (1991) 'Modeling purchase-timing and brand-switching behavior incorporating explanatory variables and unobserved heterogeneity', *Journal of Marketing Research*, February: 29–41

Yudelson, J. (1999), 'Adapting McCarthy's Four Ps for the twenty-first century', *Journal of Marketing Education*, 21 (1): 60–7

Zaichkowsky, J. L. (1991) 'Consumer behavior: yesterday, today and tomorrow', *Business Horizons*, 34 (3): 51

5 The identity approach

with a commentary by Professor Majken Schultz, Copenhagen Business School, and Professor Emerita Mary Jo Hatch, University of Virginia

Learning objectives

The purpose of this chapter is to:

Understand the assumptions of the identity approach
- The brand should express one unified and coherent identity, internally as well as externally, by using the visual and behavioural identity of the corporation to build the brand

Understand the theoretical building blocks of the identity approach
- The four supporting themes of brand identity: corporate identity, organizational identity, image and reputation
- The two frameworks: the corporate brand tool kit and the AC2ID model are useful for the alignment of corporate identity, organizational identity, image and reputation to create a coherent brand identity

Provide insights into the methods of the identity approach
- In the identity approach a mix of methods is used. Internally, focus is on corporate identity (visual and strategic) and organizational identity (behaviour and culture) rooted in ethnographic and anthropological methods. Externally, the element's image and reputation combine methods stemming from cognitive and social psychology

Understand the managerial implications
- Understand the complexity of managing brand identity by ensuring alignment of corporate identity, organizational identity, image and reputation

In 1907, AEG appointed Peter Behrens to be what at the time was called 'Artistic Consultant'. His job turned out to be the first corporate engagement in the conscious management of identity. Peter Behrens's philosophy was simple – the products, design and communication should express one unified identity. To accomplish this, he created products, logos, advertising material and company publications with a consistent, unified design. This unified design and visual expression of identity make Peter Behrens and AEG the founders of the rationale behind the identity concept and corporate identity management programmes in practice. Identity programmes have since been an integral part of marketing.

In the late 1980s and early 1990s, this line of thought began to take shape in the context of brand management, laying the ground for the identity approach. Abratt (1989) elaborated on the conceptual development of the approach by adding an in-depth study of the dimensions that link the interior processes (corporate identity) with the exterior-focused activities (corporate image). A new stream of research has, especially in a European context, during the 1990s led to a conceptualization of brand identity, where the interplay between corporate identity, organizational identity, image and reputation provides the elements for brand identity.

In brand management, the identity construct has grown increasingly popular, because it is a powerful and complex concept with the potential of strengthening competitive power significantly. Most companies today build and manage identity to ensure that the brand identity expresses an exact set of values, capabilities and unique sales propositions.

Unlike several of the other brand management approaches described in this book, the conceptualization and evolution of the identity approach in brand management is primarily practitioner-led. This means that the core definitions and conceptualization of the identity approach are not the result of a single comprehensive breakthrough study (as is the case in the consumer-based, the personality, the relational and the community approaches), but rather based on practical experience from the use of the identity concept as a management tool. There are, however, many influential articles and books worth mentioning in relation to the identity approach. We will refrain from listing the complete selection but mention two collections that in particular have set the scene in the recent perspectives on brand identity. *The Expressive Organization* by Schultz *et al.* (2000) is a selection of articles exploring the identity domain from multiple academic fields, with the aim of discussing the relational differences between identity, image and culture in organizations with the aim of clarifying and articulating the theoretical domain of identity (Schultz *et al.* 2000). *Revealing the Corporation: Perspectives on Identity, Image, Reputation, Corporate Branding, and Corporate-level Marketing* (Balmer and Greyser 2003) is another important collection guiding the reader through influential classics and contemporary academic articles shedding light on different perspectives on identity, image, reputation and corporate branding.

This chapter offers an overview of the essence of the identity approach, by providing insights into the assumptions, theoretical elements and methodologies underlying the identity approach. Finally, the chapter describes and discusses the

Figure 5.1 Sources of brand identity. The corporation is pivotal for the creation of brand equity in the identity approach

managerial guidelines that can be accumulated from the most prominent research publications and key non-research literature, supplemented with illustrative cases of how companies have dealt with the management of brand identity in practice.

Assumptions of the identity approach

The economic approach assumes that attributes related to the Four Ps of marketing (product, price, placement and promotion) are the main mechanisms behind the creation and management of brand equity.

The identity approach brings into focus the creation of a unified, visual and behavioural identity. It is assumed that consumers attribute identity characteristics to *companies* and that people form images of companies based on the *total experience of the company*. This places the corporation and its employees at the centre of brand equity creation. The identity approach hence adds the importance of the identity of the corporate branding to the theoretical domain of brand management.

The corporate identity perspective

As mentioned in the introduction, the identity concept has a long history from the field of marketing (both in research and in practice) and many of the concepts used and studied in marketing have been applied to the use of the identity concept in brand management. The identity approach is hence multidimensional and draws on a selection of very diverse academic fields such as graphic design and strategic management, organizational culture studies and organizational behaviour. Before seeking a proper understanding of the assumptions underlying the identity approach it is therefore necessary to know how the identity concept has been played out in the field of marketing prior to its adaptation to a brand management context.

Box 5.1 The identity concept adopted from marketing

There were two main streams of practical use of and research in the identity concept in marketing before it became important in a brand management context. One focused on visual identity while the other focused on behavioural identity. These two concepts and their conceptualization in marketing will be explained here:

Visual identity
Wally Olins is a brand identity pioneer. In his first big publication about corporate brand identity, *The Corporate Personality: An Inquiry into the Nature of Corporate Identity* (1978), he described the rationale of the identity concept. Olins advocates the importance of identity for corporate entities and poses two questions that are still considered pivotal in the identity approach today: *What are we?* and *Who are we?* Olins focuses on answering these questions primarily through a visual expression of the essence of the identity. Still, he acknowledges that identity is not only about appearance but also about behaviour. Olins advocates that corporations use systems of visual identification to build identity as a communication vehicle. The communication should uphold a consistent visual expression while still ensuring that the brand remains fashionable by undergoing continual adaptation to emergent changes.

Behavioural identity
Kennedy laid the ground for the conceptualization of behavioural identity in 1977. She hypothesized that consumers base consumption decisions on their perceptions of company personality to a much greater extent than on rational evaluation of attribute functionality. Consumer perception of identity is, according to Kennedy, based on the total experience of the company the consumer gets through all the contacts consumers have over time with the brand/company. This line of thought adds the employees and their behaviour as a key factor when building identity.

In a brand management context, the key assumption of the identity approach is that all marketing and communication activities should be integrated, aligned and elevated from a product-focused and tactical level to a strategic, corporate level. Only in that way will it be possible to create a coherent company experience for the consumer. It is from that assumption that the idea of corporate branding and integrated market communication stems. The notion of identity is applicable to the individual brand level, but corporate branding plays a vital role in the identity approach because alignment of all communication in one unified identity requires strategic-level brand management. Identity is something that is initiated from inside the company. Some of the questions corporations need to ask themselves are in the identity approach. Who are we? What do we stand for? What do we want to become? Brand value creation is hence dependent on finding the right answers to these questions and implementing them in every aspect of the business.

From product to corporate branding

Traditionally, the general notion of the classic brand management system has been that each individual product must have an individual and distinct product brand identity. However in the identity approach focus is often on a corporate as opposed to product level branding. The idea of corporate branding is the assumption that creating one unified (at corporate level) message across all functions will elevate brand management from a tactical operational discipline involving only the marketing and sales department to a strategic, corporate level involving the whole organization. Creating one unified message across functions hence requires one unified corporate identity.

Corporate branding implies deserting product branding with its narrow marketing-driven focus on tactical, functional processes. Product branding has been criticized for having a too narrow, external perspective, detached from the organization behind the products. Corporate branding is an attempt to accommodate these weaknesses. Product branding is based on short-term advertising ideas, while corporate branding is based on a long-term brand idea. Corporate branding also expands the parameters of differentiation by enabling companies to use their rich heritage actively to create strong brands. Corporate branding involves the whole organization and emphasises the pivotal role employees play if they are to succeed in the creation of a strong corporate brand. Values and beliefs held by employees are key elements in the differentiation strategy. Corporate branding is a 'move towards conceiving more integrated relationships between internal and external stakeholders linking top management, employees, customers and other stakeholders' (Schultz *et al.* 2005, p. 24).

Table 5.1 Product and corporate branding

	Product branding	Corporate branding
Foundation	Individual products	The company/organization
Conceptualization	Marketing, outside–in thinking	Cross-disciplinary, combines inside-out and outside–in thinking
Brand receivers	Consumers	All stakeholders
Core processes	Marketing and communication	Managerial and organizational processes
Difficulties	• Create and sustain differentiation • Involvement of employees and use of organizational cultural heritage • Limited involvement of stakeholders other than consumers	• Alignment of internal and external stakeholders • Create and communicate credible and authentic identity • Involvement of multiple subcultures internally, and multiple stakeholders externally
Brand equity comes from	Superior product attributes, good advertising and communication	The visual and behavioural identity of the corporation

Source Schultz *et al.* (2005), by courtesy of Copenhagen Business School Press.

This is why organizational and managerial processes are in focus in corporate branding: only in that way can the distinctive identity of the corporate brand be reflected in and nurtured by the way the organization works. Strategy making in corporate branding should take a multidisciplinary approach because it involves not only marketing, but multiple functions and departments.

> Alignments between the origin and everyday practices of the organization [organizational culture]; where the organization aspires to go [strategic vision]; how the organization is perceived by external stakeholders [images]; all nested in perceptions of who the organization is [identity].
>
> (Schultz *et al.* 2005, p. 24)

Corporate branding focuses on developing distinctive features of the organization through organizational and managerial processes. Breaking down the silos between marketing (externally focused) and organizational development (internally focused) and using internal organizational resources to build brand identity, image, reputation and corporate branding have increasingly become an integral part of brand management, and practitioners ascribe corporate culture as one of the most important aspects when conceptualizing the domain of identity. The case of how Lego has shifted from a focus on product branding to corporate branding is a good example of how this shift can be done in practice.

Box 5.2   From product to corporate branding at Lego

In the mid-1990s Lego – the fourth biggest producer of toys in the world – was caught in a general decline in the toy market. For most people Lego is synonymous with the Lego brick, which was also the focus internally. The product focus was perceived as an impediment to growth. Lego had to reinvent the company by implementing a shift from product branding to corporate branding. The identity (internally) and image (externally) of Lego underwent analysis. It was found that the image of Lego was indeed strong among many stakeholders as a producer of toys enhancing creativity and learning. The strategic vision of the company had to be aligned with this image. Management moved away from defining themselves as producers of Lego bricks to defining themselves as leaders in the business of creativity and learning.

> *Adapted from* 'Are the strategic stars aligned for your corporate brand' (Hatch and Schultz 2001) and 'Brand culture' (Schroeder and Salzer-Mörling 2006)

The 'brand–consumer' exchange

In the identity approach, a reliable image and reputation are assumed to be key determinants of consumers' brand choice. In the other six brand approaches, the brand–consumer exchange is key. In the identity approach, brand–consumer exchange is expanded to a focus on all potential stakeholders, and not only interaction with consumers. This broader focus and altered perception of who the receivers of brand communications are can be explained with the emphasis on trust and reputation characterizing the identity approach.

There have been countless discussions of the extent to which communication between brand and receiver (here all stakeholders) is linear or the result of a dialogue. The reason for these discussions is that scholars and practitioners involved in the field of brand identity often come from different academic backgrounds. We will run through the different points of view in order to clarify the assumptions of the brand–stakeholder exchange.

- The exchange between brand and stakeholder from a visual and strategic point of view (*corporate identity*) derives its mindset from marketing, graphic design and strategic management. The concept of corporate identity focuses on the creation of a coherent visual identity. The key determinant of success is the ability to control all communication, with the aim of creating an enduring, distinctive and stable brand identity that is communicated *linearly* to all stakeholders.
- Research into the more behavioural aspects of brand identity (*organizational identity*) has its origin in academic disciplines like sociology, anthropology and organization studies.[1] The concept of organizational identity focuses on how behaviour affects brand identity. Identity is believed to be context-dependent and both socially and individually created – hence a social constructivist view of identity, where it is assumed that identity is the result of a co-creation between brand and stakeholder.
- *Image* is defined as the mosaic of brand associations held by stakeholders, hence implying the stakeholder perspective of the exchange. Here the communication may be linear, but stakeholders' reactions are perceived to be a central element in the formation and management of identity.
- *Reputation* is a more long-term gathering of impressions and evaluations of image stored in the long-term memory of consumers and stakeholders. Reputation focuses more on relation building than linear communication.

In recent research of brand identity a multidimensional approach has been adopted where the four perspectives mentioned above are combined. The construction of the brand in the identity approach is hence, in its original form, assumed to be linear, but a social constructionist perspective where a more interaction-based perspective is dominant has come to take up more and more space in the identity approach in the recent years.

In that sense, brand identity has evolved from a rather static, narrow concept focusing on graphic design to a more dynamic, complex and social constructivist view of identity. If identity is context-dependent and socially constructed, it follows that the linear communication process assumed to characterize the 'brand–stakeholder exchange' is also challenged, because the social construction of identity implies that identity is not something that can be formed inside a company and then sent to consumers, who perceive the message exactly as it was intended. In the dynamic view of identity it is perceived that identity is something that is co-created because it is formed both internally (by the company) and externally (by the consumer). This co-creation of identity resulted during the 1990s in a new area of research, namely the research on how to ensure alignment between the *internal* corporate identity and organizational identity and the *external* expressions of brand identity image and reputation: 'To get the most out of corporate brand strategy, three essential elements must be aligned: vision, culture, and image. Aligning these strategic stars takes concentrated management skill and will. Each element is driven by a different constituency' (Hatch and Schultz 2001, p. 131).

Box 5.3 Is identity enduring?

The three characteristics of identity were defined by Albert and Wetten in 1985 as:

- *Central character.* It should capture the essence of the organization.
- *Claimed distinctiveness.* Distinguish the organization from others.
- *Temporal continuity.* It will exhibit continuity over time (enduring).

These three characteristics went unchallenged for a long time until Gioia *et al*. in 2000 challenged that an identity should be enduring and stable. They argued that an identity is relatively fluid and not stable. It is this fluidity and flexibility of the identity that is the strength of many organizations, because it enables them to accommodate rapid environmental changes (Gioia *et al*. 2000). This new perception of identity as being context-dependent and socially constructed introduces a new and more dynamic perspective on identity.

Summary

The identity approach assumes that a strong and coherent brand identity is pivotal for brand value creation. The brand must focus on finding out 'who we are' as an organization in order to facilitate expressing one coherent identity to all stakeholders. Creating this coherent identity often has a corporate rather than a product-level focus and attention has shifted from a focus on the visual representation of product brands to a focus on how organizational behaviour affects identity, and ultimately image and reputation. The perception of the consumer in the identity approach has also evolved. In the earlier days of the identity approach it was believed that brand identity could be managed and controlled entirely by the corporation; the exchange between the brand and the consumer was perceived to be linear. Recent developments have broadened that perception, it has been acknowledged that identity is not enduring but context-dependent, which implies

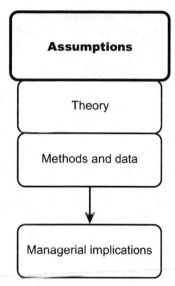

Figure 5.2 Assumptions of the identity approach

that identity cannot be communicated linearly but is the result of negotiation between internal and external shareholders

Theoretical building blocks of the identity approach

The key constructs of the identity approach have changed and broadened along with the shift in focus from product to corporate branding. The ever-continuous evolution of the conceptualization of brand identity has led to a considerable volume of concepts and frameworks of a multidisciplinary nature. Concepts are often used interchangeably and it can be difficult to gain a clear overview of the key constructs, how they relate to each other and, how they can be combined in managerial frameworks.

The core theme of the identity approach is brand identity. Brand identity is made up of four components: *organizational identity, corporate identity, image* and *reputation*. The four supporting themes can be divided into two main categories: the internal and the external elements of brand identity. Corporate identity and organizational identity are supporting themes representing theories used for the creation and maintenance and research of brand identity internally. The two supporting themes, image and reputation, represent theories used to build, manage and research brand identity externally.

Having explained the nature of the four supporting themes and the core theme, we will turn to two frameworks focusing on the alignment of the four supporting themes in a way that strengthens the core theme of brand identity. *The corporate brand tool kit* and *the AC2ID framework* take the understanding

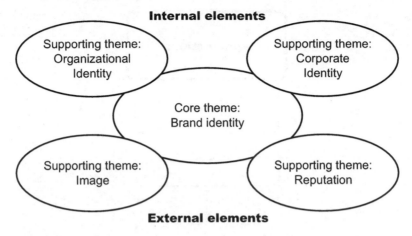

Figure 5.3 Supporting themes of the identity approach

of the theoretical building blocks further by suggesting how a corporate brand should be managed.

Supporting theme: corporate identity (internal)

The first internal supporting theme of brand identity is corporate identity. Corporate identity is an assembly of visual, physical or behavioural cues representing the company, making it immediately recognizable to consumers and other stakeholders. The academic literature forms two clusters representing two perspectives on how to create and manage corporate identity: a visual perspective using visual means to build brand identity and a strategic perspective focused on the strategic vision of the brand.

The visual identity is mainly concerned with the way the organization expresses itself visually and should ideally be outward signs and symbols of the inward commitment of the organization. The visual school focuses on tangible visual manifestations of the corporate identity and on how these manifestations can affect leadership behaviour and company structure and vice versa. This perspective has its origin in graphic design, where focus is on the creation and management of logo, the name, colour, sound, touch and smell of brand identity that ensures optimum reflection of brand identity. From the visual school's perspective, corporate identity can be aligned through graphic design, by using systems of visual identification. These systems are useful because they can act as catalysts for change, vehicles of communication, and tools to ensure that the visual expression of brand identity is up to date. Recognition is in this perspective important because it breeds favourability. The visual school has often been criticized for being too narrowly conceived and misunderstood in practice because of too much focus on the design, name and logo. Corporate identity is, however, also about merging behaviour and the visual identity; it is only when behaviour and appearance are linked that corporate identity emerges.

The fact of the matter is that when an organization has a clear idea about itself, what its business is, what its priorities are, how it wants to conduct itself, how it wants to be perceived, its identity falls fairly easily in place.

(Olins 1979, p. 60)

The visual expression of brand identity becomes much easier if identity is also embedded in a common corporate behavioural standard. Signs and symbols of identity are merely myths, but they can become reality if they also act as catalysts for change. They need to act as symbols both internally and externally of the corporate identity of the organization. Hence corporate identity can not be confined merely to the visual expression, it is also the way people who work in an organization think, behave and work. The focus is still to ensure the right expression outwards as opposed to the organizational identity, where the goal and focus are to ensure the right behaviour, culture and expression inward.

The strategic school focuses on the central idea of the organization (mission, vision and philosophy). The strategic school links the corporate strategy with brand identity; how it can be expressed and communicated to ensure that it is reflected in the corporate image and reputation. The strategic school of corporate identity focuses on defining internal aspects of the corporate identity: *who they are*; *what the core competences are*; and *how these can be utilized* to ensure the right expression of brand identity externally. The strategic school of corporate identity emphasizes that behaviour to a greater extent than appearance determines corporate identity.

Corporate identity hence contributes to brand identity in two ways. First, it ensures that input from strategic management – the vision and mission the corporation has for the brand – is implemented in the creation and management of brand identity. Second, it ensures that the brand identity is represented visually through management of product design, logo name and so on, encompassing all visual representations of brand identity. Recently the acknowledgement of the importance of behaviour has been underpinned by research pointing out how difficult it can be to translate managerial and strategic vision into brand identity. To ensure that this process is done accurately, deep insight into organizational behaviour and culture is needed. This is hence the next supporting theme of the identity approach.

Supporting theme: organizational identity (internal)

The second supporting theme of brand identity is organizational identity: it refers to the behavioural and cultural aspects affecting brand identity. Key concepts are organizational behaviour, culture and structure; these are all elements affecting how organizational members perceive *who they are* and *what they stand for* as a company or organization. The organizational identity provides a cognitive and emotional foundation on which organizational members build attachment. It also sets the scene for how employees create meaningful relationships with their organization. Organizational culture is closely linked to employee commitment and performance, which is why organizational identity is so pivotal for consumers' evaluation of brand identity.

Box 5.4 Culture in the identity approach

In the identity approach, culture is defined at micro-level (while the cultural approach highlights branding in the context of macro-level culture). In the micro-level culture definition of the identity approach, organizational culture is to be understood as a concept that provides a local context or frame for the organizational identity. The organizational culture furthermore contributes with symbolic material to the construction of corporate identity. Culture is regarded as the expression of everyday life in an organization – the values (the 'taken-for-granted assumptions'), the behaviour ('the way we do things around here') and the formal internal and external communication as well as the more informal communication of internal organizational stories.

Source Hatch and Schultz (2000)

As mentioned previously, this line of thought originates from the idea that people base their evaluations of brand identity (the brand image) on their total experience of a company. This notion makes employees the pivotal instrument for brand management. The ability of employees to deliver the content and promise of the brand in the long run creates corporate image and reputation.

The 'living the brand' construct is often used in this perspective. The concept describes how organizational members can become so attached to the brand that it becomes an important part of the creation and enhancement of brand equity. Employees are expected to 'live the brand', acting as brand ambassadors and co-creators of brand equity. The brand is brought to life in the interaction between consumer and employee, demanding a high level of commitment to the brand from the employee. In an ideal world, organizational culture is altered and nursed by embedding certain values in the culture and behaviour using tools such as storytelling, internal training and employee branding. This process aligns employee behaviour with the brand vision and brand identity. Since employees increasingly demand empowerment and a meaningful workplace, and companies demand committed employees, this approach seems like a win–win situation for both employees and companies. But in reality it is often different; the proven effect of internal employee branding (the storytelling and value-based management tools used to alter organizational culture) is questionable. Several studies conclude that the majority of employees do not really buy in on internal branding efforts long term. Once activities have died down, resistance to change and old routines win the battle. Hence, managing brand identity through the creation and enhancement of organizational identity is not an easy task, but if it is done with success, the result can be an unbeatably strong and unique brand identity. The methods of how to go about creating an organizational culture as a brand manager and some of the problems and how to overcome them are further explained in 'methods' (p. 64) and 'managerial implications' (p. 70).

Supporting theme: corporate image (external)

Images are the basic element of thought, and the concept of corporate image is key in the identity approach, since it is part of the external representation of the brand identity. The aim is to project one single image to all stakeholders, ensuring a consistent perception of brand image among stakeholders. Corporate image is a mosaic of impressions formed by a variety of formal and informal signals projected by the company. From this mosaic the recipient pieces together the corporate image. The corporate image is hence not what the company believes it to be, but exists in the mind of the audience. Corporate image is the result of a mosaic of attitudes commencing within the company with the employees and their perception of the company. Continuously measuring the corporate image is an important source of keeping track of how consumers and other stakeholders perceive and value brand identity.

Supporting theme: reputation (external)

Some scholars argue that the research and literature about reputation can be categorized as one of the schools of thought about how to create and manage the corporate image. We define the concept of reputation in a category by itself, because the mechanisms applying to this field are quite different from the mechanisms that apply to the concept of image.

During the 1990s the concept of reputation gained popularity particularly in practice. As opposed to the image concept it takes a long time to form a reputation, because it is based on what the company has done over time and how it has behaved, rather than being a result of short-term communication and advertising as is the case for the formation of image. The corporate reputation construct is mainly used externally to measure consumer evaluations of brand identity, but can also be used internally to guide employee behaviour. Corporate reputation can also reveal the standards that govern organizational behaviour. So how does a company ensure a good reputation? Too often it does not – because reputation management is often not considered unless the reputation is threatened.

The key drivers of reputation are PR and the communication and accentuation of corporate stories of success and corporate social responsibility. Reputation can be enhanced through corporate communication, but is more effective when communicated by an independent third party. This is one of the reasons why increasingly higher percentages of company expenditure are invested in the building of PR and good relations with key players in the media. PR can be estimated by analysing the brand's position in the market place measured by competitive effectiveness and market leadership.

Core theme: brand identity

An in-depth understanding of the four supporting themes adds up to the core theoretical concept of the identity approach; namely brand identity. By

Table 5.2 The internal and external supporting themes adding up to brand identity

Internal	*Corporate Identity* • Visual expression of brand identity • Strategic vision of brand identity • Top management	*Organizational Identity* • Behavioural aspects of brand identity • Organizational culture • Employees

External	*Image*
	• Short-term
	• Mosaic of stakeholder associations
	• Exists entirely in the minds of
	   stakeholders
		Reputation
		• Long-term evaluation of brand
		   identity
		• Stakeholder evaluations of brand
		   actions
		• Key tools: PR and personal relations

combining all components in figure 5.4 you will have a clear picture of the components of brand identity.

After having gained a sound understanding of the elements that comprise the brand identity construct, the next section will elaborate on how these elements, in interplay, can be managed to construct and enhance brand identity. 'Alignment' is the key word if the management of all four elements is to result in a unified communication of a coherent brand identity to all shareholders.

Aligning brand identity

This section will explain how the elements of brand identity (corporate identity, organizational identity, image and reputation) in interplay form brand identity through proper alignment. It offers an introduction to two key theoretical frameworks used to manage and align the elements influencing brand identity. The two frameworks selected and described here have been chosen because they express the key concern that most recent frameworks for the management of brand identity have in common,

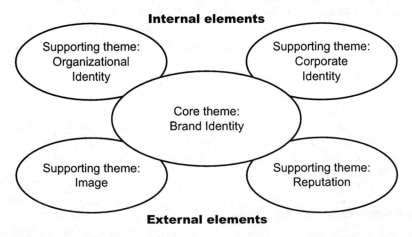

Figure 5.4 Brand identity: the core theme and alignment frameworks of the identity approach

namely the alignment of identity, culture, image and reputation. This alignment is the pivotal task in the brand identity management process. The *corporate brand toolkit* developed by Hatch and Schultz is based on research in more than 100 companies over more than ten years. The toolkit was published in *Harvard Business Review* in 2001. Balmer (Balmer and Greyser 2003) developed another influential framework, the *AC2ID framework*. Like the corporate brand toolkit, it focuses on the identity types present in a company and how these identity types should be managed in order to ensure alignment. The AC2ID framework is based on extensive research in the corporate industry field, but has also incorporated recent trends from the academic literature. It was first published in *California Management Review* in 2002.

The corporate brand toolkit

The corporate brand toolkit identifies strategic vision, organizational culture and stakeholders' images as the strategic stars of the organization.

- *Strategic vision*: central idea behind what the company does. The strategic vision expresses future management aspirations.
- *Organizational culture*: internal values and beliefs. Basic assumptions that embody the heritage of the company, manifested in the ways employees feel about the company across rank, reflected in behaviour.
- *Stakeholders' images*: how external stakeholders perceive the company, in other words, it is the outside world's overall impression of the company.

The alignment of these stars is the means to the creation of a strong and successful corporate brand identity. These elements are comparable to the four supporting themes: strategic vision equals corporate identity, organizational culture and organizational identity share common perspective, and stakeholder images are equivalent to the two external supporting themes, image and reputation.

The alignment of the three strategic stars requires that attention be paid to all three elements simultaneously. Misalignments can be detected by a series of diagnostic questions to all stakeholders internally as well as externally, uncovering the relationship between the three elements and potential gaps.

The aim with this series of questions is to uncover gaps between either of the elements, represented by, respectively, employees, management and external stakeholders. It is a way to see whether if the strategic vision of top management is in line with consumer demands and if there is sufficient internal employee support for the strategic vision. Analysis of identity gaps should ideally be conducted concurrently to ensure ongoing alignment of the strategic elements that are key to the creation of brand identity. After having identified any identity gaps, it is essential that the information gathered is used to make an action plan for how vision and image can undergo a process of realignment. If the problem is misalignment between vision and organizational culture, then the consequences could be a brand identity promising too much compared with what employees are prepared or able to deliver. This type of misalignment problem requires that either

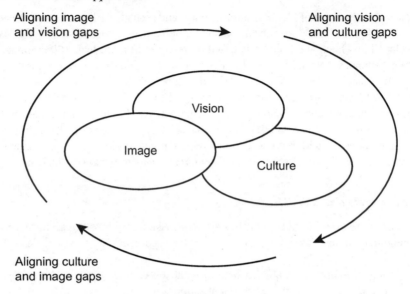

Figure 5.5 Alignment of the strategic stars of brand identity; from Hatch and Schultz, 'Are your strategic stars aligned for your corporate brand?' *Harvard Business Review*, February 2001, reprinted by permission of *Harvard Business Review*, copyright © 2001 by the Harvard Business School Publishing Corporation; all rights reserved

the strategic vision is downplayed or that an organizational culture in line with the strategic vision of the company is nurtured and developed. The identification and analysis of gaps between the strategic stars of brand identity lay the foundation for a customized strategy for aligning identified gaps that can ensure the continuous alignment of the elements of brand identity (Hatch and Schultz 2001).

The AC2ID framework

The AC2ID framework developed by Balmer and Greyser (2003) focuses on the alignment of five identities in the corporation. The assumption is similar to that of the corporate brand toolkit, since it is that multiple identities do indeed exist and only when they are aligned continually can a strong brand identity emerge and strive. Dissonance between the five identity types will weaken the overall brand identity and ultimately corporate performance. AC2ID is an acronym for the five identity types Balmer in the framework identifies as key for brand identity.

- *Actual*: the actual identity, organizational behaviour and everyday reality of the corporation.
- *Communicated*: the brand identity expressed through all sources of communication.
- *Conceived*: refers to the image/reputation of the corporation – how do stake-holders conceive brand identity?

- *Ideal*: represents the optimum positioning of the organization in the market at any given time.
- *Desired*: lives in the hearts and minds of the corporate leaders – equivalent of the strategic vision.

In the AC2ID framework the four supporting themes are also reflected in the five identity types since the desired and communicated identity cover the same topics as the supporting theme of corporate identity. The actual identity and the organizational identity are comparable and the conceived identity and ideal identity cover the external elements equivalent to the supporting themes of image and reputation. Management should on a continuous basis ensure that these identities are aligned, meanwhile also updating the ideal and desired identity according to changes and developments in the business environment. Overlooking or not monitoring the multiple identities of a brand can have fatal consequences. The AC2ID framework can assist top management in the research and management of multiple identities and guide the company through identity changes and realignment processes of brand identity. Especially in situations where identity is challenged (e.g. mergers or acquisitions) brand identity management is crucial.

Box 5.5 Misaligned identities: the case of Body Shop

The founder of the Body Shop, Anita Roddick, from the beginning ran the Body Shop according to her environmental and socially responsible values. Her personal values (desired identity) had a significant influence on the positioning and branding of the Body Shop as a socially responsible company against animal testing, etc. An investigation of whether the actual practices of the corporation could live up to these values led to accusations that it did not live up to its own standards. This is clearly a case of misalignment of the desired identity in relation to the actual identity. Media attention led to consumer suspicion, with the result that the conceived identity also became misaligned with the desired identity. The misalignment of identities in the case of Body Shop is a good example of what often happens when small companies grow fast, and the growing distance between the ideals and dreams of the founder and the actual behaviour is inevitable if well managed brand identity-building activities are not in place to make up for this lack of presence in every day procedure by the founder.

Adapted from 'Multiple identities of the corporation'
(Balmer and Greyser 2003)

Summary

The theoretical building blocks of brand identity consist of the four supporting themes behind the core concept of brand identity. Two of these cover internal aspects: corporate identity, representing the visual and strategic elements of brand

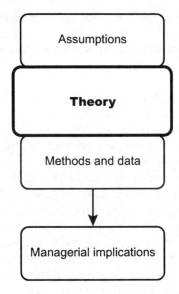

Figure 5.6 Theory of the identity approach

identity, and organizational identity, representing the behavioural and cultural aspects. The two supporting themes covering the external aspects are: image and reputation. Image is the short-term mosaic of images perceived by the consumer. The reputation is a long-term compilation of all image evaluations of brand identity made by the consumer. These four supporting themes each contribute to the brand identity construct. Pivotal in the recent theoretical frameworks for the management of brand identity is the alignment of the multiple identities of the corporation. Two key frameworks are the *corporate brand toolkit* focusing on the alignment between vision/organizational culture and image. The *AC2ID framework* works with the alignment of actual, communicated, conceived, ideal and desired identity.

Methods and data of the identity approach

The methods and data used in the identity approach are diverse and have their origin in different research traditions, due to the different focus (internal and external) and origins of the four supporting themes of the brand identity construct. The methods used to collect data about organizational identity stem from anthropological and culture studies, while the study of corporate identity has a more heuristic approach deriving material from strategic management, the visual expression and history of the corporation. Researching the image element of brand identity requires insights into the cognitive processes that consumers and stakeholders go through when evaluating a brand identity and requires methods from cognitive psychology. Finally, the reputation element requires more focus on the long-term interaction between the brand and the consumer or stakeholder. In the attempt to make the overview of these diverse methods more comprehensible, the section is divided into two main parts. The first part accounts for the methods and data used when researching corporate identity and organizational identity. The second part offers an overview of the methods and data used to research image and reputation.

The internal elements of brand identity: methods for the study of corporate identity and organizational identity

How to uncover corporate identity

Corporate identity is an expression of the strategic aspirations top management has for the brand in the shape of, for instance, a strategic vision for the brand or the corporation as a whole. The corporate identity also refers to the visual identity of the brand. The methods for gathering data about the two differ:

- When uncovering the strategic perspective on corporate identity, it is mainly historical sources about the development of the vision and strategy of the company and brand specific historical records that are used to get an overview of the corporate identity and its development. Semi-structured interviews, storytelling methods and heuristic analysis are the more specific methods used as a supplement to the more formal records of how the strategic vision has developed over time.
- Data about how the visual expression of the corporate identity has evolved over time must also be researched when uncovering corporate identity.

After having uncovered these two sources of visual and strategic identity representing the more formal aspects of identity expressed by the company, the behavioural and cultural aspects of identity must also be uncovered.

How to uncover organizational identity

Research into organizational identity (organizational culture and behaviour) draws on methods from various research traditions, such as anthropology, sociology, cultural and organizational studies. In the academic milieu there has been a fierce discussion about how organizational culture ought to be perceived and studied. However, during the last decade methods using a multi-paradigm approach, combining the different views and starting points, have emerged. High-performing brands often share the characteristic that they use organizational culture as a tool to nurture high employee commitment and loyalty. A strong organizational culture is consistent over time and values and norms guide action and language. There are several sources of a strong organizational identity: the style of top management, everyday organizational behaviour, and embedded norms and values. How these elements contribute to organizational identity is the subject of analysis when uncovering organizational culture.

The basic perception of organizational identity has evolved from a static and functionalistic view to a more dynamic constructivist one. In the functionalist view, understanding culture is about identifying and categorizing cultural stereo-types. From a symbolic and interpretive approach, culture is embedded in and expressed through people's actions and language. Finally, in the constructivist view of culture, the strength of organizational culture is defined by its ability to adapt to changes in the environment. In this view the strength of an organizational culture is found in its ability to learn, change and adapt to market demands. This evolution is reflected in the recent multi-paradigm methods of studying organizational culture. One of the key frameworks for the study of organizational culture offers a three-perspective approach. The three perspectives reflect the inherent ambiguity and forces of organizational culture.

The *integration* perspective represents the functionalist perspective and the forces in the organization oriented towards consensus and consistency. This

Table 5.3 Three perspectives on organizational culture

Characteristics	Integration	Differentiation	Fragmentation
Level of consensus	Organization-wide consensus	Subcultural consensus	Consensus appears only temporarily in clusters
Consistency of cultural manifestations	Consistent	Inconsistent	Complex
How ambiguity is perceived	Ambiguity is excluded and avoided	Ambiguity between subcultures is acknowledged	Ambiguity rather than consensus is assumed
The primary creators of culture	Founder or top management	Groups of subcultures	Individuals
Where to look for organizational culture	The formal culture dispersed by top management	The different levels of culture are played out in different functions or other groupings: a mix of formal and informal culture	Culture exists at an individual level
How to uncover organizational culture	Join all meetings and go through all internal communication and formal activities for employees	Get in deep with every function/ department or subculture to learn how they are diverse	It is by getting to know the individual employee that culture can be uncovered because it is assumed that there are as many interpretations of organizational culture as there are individual employees

Source Adapted from Martin (2002).

perspective is usually found in the messages and activities initiated by top management to create and enhance organizational culture.

The *differentiation* perspective represents a more interpretive approach. The differentiation perspective assumes that cultural consensus exists within different subcultures and groupings, but not on an organization-wide level. The manifestations of organizational culture are hence not consistent throughout the organization. Ambiguity and the drivers of organizational culture are to be found in the consistency within subgroups and in the ambiguity distinguishing these different subgroups.

In the third, and last, perspective of fragmentation the more constructivist perspective is represented. Here, it is assumed that an organizational culture can display a multitude of views. In the fragmentation perspective, there is no consensus and the relation between manifestations of organizational culture is complex. Only a combination of the three levels – the whole organization, subgroups and individual level of research – can give an accurate and complete snapshot of the cultural web and drivers of organizational culture.

In practice, the data collection focuses on the manifestations of organizational culture expressed through a combination of different elements. These elements illustrate that not only is it essential to encompass different perspectives in a research plan to ensure a deep and full understanding; grasping organizational culture also requires breadth. The manifestations form the cultural web of manifestations that in combination define a specific organizational culture.

Organizational culture is best studied qualitatively and through embedding oneself in the cultural settings. The researcher must seek detailed and holistic descriptions based on intensive fieldwork to ensure understanding of how the cultural manifestations express a certain organizational identity. Since intensive fieldwork can be time-consuming, the ethnographic approach can adopt a clinical

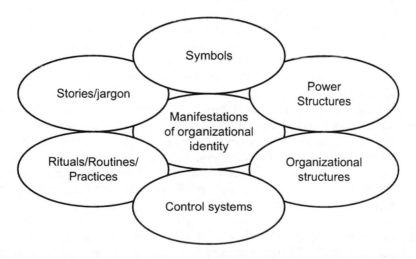

Figure 5.7 Manifestations of organizational identity (culture)

perspective, where qualitative interviews are the main research instrument. But in order to really understand a culture and interpret manifestations correctly, interviews and observation may not always be enough. Interaction with and immersion into the culture can be necessary to ensure the right interpretation (refer to chapter 9 for a fuller description of ethnographic methods).

The external elements of brand identity: methods for the study of image and reputation

The object of analysis when collecting data and learning about image and reputation is, on the one hand, the positioning of the company image in relation to competitors and, on the other hand, research of image from the receivers' point of view. When studying the image and reputation of a brand in relation to competitors, surveys and laddering techniques are frequently used. But in order to get a deep understanding of how and why consumers associate a certain image with a brand, methods from cognitive and social psychology are used to investigate consumer perceptions and evaluations of image and reputation. Attitudes and perceptions are key elements when trying to understand the formation of an image and the mechanisms behind how image and reputation can be studied:

- *Perception.* Human beings perceive through sensory processes involving sight, sound, taste and hearing. After having absorbed inputs with our senses, it is time to perceive them. Perception is the process of meaning creation where the brain identifies input patterns and recognizes certain elements as being intertwined.
- *Cognition.* Before being able to think about sensory inputs and messages, they must be perceived and recognized. Consumers construct mental representations (images) and develop an understanding of what they have perceived – recognition process. This process takes place through abstract cognitive units rather than in language based units. These cognitive units are created through the use of images, words and symbols. Cognitive units link object (apple) and attribute (green), and action (donation of money to charity) to subject (a corporation). The cognition process is hence mental images capturing spatial relationships and ensuring recognition.
- *Attitudes* are the general evaluations people make of themselves, other people, objects and issues. Attitudes are emotional and influence how people behave. Attitudes can make people react. (In brand management it is important to know exactly which brand initiatives make consumers react = consume.) It is difficult to predict to what extent attitudes affect action, but one thing is sure: people are more predisposed to act when some kind of change of circumstance causes them to evaluate their attitudes.

Understanding how cognitive units work and what makes consumers change their attitudes and maybe change consumption patterns is very valuable when researching brand image and reputation. Any research design for the investigation of the external elements of brand identity should reflect this knowledge about how consumers perceive, form attitudes and ultimately act. Image is the result of short-term advertising or other communication efforts and reputation is formed based on a more long-term evaluation of brand actions and how the consumer interprets these and the motives behind them. Analysis of the contact points between brand and receiver is more important when collecting data about reputation. However, no matter whether the subject of analysis is image or reputation, knowledge about how consumers perceive and ultimately evaluate brand interaction is essential.

Box 5.6 Doing a study of brand identity yourself

- Since the four elements of brand identity are studied with very different methods, make sure that you differentiate and carefully select the right methods to study each of the four elements of brand identity.
- Initiate a long-term continuous research of reputation. Use a combination of surveys, questionnaires and in-depth interviews.
- For the study of image initiate the research with explorative qualitative methods, where free association methods subtract all potential feedback and associations. Finalize and make the results useful to guide managerial decisions by using quantitative methods to uncover the salience of the complete list of feedback until narrowed down to a few central insights.
- For the study of the internal elements, plan the research, ensure full access to all meetings and processes. Without full access you will not get a complete and accurate picture of the organizational identity or the corporate identity.
- Immerse yourself in the everyday environment of the objects: watch, listen, learn and act.
- Initiate the process of changing the object that is observed (mainly organizational identity) according to the observations made already. Changes should not be stand-alone activities, but should be implemented in every day processes.
- Observe how existing routines or other manifestations of organizational identity are affected.
- Make sure to include all levels and functions in all actions and observations, not only in the process of collecting data, but also in the data interpretation process. This will ensure a more accurate and deep understanding of organizational identity and its interplay with the corporate identity
- Reflect on how the initiated changes were received, what can be done differently to improve results. What have you learned about the organizational culture that is new and requires new methods of observation and maybe new actions?
- Make sure that all the four elements are studied simultaneously and that the results from the four studies are merged in an overall plan for how to respond to the results

Summary

The methods used and the data collected in the identity approach vary depending on which of the four supporting themes is the subject to be studied. Data about corporate identity are collected with the use of heuristic methods. The aim is to study the historical and current strategic development and visual expression of brand identity. When researching organizational identity, the methods draw on inspiration from anthropology and cultural studies, where participation, immersion and extensive fieldwork are a prerequisite for gaining the deep and rich insights necessary to understand the underlying drivers of the cultural manifestations. Image is best studied by using a combination of qualitative methods for the explorative phase, supplemented by a quantitative phase making the results managerially useful. The methods originate from cognitive and social psychology and the focus is on consumer/stakeholder perception, cognition and attitudes formed in the process of continuous evaluation of brand image and reputation.

Managerial implications

A strong brand identity can be the source of competitive and financial strength. However, building and managing brand identity is a complex and difficult management task. Research and management of the four supporting themes adding up to brand identity require very diverse data collection methods and a variety of skills and processes to implement in practice, because they respond to very different constituencies. This underpins the need for a carefully planned strategy and sensitive approach when managing brand identity.

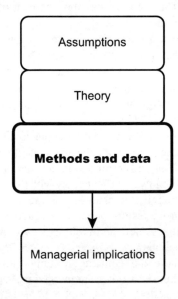

Figure 5.8 Methods and data of the identity approach

Where most companies fail is getting the organizational identity right, aligned with the remaining three supporting themes. Also, 'Ignoring issues of identity is not a feasible option, particularly for managers. Indeed, it only tends to exacerbate the problem. Identity does not go away, and can surface with a vengeance' (Balmer and Greyser 2003, p. 34). The involvement of employees in the co-creation of brand identity is extremely difficult and requires great skill and persistence. This section introduces the reader to the managerial guidelines of how the four supporting themes – corporate identity, organizational identity, image and reputation – can be managed and aligned into a coherent brand identity.

Aligning vision and culture in practice

Any management process and activity, big or small, requires the right insight into the elements that are to be managed. In the case of brand identity, the goal is not to get information about the supporting themes separately, but to observe and analyse the interplay between them. As described in the section on theoretical building blocks, it is their alignment that is the key to a strong brand identity. The pivotal goal of brand management in the identity approach is therefore the alignment of the four supporting themes: image, reputation, corporate identity and organizational identity. In practice, these elements have different constituencies and different drivers; top management drives the vision (corporate identity), while the employees are drivers of culture (organizational identity). The drivers of image

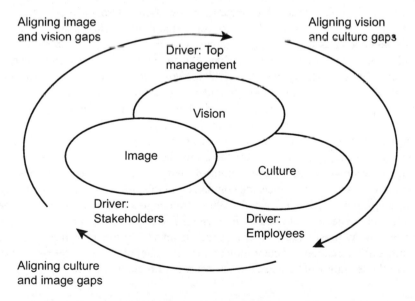

Figure 5.9 Drivers of the alignment process of brand identity; from Hatch and Schultz, 'Are your strategic stars aligned for your corporate brand?' *Harvard Business Review*, February 2001, reprinted by permission of *Harvard Business Review*, copyright © 2001 by the Harvard Business School Publishing Corporation; all rights reserved

and reputation are all stakeholders. These different constituencies require that information is gathered from multiple sources and a variety of methods are used before misalignments or opportunities are uncovered.

Gaps between vision and culture occur when the strategic vision top management plans for the organization is not in line with the reality (organizational identity) of the corporation – when employees are not able or willing to live up to the ambitious goals set by management. To uncover these gaps between vision and culture, it must be investigated if and to what extent employees support the visions planned by top management. It is also essential to uncover if all functions or subcultures (from R&D across production, marketing and eventually the sales force and pre-sales service function) in the organization approve and support the vision. If not all subcultures or groupings of an organization work to achieve the same goal it is very difficult to build a coherent brand identity. Since the vision and culture are the primary drivers of difficult-to-imitate differentiation, it is also important to investigate the vision and culture of the corporation stand out compared with the competition and hence deliver sufficient grounds for the differentiation of brand identity. A general tendency is that management practices have evolved from focus on control mechanisms and extensive identity programme manuals to focus more on empowerment, the use of experience and story telling to build commitment and cultural affiliation.

Detecting identity gaps

Gaps between image and culture occur if employees do not deliver on the brand promise and thereby disappoint consumer expectations. Here, the focus of investigation is on the extent to which employees' perception of brand identity is in line with stakeholder associations and evaluations of brand image and reputation. It is vital to uncover how brand stimuli and the interaction between employees as carriers of brand identity and stakeholders contribute to the formation of brand image. Finally, gaps between image and vision are an expression of a situation where top management is alienated from what consumers expect and perceive of the brand identity. Misalignments between vision and image can result in consumers rejecting new product launches or marketing activities if they do not feel that it is the right direction for the brand. Misalignment between vision and image is serious and can be a symptom of inertia or lack of sufficient consumer intelligence. As a consequence, the company will miss out on market potential and consumer loyalty. To detect whether there are dangers of misalignment between vision and image, it must be identified who the primary stakeholders of the brand are and what these stakeholders expect from the brand identity. Effective, continuous interaction and communication with stakeholders are required in order to avoid misalignment between the two sources of brand identity.

Aligning identity gaps

In practice, brand managers can use knowledge about the multiple identities and their alignment to manage the brand in a direction that is in line with consumers'

Table 5.4 Detecting identity gaps

Gap between (according to the corporate brand toolkit):	Vision/Culture	Culture/Image	Image/Vision
Theoretical elements	Corporate identity and organizational identity	Organizational identity and image	Image and corporate identity
Gaps between (according to the AC2ID framework):	Desired and ideal identity misaligned with the actual identity	The actual identity misaligned with the communicated and conceived identity	The conceived identity misaligned with the desired and ideal identity
Constituencies	Top management and employees	Employees and stakeholders	Stakeholders and top management
Questions	• Does the everyday reality reflect the values the vision requires? • Is the vision supported by all functions and subcultures of the company? • Are vision and culture sufficiently differentiated from competition?	• What perception of image do stakeholders express? • How do employees perceive company image? • How do stakeholders and employees interact?	• Who are the stakeholders of the company? • What do the stakeholders want and expect from the company? • How well is knowledge about stakeholders' images communicated to top management and vice versa?
How to solve misalignment	Ensure that not only communication but also out-of-the-box activities and continuous training ensure that employees understand and support the corporate identity	Set up organizational identity in a way that supports the image and reputation of the brand identity. Measure all contact points between stakeholders and employees against image and reputation	Make sure that top management is informed by customer insights and new tendencies are detected. Avoid inertia and self-consumed irrelevant brand launches or activities by taking image perceptions seriously

perceptions of image, the strategic visions and hope for what the brand should achieve in the future, and the actual behaviour and organizational culture of the brand. After having uncovered the state of the image, corporate identity and the organizational identity and their respective alignment issues, a process of enhancing and alignment must take place. The tools used to manage this process can be divided into five cyclical steps:

- *Stating.* State the vision and identity of the corporate brand. (Who are we and what do we want to become?) Articulating core values and identity behind brand *establishes the corporate identity.*
- *Organizing.* Link vision with culture and image practices. How can we reorganize to achieve fit? Cross-functional structure and process changes *establish the frame for developing the appropriate organizational identity.*
- *Involving.* Involve stakeholders through culture and image. Engage employees in execution and involve consumer images. Get input from multiple sources.
- *Integrating.* Integrate culture and image around a new brand identity. Align the organization behind the brand. *Align the multiple identities across internal functions.*
- *Monitoring.* Track corporate branding gaps and brand performance.

Challenges when building brand identity

Brand-building activities based on the line of thought behind the identity approach are often criticized for being an ego-stroking waste of time with no relevance for either consumers or stakeholders. To avoid this identity trap and

Table 5.5 Aligning identity gaps

Activity	Cycle 1: State	Cycle 2: Organize	Cycle 3: Involve	Cycle 4: Integrate
Key process	State the identity for the corporate brand and link this identity to corporate vision	Link corporate vision to organizational culture and the image	Involve stakeholders through organizational culture and the image	Integrate corporate vision, organizational culture and the image around the new brand identity
Key question	Who are we as an organization and what do we stand for?	How can we reorganize the corporate brand?	How can we involve internal and external stakeholders in the corporate brand?	How can we integrate corporate vision, organizational culture and the image of the corporate brand?
Key concerns	• Make company wide audit of brand expression • Revisit brand cultural heritage • Analyse brand images among stakeholders	• Create a coherent brand organization • Provide managerial foundation for implementation processes	• Does the company have a shared cultural mindset? • Ensure active inclusion of global stakeholders perceptions	• Integrate the brand across markets and business areas

Source Adapted from Schultz *et al.* (2005).

enhance the probability of success, the objectives of the brand identity building campaign must be clearly defined and results must be carefully measured against objectives. Is the object to create awareness, the creation of favourable attitudes or the enhancement of organizational identity, and why? Is the goal externally oriented or is the focus more internal, with the aim to increase employer motivation and attract better recruits? No matter what the goal is, it is important to be very clear on why brand identity activities are needed and what the company wishes to achieve with such activities.

It is also necessary to consider whether the organizational structure of the company suits the aims of brand identity. It is important to understand the forces that drive particular types of organizations. Having established goals and organizational structure, it is time to involve employees in the brand identity project. Often, too much energy is used on attempts to change employee attitudes and behaviour in practice. Best-practice cases have indicated that efforts ought to focus on the translation of brand values into real-life experiences that can be used on any occasion. It is often difficult to get all employees to actively support brand identity programmes. A good way to ensure daily involvement and commitment can be to give employees 'out of the box' experiences on a regular basis through events and sponsorships; this can provide real-life experiences, building commitment and sharing. Instead of trying to implement and align identities through communication only, these real-life experiences can inspire employees to activate the brand promise in their everyday working environment. Sharing of real-life experiences among employees is a good way to bring the brand identity to life internally and ensure that employees live the values and the organizational identity of the brand.

Box 5.7 Living the brand: all about the people of Quiksilver

'Living the brand' is a construct that describes brands building on ideas that are so powerful that employees engage to such an extent that they are not only employed by, but 'live the brand'. These brands build unforeseen employee involvement and commitment. Employees internalize brand values: brand values, symbols and stories keep employees' behaviour aligned with the values of the brand. This enables them to deliver the brand promise to consumers, hence acting as key co-creators of brand equity. The companies succeeding in this benefit in terms of higher productivity, enhanced financial performance and greater intellectual capital.

Australian surfers Alan Green and John Law founded Quiksilver in 1970. Greenie and Law started Quiksilver by redesigning the surfer's board shorter using a fabric that dried rapidly, with Velcro and snap closure. These features were exactly what board riders demanded and the product became a huge success. The founders had insights into the needs of board riders because they themselves were part of that environment. This insight was what laid the foundation for the company. This foundation and the implied closeness to the environment of their consumers is still a priority. Today, Quiksilver call themselves a board-riding company, indicating that employees share the passion for board riding. Consumer involvement is underpinned by much sponsorship of surfers and of board-riding events that Quiksilver supports or arranges around the world. Employees at Quiksilver live the Quiksilver brand, getting actively involved in board-riding communities.

The cultural and historical heritage of a company can also be used to build brand identity. The company does not necessarily need to have been in business for many years before it is able to use history or culture actively in the building of brand identity. Also a unique organizational identity or a charismatic CEO can be the source of corporate and organizational identity.

Box 5. 8 Do's and don'ts of the identity approach

Do	Don't
Disperse shared vision	Don't neglect diverse interpretations and loose vitality and dynamics
Disperse shared organizational culture	Don't get stuck in the pitfall of group-think and path dependence
Management should be strong, visible, and provide guidance	Don't neglect subcultures and diverse organizational functions
Be cross-functional, involve the whole organization	Don't cut off innovation and new ideas that require deep insight and exploration of new paths
Incorporate change	Don't jeopardize the distinctiveness of brand identity
Listen to the market and be open to co-creation of brand identity	Don't go with short-term market trends and lose core competences
Embed brand identity management strategically	Don't leave brand management to top management solely
Align corporate identity, organizational identity, image and reputation continuously	Don't overcomplicate matters and get lost in complexity
Make sure that brand identity evolves continuously	Don't revolutionize brand identity

Run campaigns internally before they are run externally	Don't fail to communicate and activate to ensure real life experiences internally before brand activities are initiated externally

Summary

The primary task of the brand manager in the brand identity approach is to ensure that consumers and stakeholders experience a strong and coherent brand identity through all contacts with it. In order to achieve this, it is essential that the identity types or the theoretical building blocks of organizational identity, corporate identity, image and reputation, are aligned. This requires a multidimensional approach where the detection and alignment can take place across all functions and subcultures in the organization. After careful analysis of identity gaps the brand identity can be developed and enhanced through a process of cyclical steps. In this process, the brand identity is stated, more information about identity types is gathered and core values are articulated. Secondly the brand identity is organized – how can the stated brand identity be implemented to kick in all identity types? The third process ensures that all stakeholders are involved in the creation and implementation of brand identity through dispersing information and brand identity-building activities. The final process integrates all the identity types in one coherent brand identity.

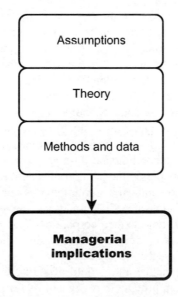

Figure 5.10 Managerial implications of the identity approach

Comments from the 'founding fathers' (1)

The value of the identity approach to the study and management of brands

Majken Schultz, Copenhagen Business School, and Mary Jo Hatch, University of Virginia

Branding is constantly on the move, both in theory and in practice. Since the early days, when it was rooted in the marketing discipline, branding has become a strategic concern for corporations which requires a much more integrative approach than marketing alone can provide. A range of different disciplines and organizational functions need to be engaged and inspired so that the organization is motivated to deliver the brand promise throughout all activities. The recent development of what here is called the identity approach is an example of this shift in the foundation for analyzing and managing brands.

Originating from corporate identity with its focus on the expressive side of branding, the identity approach draws on insights from organization studies, social psychology and stakeholder theory. Through these influences, the approach embraces the relational and dynamic nature of identity, claiming that, when corporate branding works, it is intimately tied into the organization's identity, continuously arcing between the poles of 'Who am I?' and 'What do others think about me?' Knowing what creates the sense of 'we' allows organizations to authentically tell others what they stand for. But knowing who you are also requires intimate knowledge of how stakeholders see your organization. This is because external images interact with the ways in which employees think about their organization and the organizational culture that helps them make sense of what they hear and know about the organization. Together, what they know themselves to be through direct experience and contact with the images of others creates an identity dialogue that provides the foundation for branding.

We claim that strong brands are based in the alignment between strategic vision, organization culture and stakeholder images. This is represented in chapter 5 as the corporate branding toolkit. As with most conceptual models, this is an ideal to aim for. The reality for most companies is that they continually struggle to maintain alignment through most of their lives, at times confronting significant gaps in the relationships between vision, culture and images that require more radical intervention. It is our experience that what makes the difference between leading brands and the rest is their willingness and ability to pose questions to their corporate brands – and use the answers in their continuous development of their vision, their culture and their images. This is a process that never ceases.

Meanwhile, as a practice and a field of study, branding continues to evolve from its roots in product thinking and its further development as a corporate-wide endeavour. As a consequence the ways in which companies engage in brand management continue to change. Branding began as a marketing endeavour to create and manage the relationship between *products and consumers*. This might have worked well at the product level, but it implied that corporate brands often were treated as if they were giant economy-sized product brands that can be created with advertising campaigns.

When the term *corporate* started to receive more attention in corporate branding, brand management became a multi-functional activity. This meant that HR, corporate communication, investor relations, and all the other communication functions joined with marketers to manage the corporate brand. This ultimately spawned cross-functional task forces and teams whose job was to co-ordinate all the corporate brand efforts going on around the company and to bring corporate brand thinking to other projects and programmes as well. Corporate branding led to such innovations as employer brands and a plethora of brand activation and renewal programmes – each designed, orchestrated and led by different groups within the corporation. Over time, this activity contributed to fragmentation and confusion as different groups claimed their piece of the branding puzzle and the resources that came along with them.

In the context of the stakeholder society, a new wave of *enterprise* branding is evolving to respond to these gathering forces and balance the identity conversation by positioning the corporate brand to be the voice, not just of the company, but of the stakeholders that comprise the enterprise. This newly emerging framework holds out hope not only that corporate branding will resolve internal integration problems, but that it will reaffirm the strategic approach to managing the expectations of those stakeholders who make up the enterprise of which the company is but a part.

As a result the next generation of brand managers will spend increasing amounts of time looking at the brand through the eyes of their multiple stakeholders. Participation in brand community events will feature prominently on their schedules, and every interaction inside the firm and out will become much more of a two-way communication process. Brand managers will bring some of these stakeholders into the management process, making use of their ideas and skills in internal company activities. They will design new activities that get employees to work alongside even more stakeholders doing things that give all of their lives greater meaning.

Student questions

1 How is the identity approach different from the economic approach?
2 What are the differences between product branding and corporate branding?
3 How can companies benefit from corporate branding?

4   What elements are pivotal when creating brand equity in the identity approach?
5   What methods are used to uncover the internal elements, corporate identity and organizational identity of brand identity?
6   How are the methods used to study organizational identity different from those used when studying image and reputation?
7   Why can a misalignment in identities weaken the brand?
8   How can misalignments between multiple identities be identified?
9   How can 'living the brand' be implemented in practice?

References and further reading

Key readings are in **bold type**.

Aaker, D. A. (1991) *Managing Brand Equity*, New York: Free Press Business

Aaker, D. A. and Joachimsthaler, E. (2000) *Brand Leadership*, New York: Free Press Business

Abratt, R. (1989) 'A new approach to the corporate image management process', *Journal of Marketing Management*, 5 (1): 63–76

Albert, S. and Whetten, D. (1985) 'Organizational identity', *Research in Organizational Behavior*, 7: 263–95

Argenti, P. A. (1998) 'Strategic employee communications', *Human Resource Management*, 37 (3–4): 199–207

Balmer, J. M. T. (1995) 'Corporate branding and connoisseurship', *Journal of General Management*, 21 (1): 24–46

Balmer, J. M. T. (1998) 'Corporate identity and the advent of corporate marketing', *Journal of Marketing Management*, 14 (8): 963–96

Balmer, J. M. T. (2001a) 'The three virtues and seven deadly sins of corporate brand management', *Journal of General Management*, 27 (1): 1–17

Balmer, J. M. T. (2001b) 'Corporate identity, corporate branding and corporate marketing; seeing through the fog', *European Journal of Marketing* (special edition on corporate identity): 35 (3–4): 248–91

Balmer, J. M. T. and Greyser, S. E. (2003) *Revealing the Corporation: Perspectives on Identity, Image, Reputation, Corporate Branding, and Corporate-level Marketing*, London: Routledge

Berens, G., van Riel, C. B. M. and van Bruggen, G. H. (2005) 'Corporate associations and consumer product responses: the moderating role of corporate brand dominance', *Journal of Marketing*, 69 (3) (July): 35–18

Bernstein, D. (1984) *Company Image and Reality: A Critique of Corporate Communications*, Eastborne: Holt, Rinehart & Winston

Chernatony, L. De (1999), 'Brand management through narrowing the gap between brand identity and brand reputation', *Journal of Marketing Management*, 15: 157–59

Collins, J. C. and Porras, J. I. (1994) *Built to Last: Successful Habits of Visionary Companies*, New York: Harper Business

Fombrun, J. C. and van Riel, C. B. M. (1998) 'The reputational landscape', *Corporate Reputation Review*, 1 (1): 5–13, reprinted in J. M. T. Balmer and S. Greyser, (eds) *Revealing the Corporation: Perspectives on Identity, Image, Reputation, Corporate Branding, and Corporate-level Marketing*, London: Routledge (2003)

Gioia, D. A., Schultz, M. and Corley, K. G. (2000) 'Organizational identity, image and adaptive instability', *Academy of Management Review*, 25 (1): 63–81

Gotsi, M. and Wilson, A. (2001) 'Corporate reputation management: living the brand', *Management Decision,* 39: 99–104

Gray, E. R. and Balmer, J. M. T. (2001), 'The corporate brand: a strategic asset', *Management in Practice,* 4: 1–4

Gray, E. R. and Schmeltzer, L. R. (1987) 'Planning a face-lift: implementing a corporate image programme', *Journal of Business Strategy,* 8 (1): 4–10

Grunig J. (1993), 'Image and substance: from symbolic to behavioral relationships', *Public Relations Review,* 19 (2): 121–39

Hackley, C. (2003), *Doing Research Projects in Marketing, Management and Consumer Research,* London: Routledge

Hatch, M. J. and Schultz, M. (1997) 'Relations between organizational culture, identity and image', *European Journal of Marketing,* 31 (5–6): 356–65

Hatch, M. J. and Schultz, M. (2000) 'Scaling the tower of Babel: relational difference between identity, image and culture in organizations', in M. Schultz, M. J. Hatch and H. Larsen (eds) *The Expressive Organization: Linking Identity, Reputation and the Corporate Brand,* Oxford: Oxford University Press

Hatch, M. J. and Schultz, M. (2001) 'Are the strategic stars aligned for your corporate brand?' *Harvard Business Review,* February: 129–34

Hatch, M. J. and Schultz, M. (2003) 'Bringing the corporation into corporate branding', *European Journal of Marketing,* 37 (7–8): 1041–64

Hatch, M. J. and Schultz, M. (2008) *Taking Brand Initiative: How Companies can align Strategy, Culture, and Identity through Corporate Branding,* San Francisco: Wiley

Ind, N. (1992) *The Corporate Image,* London: Kogan Page

Ind, N. (1997) *The Corporate Brand,* New York: New York University Press

Ind, N. (1998) 'An integrated approach to corporate branding', *Journal of Brand Management,* 6 (5): 323–9

Ind, N. (2001) *Living the Brand,* London: Kogan Page

Kapferer, J-N. (1997), *Strategic Brand Management: Creating and Sustaining Brand Equity Long Term,* London: Kogan Page

Karmark, E. (2005) 'Living the brand', in M. Schultz, Y. M. Antorini and F. F. Csaba (eds) *Corporate Branding: Purpose, People, Process,* Copenhagen: Copenhagen Business School Press

Keller, K. L. (1997), *Strategic Brand Management: Building, Measuring, and Managing Brand Equity,* Englewood Cliffs NJ: Pearson

Kennedy, S. H. (1977) 'Nurturing corporate images', *European Journal of Marketing,* 1 (3): 119–64

King, S. (1991) 'Brand building in the 1990s', *Journal of Marketing Management,* 7: 3–13

Martin, J. (2002) *Organizational Culture: Mapping the Terrain,* Thousand Oaks C A: Sage Publications

Mitchell, A. (2004) 'Getting staff to live the brand: work in progress', *Marketing Week,* 2 September: 30

Mitchell, C. (2002) 'Selling the brand inside: you tell customers what makes you great. Do your employees know?' *Harvard Business Review,* January: 99–106

Olins, W. (1978), *The Corporate Personality: An Inquiry into the Nature of Corporate Identity,* London: Design Council

Olins, W. (1979) 'Corporate identity: the myth and the reality', *Royal Society of Arts Journal,* March

Olins, W. (1989) *Corporate Identity: Making Business Strategy Visible through Design,* Boston MA: Harvard Business School Press

Olins, W. (2001), 'How brands are taking over the corporation', in M. Schultz, M. J. Hatch and M. H. Larsen (eds), *The Expressive Organization: Linking Identity, Reputation and the Corporate Brand,* Oxford: Oxford University Press

Petty, R. E. and Cacioppo, J. T. (1986) *Communication and Persuasion: Central and Peripheral Routes to Attitude Change,* New York: Springer

Scott, W. A., Osgood, D. W. and Peterson, C. (1979) *Cognitive Structure: Theory and Measurement of Individual Difference,* New York: Wiley

Schmitt, B. and Simonson, A. (1997) 'Looks count', *Entrepreneur,* 25 (9): 166–70

Schroeder, J. E. and Salzer-Mörling, M. (ed.) (2006) *Brand Culture,* London and New York: Routledge

Schultz, M., Antorini, Y. M. and Csaba, F. F. (2005) *Corporate Branding: Purpose, People, Process,* Copenhagen: Copenhagen Business School Press

Schultz, M., Hatch, M. J. and Larsen, M. H. (eds) (2000), ***The Expressive Organization: Linking Identity, Reputation and the Corporate Brand,*** **Oxford: Oxford University Press**

Websites

www.aeg.com
www.lego.com
www.quiksilver.com

6   The consumer-based approach

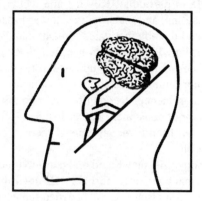

with a commentary by Professor Kevin Lane Keller, Tuck School of Business, Dartmouth College

---

Learning objectives

The purpose of this chapter is to:

Understand the assumptions of the consumer-based approach
- The brand is a cognitive construal in the mind of the consumer
- The brand resides in the mind of the consumer, but the marketer is still able to control brand value creation

Understand the theoretical building blocks and how they are connected
- The cognitive consumer perspective
- The information-processing theory of consumer choice
- Customer-based brand equity

Provide insights into the variety of methods used to inquire into the cognitive aspects of the consumer
- Input–output methods to understand how consumer decisions change if stimuli are changed
- Process-tracing methods to understand the process of brand choice
- Measuring customer-based brand equity

Understand the managerial implications
- The 'dualist' nature of the approach
- Superior outside–in capabilities
- The marketer should stress brand congruency and consistency

In the early years of brand management the focus was on the 'sender end' of brand communication. In the year of 1993 brand management was profoundly changed by one research article in particular. Kevin Lane Keller published the article 'Conceptualizing, measuring, and managing customer-based brand equity' in the *Journal of Marketing* and thereby instigated a major change in the field of brand management. Customer-based brand equity is based on the premise that the brand resides in the minds of consumers as a cognitive construal, which is why we have chosen to name it the consumer-based approach. Consumer research was, at this point in time, very much influenced by cognitive psychology and the related information-processing theory of consumer choice. Insights from these veins of literature were adapted to brand management theory by the birth of the consumer-based approach.

The 1993 article introduced a new brand and consumer perspective, thus giving birth to a new brand management approach. Besides that, it also played an extremely important role as it discussed and clarified some central notions of brand management. At this time, the discipline of brand management suffered from a lack of independence in relation to the parent discipline of marketing. Research articles on branding were often difficult to tell from articles on advertising research and other marketing phenomena. The key notion of brand equity often was not even mentioned and certainly not defined. All in all, the academic discipline of brand management appeared rather immature and scientifically incomplete. All this changed after the introduction of customer-based brand equity. One of the very important contributions of the Keller publication was that the article instigated a new way of relating to the more and more independent scientific discipline of brand management by its thorough discussion of the key term of brand equity. Before 1993 academic articles rarely mentioned brand equity while the vast majority of post-1993 articles start out by relating their subject of choice to different definitions of brand equity (read about brand equity in chapter 2).

Since the launch of the consumer-based approach, the mindset behind it has been widely adopted as the most influential way of thinking about brands and branding: 'Keller's exposition of the customer-based brand equity model offers the most widely accepted and comprehensive treatment of branding in American marketing' (Holt 2005, p. 277). The initial impact of the theory as presented in 1993 has been followed up by the great importance of Keller's book *Strategic Brand Management: Building, Measuring, and Managing Brand Equity* (1998 and 2003).

As it is our aim to make a side-by-side presentation of the seven schools of thought, they are presented as ideal types. Therefore, we focus on the original cognitive brand and consumer perspective in this approach (by focusing on the founding article and the literature relating to it). How the approach has further developed will be discussed and compared with the new approaches in a final section.

Assumptions of the consumer-based approach

The two prior approaches – the economic approach and the identity approach – are both primarily focused on the *sending end* of brand communication. The economic approach (chapter 4) focuses on the way a marketer can influence brand value creation through adjusting the components of the traditional marketing mix. The primary focus of the identity approach (chapter 5) is the brand in an organizational perspective. In the consumer-based approach, the brand is analysed as residing *in the mind of the individual consumer* as a cognitive construal.

The consumer has thus become the main point of interest in this approach. He or she is suddenly considered the 'owner' of the brand. Where the two prior approaches stressed an inside–out perspective on brand value creation, the consumer-based approach introduces an outside–in approach to brand management. The approach thereby embraces an external strategy formation opposed to the internal formation of the two prior approaches.

Brand value creation takes place by moulding the brand associations held in the consumers' minds. Understanding the consumer is hence central in this take on brand value creation; but it is important to notice that the approach implies a specific view on the consumer. The consumer is analysed by means of theories adopted from cognitive psychology and the information-processing theory of consumer choice.

The 'brand–consumer exchange' and the cognitive perspective

In the other approach chapters we have outlined the assumed characteristics of the brand–consumer exchange first and then introduced the scientific tradition from which the approach stems In this section we will, however, introduce the two themes jointly as it does not make sense to talk about the brand–consumer exchange without also talking about the specific consumer perspective.

In the consumer-based approach, brand strength equals strong, unique and favourable associations in the minds of its consumers. The fact that the brand is a cognitive construal in the mind of the consumer makes one jump to the conclusion that the consumer 'owns' the brand and thereby controls brand value creation.

The marketer is, however, assumed to be very much in control with brand communication as the approach rests upon an assumption of the consumer as a *cognitive man*. The consumer is seen and analysed through a lens grounded in cognitive psychology and information economics. As we describe in further detail in the next section, the cognitive perspective implies a view of man that still grants managers control over brand image creation. Even though the brand is analysed as a mental construal in the mind of the consumer, it still makes sense to talk about the communication of intended meaning. This notion of linear communication

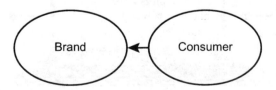

Figure 6.1 The brand resides in the mind of the consumer

means that the recipient of a message understands the message as intended by the sender. In cognitive psychology, the dominant man metaphor is that of the computer and the human mind is supposed to process sensory data in much the same way a computer processes binary data.

In cognitive psychology, an if–then logic applies. *If* the marketer feeds the 'consumer computer' with the most appropriate information, *then* the consumer will do as intended and choose the brand. One is able to programme a computer into doing the same thing every time and this logic applies to the brand–consumer exchange of this approach. In other words, the consumer is the focal point in this approach, but the marketer is still assumed to control the brand. The approach assumes the linear interaction between sensory input → consumer → brand choice.

At a first glance, the consumer appears to be all-powerful in the brand–consumer exchange in this approach. But the consumer 'ownership' of the approach is paradoxical; even though the consumer 'owns' the brand, he or she is still treated as a generic entity that the skilled communicator is able to 'programme' into intended action. The chaotic, unpredictable and 'autonomous' aspects of consumer behaviour that are taken into consideration in the later approaches (the relational, the community and the cultural approaches) are not considered in the consumer perspective in this approach.

Summary

The consumer-based approach assumes that the brand is a cognitive construal residing in the mind of the consumer.

This assumption indicates that the consumer is very much in control of the brand–consumer exchange. This is, however, not entirely the case. The consumer is seen through a lens borrowed from cognitive psychology and the main metaphor for man in this perspective is that of the computer.

And just like a skilled computer programmer is able to programme the computer into doing as intended, the marketer who is willing to map out the brand construal in the mind of the consumer, will be able to choose exactly the right brand elements and communicate them to a consumer who will respond accordingly. These, seemingly contradictory, assumptions are what lie behind the consumer-based approach.

Sensory input ⟶ the information processing consumer ⟶ Brand choice

Figure 6.2 The computer is the central metaphor of man in cognitive psychology

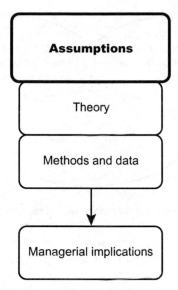

Figure 6.3 Assumptions of the consumer-based approach

Theoretical building blocks of the consumer-based approach

As mentioned in the introduction, the consumer-based approach is founded on one research article presenting the customer-based brand equity framework. This framework is the core theme of the consumer-based approach.

Behind the framework is the information-processing theory of consumer choice, and *behind* this theory we find the cognitive consumer perspective. In this section we will move forwards, starting out with a brief introduction to the cognitive consumer perspective. From here, we move on to a short review of the information-processing theory of consumer choice. Both topics are extremely comprehensive and quite complicated and going into depth with them is beyond the scope of this book. Still, having become acquainted with important characteristics of these two topics, the reader will be better equipped to fully understand the core theme: that of customer-based brand equity.

Figure 6.4 depicts how the customer-based brand equity framework builds on insights from both the cognitive consumer perspective and the information-processing theory of consumer choice and that this theory also draws on the cognitive consumer perspective.

The cognitive consumer perspective

In the assumptions you have already been introduced to some of the key characteristics of cognitive psychology. The main metaphor for man (the consumer) is that of the computer; cognitive psychology focuses on the process from a consumer being exposed to stimuli from his or her environment (input, information), how

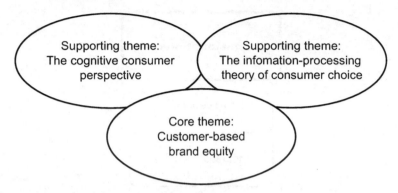

Figure 6.4 Supporting themes and the core themes of the consumer-based approach

these stimuli enter the mind via the senses, and how they lead to action (choice). It is also fundamental to understand the if–then logic that applies to this consumer perspective.

Cognitive psychology is concerned with the higher cognitive processes, namely memory, language, problem solving, imagery, deduction and induction. In other words, the cognitive research tradition deals with aspects such as reasoning, intelligence and learning, and tries to answer questions like 'How do we learn?' 'How do we remember?' 'What makes us pay attention?' 'What makes us react?' As we grow up, we develop greater cognitive structure; meaning that we become still better at discriminating among stimuli and organizing stimuli into meaningful constructs.

The cognitive research tradition deliberately neglects emotional factors as well as historical and cultural aspects when studying how human beings function and behave. Relevant to this approach is how we store knowledge, how we remember, and how our attention is captured. The sum of this process is to understand how this process leads to action, in our line of interest: brand choice.

We store enormous amounts of knowledge in our memory. Memory is activated (by a sensory input) and spreading activities begin. Thereby, knowledge is retrieved from memory. Knowledge in memory consists of nodes and links and is structured into associative networks. Nodes are the stored information connected by links in associative networks. The nodes vary in strength; some associations are stronger than others. Environmental stimuli (e.g. a commercial message) trigger a node that through the 'spreading activity' triggers new nodes associated with the first one. An example of this spreading activity might be the word Volkswagen. The retrieval of the node Volkswagen triggers a spreading activity that potentially could look like figure 6.5. The associations can continue in all directions until they have lost relevance for the node Volkswagen. The fact that some links are empha-sized shows that some associations are more direct and are thus retrieved more easily than others (they are *stronger* associations).

A node is a mental representation. Cognitive research aims at deepening the understanding of mental representations as a level of description, separable from,

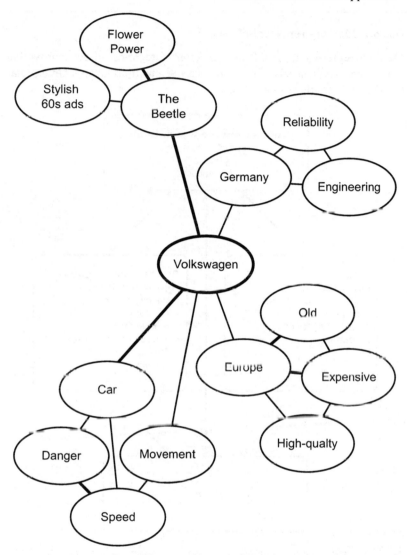

Figure 6.5 Simple associative network spreading from the node Volkswagen

respectively, neurological and socio-cultural aspects. Mental representations are abstractions we all perform at any given time as a way of 'stocking' information in memory. We cannot 'stock' items the way they really are, and therefore we 'catalogue' them in certain systems. (We cannot store the phenomenon of a 'Volkswagen' in its totality.) One of the fundamental challenges of cognitive psychology is that human beings under study have to 'translate' their memory representations into language even though we do not necessarily 'stock' memories by means of language.

Box 6.1 Memory representations

Memory representations fall into different categories: direct, non-verbal representations (sensory), propositional representations (abstract interpretations) and linguistic representations.

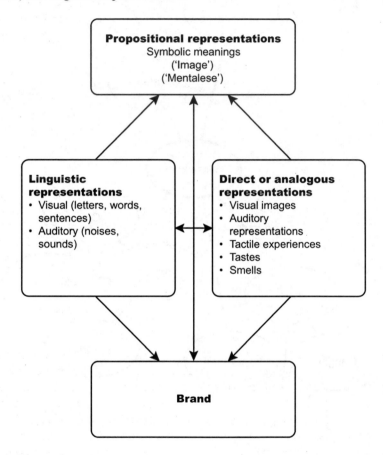

Figure 6.6 The three forms of cognition applied to brands; from G. Franzen and M. Bouwman, *The Mental World of Brands* (2001), figure 10.1, p. 178, reprinted by permission of World Advertising Research Centre, Henley on Thames (www.warc.com)

- **Direct or analogous representations** are direct (non-verbal) sensory sensations such as: what does a brand look like or how does it feel? Sensory representations also include how packaging and advertisements look. For example a Volvo is a large, rather square car and most often a station wagon.

- **Propositional representations** are interpretations of the brand. They are non-sensory, abstract brand meanings derived from the sensory brand experiences. For example a Volvo is often interpreted as a car for a well-off and rather intellectual family.
- **Linguistic representations** are words and sentences used to express brand meaning and experiences with the brand. These can be lengthy accounts or so short that they almost become analogous representations of the brand. For example Volvo = safety.

These three categories are worth considering when investigating brand associations in the memories of consumers as important brand associations emanate on all levels.

Source Franzen and Bouwman (2001)

In cognitive psychology, memory is considered very durable. Things we store in memory tend to stay there for a long time. In cognitive consumer research, repeated exposure to a commercial message is therefore considered very important. Perceptual enhancement of a concept can actually lead to more or less permanent memory codes.

This brief introduction to cognitive psychology is by no means exhaustive but has mentioned the key characteristics that are most important for understanding the background as well as the implications of the consumer-based approach.

The information-processing theory of consumer choice

The information-processing theory of consumer choice has cognitive psychology as its point of departure and focuses on explaining how consumers process information before reaching a consumption choice. Here, choice provides the focal point: 'the consumer is characterized as interacting with his or her choice environment, seeking and taking in information from various sources, processing this information, and then making a selection from among some alternatives' (Bettman 1979, p. 1).

Consumers make an enormous number of choices, and make choices at many different levels. Should I buy a particular brand? Should I examine info or not? When should I make the purchase? Where should I make the purchase? How should I pay for it? These are examples of the countless number of choices we all go through before leaving a store with a purchase. A key assumption in this theory is that choice is a process. The marketer should seek an understanding of these choice processes in order to fine-tune marketing communication to make the consumer choose as intended. (Read about process-tracing methods in the methods and data section.)

In this theory, the following factors – processing capacity, motivation, attention, perception, information acquisition and evaluation, memory decision processes, and learning – influence the process. The information-processing theory of consumer choice displays a belief that behaviour is caused and hence (in principle) explainable (the if–then logic of cognitive psychology).

In the economic approach, the consumer was supposed to be an economic man, able to take into consideration all relevant information and rationally evaluate different options in a choice situation. The view of the consumer in the information-processing theory of consumer choice is somewhat different. The consumer is assumed to be exposed to a constant information overload and the mind an inadequate container in an over-communicated society full of commercial messages. 'The computer' is in other words not capable of processing all the data that are fed to it. Therefore, the human mind economizes on processing capacity by choosing not to process all information. These simplifying strategies that economize on processing capacity (heuristics) are also central to understanding the information-processing theory of consumer research and the further implications for and of the customer-based brand equity framework.

Box 6.2 Heuristics are important in low-involvement categories

Consumers take more brand alternatives into consideration during a consumption choice process if either the perceived risks or the perceived benefits are high.

Choosing a mundane, low-involvement brand involves a simpler process of choice where heuristics are more easily applied.

Heuristics take on different forms. Below are two examples:

- *Lexicographic* heuristic: 'I buy the least expensive brand'.
- *Familiarity* heuristic: 'I buy the brand most familiar to me'.

Especially in low-involvement categories, it is hence worth while investigating which heuristics are typically applied in choice processes.

Source Kardes (1994)

Customer-based brand equity

'Customer-based brand equity is defined as the differential effect of brand knowledge on consumer response to the marketing of the brand' (Keller 1993, p. 2). It is also a conceptual model of brand equity seen from the perspective of the individual consumer: The 'marketing' of the above definition relates to the marketing mix, but the point of view is reversed in comparison with the economic approach (chapter 4) – it is consumer reactions to marketing actions that are in focus.

The global understanding of the brand in the mind of the consumer is conceptualized as 'brand knowledge', which is divided into 'brand awareness' (brand recall and brand recognition) and 'brand image' (the set of associations linked with the brand). Memory principles and structure from cognitive psychology are the background of brand knowledge. As explained in the above sections, memory and knowledge consist of a set of nodes and links. Nodes are stored information and links are what bind them together. The links vary in strength depending on how well the association is stored in long-term memory.

In order to measure whether a brand has customer-based brand equity, brand knowledge has to be mapped, implying that brand awareness and brand image – in the mind of the individual consumer – have to be measured. Brand awareness is a prerequisite for customer-based brand equity. If the consumer is not aware of the brand, it is not relevant to talk about brand equity in the first place; then the company competes on the product rather than the brand. Brand awareness consists of brand recognition and brand recall.

- Brand *recognition*. Does the consumer recognize the brand name? The consumer must confirm having had prior exposure to the brand.
- Brand *recall* is a bit more demanding of the consumer. Here, the brand has to be recalled on the mention of a cue (e.g. the product category).

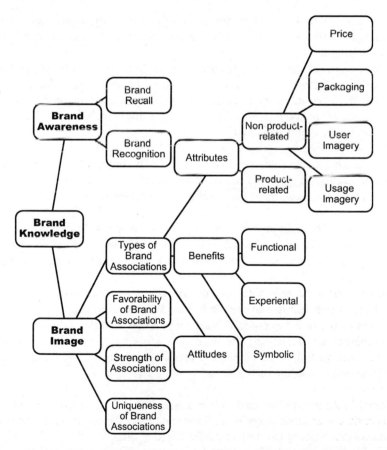

Figure 6.7 Dimensions of brand knowledge; reprinted with permission from *Journal of Marketing*, 57 (1993), published by the American Marketing Association, K. L. Keller, 'Conceptualizing, measuring, and managing customer-based brand equity', p. 7

But being able to retrieve the brand from memory is only the foundation for having customer-based brand equity. A thorough conceptualization of brand image is also a part of customer-based brand equity. Brand image is 'perceptions about a brand as reflected by the brand associations held in consumer memory. Brand associations are the other informational nodes linked to the brand node in memory and contain the meaning of the brand for consumers' (Keller 1993, p. 3).

Until 1993 the term brand image became increasingly used and the need for managing the brand image over time became emphasized: 'The relationship between a brand's concept and its image must be managed throughout the life of the brand' (Park *et al.* 1986, p. 137). Despite growing interest, it was quite unclear what brand image was. In the customer-based brand equity framework, the associations related to brand image consist of several types of associations relating to *attributes*, *benefits* and *attitudes*.

Attributes are descriptive features characterizing a product or a service.

- Product-related attributes are associations directly associated with the product or the service. It could be the physical appearance of a car and the feel of driving it.
- Non-product-related attributes are external aspects related to its purchase or the consumption of it. There are four groups of non-product-related attributes that are taken into account: price information, packaging, user imagery (an impression of the type of person that consumes the brand) and use image (impressions of the context of brand use).

Benefits are personal values attached to the brand by the consumer. They are idiosyncratic evaluations or expectations of what the brand can do for the consumer. Benefits fall into three categories; functional, experiential, and symbolic.

- *Functional* benefits are personal expectations of what the product can do for consumers. They correspond to the product-related features but are more personal evaluations; the functional benefits are thus less objective than the product-related attributes.
- *Experiential* benefits relate to the sensory experience of using the brand. What does it feel like to use the brand? What kind of pleasure will I obtain from consuming the brand? This aspect provides variety for the consumer and satisfies hedonic consumption needs.
- *Symbolic* benefits are about self-expression and the way we signal to others by means of consumption objects.

Brand attitudes are the last class of brand associations in the map of brand image. Brand attitudes are consumers' overall evaluations of the brand. This overall evaluation is very important as it often guides brand choice.

To recapitulate, a brand (of which the consumer is aware) is a node in an associative network of brand knowledge. The brand name triggers a spreading activity and associations pop up. Some associations pop up faster and more immediately than others; they are connected to the brand node by a stronger link and are, thus, more powerful associations than the ones connected more loosely to the main node. The associations appear as different kinds of mental representations, as all associations are interpretations made by our cognitive mindsets. Some associations are of a more visual nature and some are of a more verbal nature that others.

The basis for talking about customer-based brand equity is, as already mentioned, brand awareness. If brand awareness can be stated, the further process is to create a map of consumer associations consisting of the above-mentioned elements. These customer associations paint an accurate picture of the content of brand image.

Content is one thing, but customer-based brand equity also expresses a value that can be measured against that of competitors. For a brand to have *high* customer-based brand equity (in other words to be a strong brand), the consumer associations need to be more *favourable*, *strong* and *unique* than the image associated with competing brands.

- *Favourability* corresponds to whether the consumer's overall brand associations are more or less favourable than those associated with competing brands. Is the overall brand attitude so favourable that it will likely affect consumption behaviour?
- *Strength* of brand associations corresponds to the way associations spread in the associative web activated by the brand as node. Strong associations appear fast (the accentuated links in figure 6.5) and demand attention. (Make the consumer pay attention to the information stored in the association.)
- *Uniqueness* of associations. A brand with desirable customer-based brand equity can also claim some unique associations. Some central associations should ideally not be shared by competing brands. Unique associations are the unique selling point of the brand.

Customer-based brand equity has a comparative framework and can also be negative:

a brand is said to have positive (negative) customer-based brand equity if consumers react more (less) favourably to the product, price, promotion, or distribution of the brand as they do to the same marketing mix when it is attributed to a fictitiously named or unnamed version of the product or service.

(Keller 1993, p. 8)

As the customer-based brand equity is a conceptual model, it does not build on a research project, but is rather an application of the established knowledge about consumer behaviour to branding. It gives birth to a new approach to brand management (which to date has proven the most tenacious) and opens up for a clarification of brand image and brand equity. Now:

brand equity should be thought of as a multidimensional concept that depends on (1) what knowledge structures are present in the minds of consumers and

(2) what actions a firm can take to capitalize on the potential offered by these knowledge structures.

(Keller 1993, p. 14)

Box 6.3 How to structure brand associations

The association map below depicts associations spreading from the node '7-Up'. The map is based on a limited number of interviews of Dutch consumers and the brand name is the only stimulus (Franzen and Bouwman 2001). The stronger associations are emphasized, but whether the associations

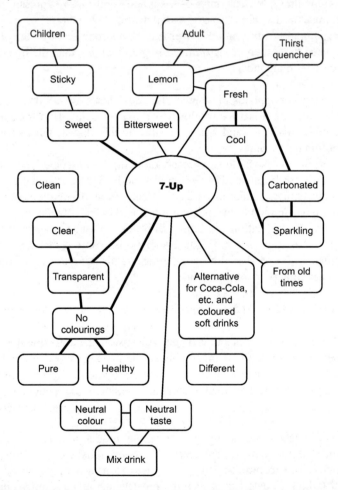

Figure 6.8 Associations spreading from the node 'Seven up'; from G. Franzen and M. Bouwman, *The Mental World of Brands* (2001), figure 10.2, p. 179, reprinted by permission of World Advertising Research Centre, Henley-on-Thames (www.warc.com)

are *strong, favourable* and *unique* are not investigated, nor is brand awareness measured. Therefore the association map is a 'messy' picture of brand image. Below, the association map is structured according to the brand image elements.

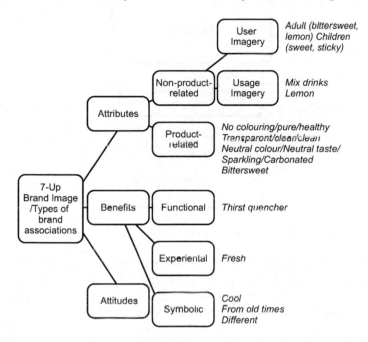

Figure 6.9 '7-Up' brand associations adapted to the customer-based brand equity framework

The process of structuring association maps arranges the content of brand image well arranged. It becomes clear which associations are linked with the product and which are more abstracted. In the case of user imagery, it is interesting that the 'children' association is linked with 'sweet' and 'sticky' while the 'adult' user imagery is linked with 'bittersweet' and 'lemon'. In that sense, the association map turned into brand image provides great insights to be elaborated on in the further planning of marketing activity.

Summary

Cognitive psychology applied to consumer research, and the associated information-processing theory of consumer choice, serve as supporting themes for the core theory of customer-based brand equity. In cognitive psychology, man is presumed to function much like a computer and the focus is on how knowledge (in the form of mental representations) is stored in and can be retrieved from memory.

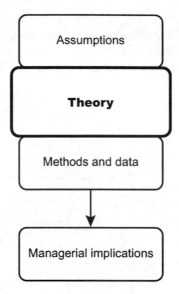

Figure 6.10 Theory of the consumer-based approach

The information-processing theory of consumer choice focuses on explaining the process of choice. Man is supposed to have limited processing capacity, which is why the marketer should be aware to make the most efficient communication.

The customer-based brand equity framework is a brand management theory that draws upon the two above themes. This framework maps brand knowledge as a cognitive construal. In order to be able to talk about customer-based brand equity, brand awareness has to exist in the minds of consumers. The brand has to be recalled and recognized. If this is the case, brand image can be mapped. Brand image consists of consumer associations depicting tangible as well as intangible aspects of the brand, also depicting attributes, benefits and attitudes. Customer-based brand equity is a comparative framework by which the favourability, strength and uniqueness of brand association can be measured against those of competing brands.

Methods and data of the consumer-based approach

As described in the introduction to this chapter, the cognitive consumer perspective and the consumer-based approach have become very dominant both in the fields of consumer research and brand management. Therefore, there is an abundance of methods that can be used for researching consumers along this line of thought. In this section we will present a few of the most widely applied methods for gathering knowledge of the cognitive consumer and his or her choice processes. These methods provide an insight into the way consumers are investigated when the researcher aims at understanding the cognitive mechanisms activated during consumption choices.

The customer-based brand equity framework also encompasses methods and directions for measuring customer-based brand equity. These methods will conclude this section.

Gathering data in the information-processing consumer perspective

As described in the sections on assumptions and theoretical building blocks, the theories based on the cognitive consumer perspective tries to explain how stimuli entered into the 'computer' consumer are economically processed and then lead to a consumption choice. In order to map out these processes, two main categories of methods are applied; namely *input–output* and *process-tracing* approaches.

Input–output methods are experiments where input factors are manipulated and the change in the output of the process is then measured. These methods correspond to the if–then logic that is so fundamental to the cognitive consumer perspective. There are in effect no limits to which inputs can be altered in order to test output. The respondent can be presented to different advertising methods, consideration sets can be differentiated, different price information can be applied to the same brand, etc. By testing consumer reactions to different inputs, the best (most predictable) marketing action can be planned.

In the information-processing theory of consumer choice, choice is seen as a process following explainable paths in consumers' minds. The *process-tracing* approaches aim at understanding and explaining this process. They are attempts to monitor the sequence of information acquired and the choices they lead to. There are many different ways of understanding this process, below are some examples:

- *Verbal protocols.* The respondent thinks out loud during the performance of an actual task. For instance, a consumer goes shopping equipped with a voice recorder. Thoughts are verbalized and recorded as they occur. In this fashion, the process of making a brand choice is recorded. For the researcher, this technique is rather time-consuming as he or she has to sort through large amounts of data.
- A similar method is the *prompted protocol*. A consumer is (willingly) video-filmed during a shopping experience. After the shopping experience the consumer comments on the video film, and thereby explains which decision processes he or she went through during the shopping experience.
- *A matrix array* is another way of understanding a choice process. Here, a matrix is constructed reflecting as many of the factoras possible, which are parts of a choice process. For example, the matrix can be constructed with brands in rows and attributes in columns. In each case of the matrix the respondent can take an information card (e.g. the price of the Toyota on information card n, or the size of the engine of the Fiat on information card t; a few examples are provided in table 6.1). This method simulates the examination of choices a consumer goes through – one at the time – leading to the final choice. The consumer researcher will get as data the sequence of cards selected and the amount of information acquired before the consumer feels ready to commit to a choice. The data will contain rich information providing insight into central

processes of choice and will answer questions like 'How many information cards are necessary before making a choice?' 'Which cards are the most important?' 'Are some information cards revisited?' 'Which piece of information turns out to be the decisive one?' Imagine the matrix in table 6.1 as a mini-bookcase with information cards on the shelves. The respondents then pick the cards necessary for reaching a consumption choice at their own pace.

- *Chronometric analysis* is an analysis of response time. The cognitive consumer perspective is much occupied with understanding the pace of memory. In a chronometric analysis, the respondent is asked to complete certain tasks: answering questions or finding associations. The time it takes to complete these tasks is then measured. Mapping out the time between the presentation of a stimulus and the response to that stimulus is beneficial in order to understand the pace of memory as well as understanding how easily associations are retrieved (the 'thickness' of the links in figure 6. 5).

These are some of the methods that can be applied when wanting to understand the choice processes that take place in the mind of the 'computer' consumer. Customer-based brand equity can also be measured; how will be explained in the forthcoming section.

Measuring customer-based brand equity

There is a direct and an indirect approach to measuring customer-based brand equity. For an optimal result, these two approaches should be complemented. The indirect approach measures brand knowledge (brand awareness and brand image, figure 6.6) by assessing its sources (consumers' associations). The direct approach measures customer-based brand equity by measuring consumer responses to the brand's marketing actions.

Table 6.1 A simple version of a matrix array

	Colour	Safety	Price	Engine
Volkswagen	Information card a: Black	Information card f: 5 Euro NCAP stars	Information card k	Information card p
Ford	Information card b: Grey	Information card g: 4 Euro NCAP stars	Information card l	Information card q
Audi	Information card c Red	Information card: 5 Euro NCAP stars	Information card m	Information card r
Toyota	Information card d Green	Information card i	Information card n	Information card s
Fiat	Information card e Orange	Information card j	Information card o	Information card t

The indirect approach implies measuring customer-based brand equity *without* measuring it against something else. Here, the sources of brand knowledge and pattern of associations are identified through mapping out consumers' brand knowledge. Keller recommends that several methods are applied in order to capture as many aspects of customer-based brand equity as possible. Remember that associations are stored in the memory as different mental representations. Some methods are more suited for bringing out some representations than others.

- *Brand awareness* is assessed through aided as well as unaided memory measures. To start with, is the brand name recognized? The brand should be correctly discerned by the consumer as previously seen or heard. Brand recall can be tested through testing which brand is 'top of mind' in a brand category. The brand should be correctly identified given for instance a product category. Response times for both recall and recognition can be measured in order to depict the ease with which the brand comes to mind, reflecting attitude strengths.
- *Brand associations* can be captured in many ways. Free association tasks can be performed either individually or in focus groups to lay out the association maps fundamental to the customer-based brand equity framework. Probing (in terms of asking 'how', 'why', 'what' questions) and projective techniques can be applied in order to help reluctant respondents along. Examples of suitable projective techniques are sentence completion, picture completion, and filling in speech balloons. Individual interviews can also be conducted in order to understand the formation of associations.

Box 6.4 Projective techniques

Using projective techniques is a way to let the respondents' unconscious speak. Respondents are assumed to hold things back in order to protect their self-image in a research situation. When investigated by means of projective techniques, focus is moved away from the respondent and 'projected' at hypothetical others. Thereby, respondents are supposed to open up to the interviewer and actually reveal more about themselves than if asked directly. Below are listed different projective techniques.

- *Sentence completion* Respondents are presented with an unfinished sentence and asked to complete it
- *Picture completion* In the same fashion, respondents are asked to complete an unfinished picture
- *Speech balloons* An empty speech balloon is filled out by the respondent

The sentences, the pictures and the drawings forming the backgrounds of the speech balloons should all carefully depict a situation that is relevant to the brand in question.

The direct approach to measuring customer-based brand equity implies measuring *against* the customer-based brand equity of other brands. Here, consumer reactions to the marketing strategies of the brand are compared with reactions to the same strategies ascribed to a fictitious or unnamed brand. In these blind test scenarios, different elements of the marketing mix are compared between a named brand and an unnamed 'rival' brand. Any marketing element will do, for example the marketer can test perceptions of taste, feel, product quality, packaging and advertising. The majority of these results show that the connotations of the known brand affect the perception of all marketing methods (negatively or positively). This comparative approach to measuring customer-based brand equity can be used for all kinds of marketing methods, but it is a challenge to secure valid results from these tests. Ideally, the whole sequence of mapping brand knowledge is performed in two or more simultaneous groups where group members are exposed to exactly the same material. Remember that brand associations are mental representations of all kinds of sensory input (figure 6.6) and the research design should therefore try to accommodate the fact that some representations are more linguistic than others. The more abstract associations should also count as important data.

Box 6.5 Map out customers' brand associations yourself

- Start out by asking your respondents if they recognize the brand name.
- In another respondent pool, ask which three brands come to mind when you mention the given product category or industry.
- Ask your respondents to draw association maps.
- Expose your respondents to an appropriate set of projective techniques (e.g. finishing sentences, filling out blank speech balloons).
- Interview individual respondents and make them rate their associations.
- Ask respondents what they consider to be unique about the brand.
- Compare patterns of the results across as many respondents as possible.
- Do the same routine with the brand's closest competitors.
- Now, compare the analyses in order to know exactly which associations of your brand are the most strong, favourable and unique.

Source Keller (1993)

Summary

Building on the if–then logic of cognitive psychology and the way choice is seen as an accurate process in the information-processing perspective, the methods applied to investigate the cognitive aspect of the consumer can be divided into input–output and process-tracing approaches. In the first category, input is changed and changes in output are measured in order to capture how the human 'computer' works. In the latter approach, different choice scenarios are monitored by means of (for example) verbal protocols, prompted protocols, and chronometric analysis.

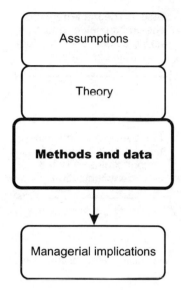

Figure 6.11 Methods and data of the consumer-based approach

Measuring customer-based brand equity can be done indirectly as well as directly. Applying the indirect techniques, brand knowledge is mapped by consumers. The results should be combined with direct comparative analyses of the brand and competing brands or through blind-testing marketing actions against a fictitiously named or unnamed brand.

Managerial implications

In the understanding assumptions section, we discussed the ownership of the brand in the consumer-based approach, which implies that brand value creation is measured in the mind of the consumer, but the view of man behind the approach still allows the idea of linear communication. This duality is reflected in the managerial implications of the approach. One aspect of the implications is a seemingly 'all power to the people' assumption, the other an assumption that the marketer is still able to control (linear) communication.

The first aspect requires closeness to the consumer. The marketer's budget should prioritize constant market monitoring in order to be at the leading edge of consumers' development. This 'market sensing' priority implies a functional or market-centred organizational form; – the consumer-based marketers must possess superior outside–in capabilities in order to succeed.

The other aspect of the consumer-based approach is that the marketer should create the optimal brand communication in order to create the strongest brand. The most skilled marketer is the best 'programmer'. It is all about making the brand known to consumers, making consumers pay attention to the brand by choosing the right brand elements, and positioning the brand through consistency in brand

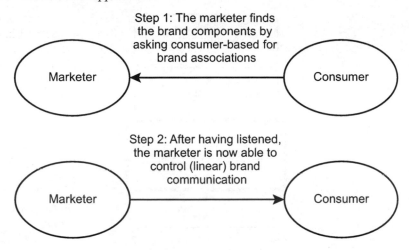

Figure 6.12 Dualistic mechanisms of the consumer-based approach influencing the managerial implications

communication. The marketer should also consider the brand a strategic corporate priority and see all marketing actions as influencing the brand in the future. Therefore, step 2 in figure 6.12 leads to the need for a new step 1, and so on and so on. Finally, it should be considered if brand image is balanced with brand identity.

Make consumers aware of your brand

The fact that the brand name ideally should spur high levels of awareness means that it is important to expose the consumer to the brand name repeatedly. Customer-based brand equity starts with brand awareness, building that meticulously is one of the important first steps to take when marketing a brand along the consumer-based line of thought. In the section about the cognitive consumer perspective we mentioned that memory is assumed to be very durable. As knowledge we store in memory tends to stay there for a very long time, repeated exposure to a commercial message is considered very important. Perceptual enhancement of a concept can lead to permanent memory codes.

Brand awareness might be the most important use of heuristics (the simplifying strategies) where consumers choose the well known brand because it facilitates the choice process. The consumer seems to be willing to pay a premium price and accept lower-quality goods for the same brand if it is a brand with high awareness. Consumers display a tendency to accept more advertising repetition by a familiar brand than from an unknown one and pioneering brands have tremendous advantages when it comes to conquering the permanent positive memory codes. So building the highest possible degree of brand awareness or familiarity is crucial for a successful brand.

When establishing brand awareness, the marketer might also pay some attention to whether brand recognition or brand recall is the most important goal for the brand in question. The recall aspect is most important in high involvement categories and when the purchase decision is made outside the store. When it comes to low-involvement categories and the purchase decision primarily is taken in-store, a high level of recognition might be enough. Here, the consumer does not need to be able to recall the brand in order to make a purchase decision. When a low-involvement brand is recognized in the supermarket, it is often the one that gets chosen.

Make consumers pay attention to your brand

After meticulously having investigated and mapped brand associations, the marketer is equipped with the tools to choose the right brand elements. The marketer has an exact overview of the types of association held in the minds of consumers, as well as the favourability, strength and uniqueness of the associations. Hereby, the marketer is aware whether the consumer-based brand equity is positive or negative.

Equipped with this knowledge, the marketer is able to make a detailed strategy by having the answers to the following questions and many more: Which elements are the most central? Which are strongest? Which are more unique? Which associations lack in favourability? Hereafter, the marketer can accurately plan where to make an effort and on which parameters the brand is strong enough. In this fashion, the marketer is able to create a detailed and well founded future work schedule.

Some elements might require special attention. The marketer can organize investigations of key elements in order to further fine-tune brand communication to accommodate the mechanisms of the cognitive consumer. Box 6.6 provides insight into the many considerations that might be taken into account before choosing the brand name. The right brand name is only one of the many important elements a marketer has to decide.

Box 6.6 Things to consider when choosing the right brand name

The brand name is a very important brand element as it is most often the key node activating the spreading activity in the associative network of brand knowledge. The brand name spurs brand awareness, which is the prerequisite for talking about brand image and customer-based brand equity in the first place.

In *Dimensions of Consumer Expertise* researchers Alba and Hutchinson (1987) list things to consider when choosing the right brand name adjusted for easy recognition.

- *The brand name should be easily read.* Consumers scan shelf displays rapidly when in a supermarket and do not take time to read carefully each name on display. In order to test the readability of a word, respondents can be exposed to the word extremely briefly or can be exposed to a name with letters missing.

- *The brand name should be easily recognized.* Studies show that pseudo-words (nonsense) words are more difficult to recognize than real words (meaning something). But as the number of exposures increases the difference seems to diminish.
- *Consider a frequently used word as brand name.* Frequently used words are more easily remembered than infrequently used words.

Other criteria apply when it comes to recalling a brand name. The inquiring reader should turn to the original source, as the above list is by no means exhaustive and meant only to indicate how many details the marketer can go into when managing the brand in the consumer-based approach.

Source Alba and Hutchinson (1987)

Position your brand

In the process of building customer-based brand equity it is also important to identify the maximum level of congruence between brand associations. Congruence means that it is beneficial to build the communication platform around the associations that are the most similar. Congruence among the different brand associations determines the cohesiveness of the brand image. A coherent brand image facilitates the spreading activity in the mind of the consumer. In other words, the 'computer' is better able to process data it does not have to retrieve in too many different places.

The need for congruence is related to the question of heuristics in the information-processing theory of consumer choice. The consumer has a limited processing capacity and lives in a world of a million commercial messages. Therefore, the consumer only pays attention to the incoming information that captures attention *and* starts a relatively easy spreading activity.

Consistency in communications is also a key aspect of the consumer-based approach. Once having established high brand awareness and the right congruent brand associations, it is assumed risky to change course. These aspects of the consumer-based approach share many characteristics with the idea of *positioning* (Ries and Trout 1983, 2001). This hugely popular theory rests upon the same key assumptions about the human mind being a computer with limited processing capabilities in an over-communicated society which is why the clever marketers are the ones repeating over and over again the commercial messages that are fine-tuned to establish a lasting mental territory for the brand. This very important aspect of the consumer-based approach is what associates it with terms like Unique Selling Proposition, brand DNA, brand mantra, and 'owning associations'.

Marketing a brand according to the consumer-based approach also requires identifying the most relevant competition. As customer-based brand equity is defined as being either positive or negative compared with competitors, there is essentially only one brand in each category with positive customer-based brand equity. In order for the marketer to make the most relevant brand strategy, it is worth while thinking about which competitors are the real threat and then conducting the comparative analyses and formulating the brand strategy in relation to them.

An emphasis on strategy

In 1993, when the idea of customer-based brand equity was first put forward, it was often difficult to distinguish between brand research and ad research. The idea of brand management being a central area of interest in corporations seemed years away. We have mentioned earlier that the publication of customer-based brand equity was extremely important in itself, and that it also had some valuable side effects, such as shedding light on the topic of brand equity and brand image. Furthermore, it lifted the brand to being a strategic priority and something else and more than advertising. In the 1993 article Keller outlines specific managerial guidelines. The guidelines are explained in box 6.7 and their implications are that the brand should be managed in a continuous process, on a strategic level, and should be conceived as much more than advertising.

Box 6.7 Six managerial guidelines

- *Adopt a broad view of marketing decisions.* Think in broad terms when you consider the many marketing actions and the many aspects of brand knowledge that can be activated and that could influence sales
- *Define the desired knowledge structures.* The marketer should be razor-sharp when making a plan for which knowledge structures will be most important to customers, and thus will build the stronger brand. Looking at the filled-out association map, which parts of the knowledge structure need the most attention?
- *Evaluate alternative tactical options regarding communication channels.* Consider the whole spectrum of potential consumer touch points and activate them systematically so that they add to the congruence and consistency of the chosen brand identity.
- *Take a long-term view of marketing decisions.* Think ahead! Every marketing action influences future marketing actions and, as the consumer is supposed to have a very long memory, every action may influence brand associations for a very long time.
- *Employ tracking studies over time.* As all marketing actions are seen as a long chain of interrelated events influencing the brand, tracking studies should be applied on a continuous basis. Here, gaps between the intended and the real brand knowledge can be detected and marketing actions can be adjusted.

- *Evaluate potential extension candidates.*[2] Management ought to consider and evaluate potential brand extensions in order to benefit from the obtained brand equity. The brand image of the main brand may serve as an efficient information base for the new product. On the other hand, associations that differ too much between the main and the extended brand may damage the main brand severely.

Source Keller (1993)

Balancing brand image with brand identity

The consumer-based approach is born and becomes influential over the same course of years as the identity approach. These two approaches are interesting to compare as they are based on completely opposite perceptions of where the brand should find its true nature, inspiration and energy. Because they are so opposite in assumptions, they illustrate each other's weaknesses neatly. In the identity approach, the brand is found inside the organization, and strategic force and inspiration hence stem from within the organization behind the brand. The main problem of managing a brand according to this approach is the risk of organizational 'narcissism' and a lack of market sensing.

It goes without saying that consumer-based management depends on superior abilities when it comes to market sensing and customer knowledge. The main problem of managing the brand according to this approach is that the focus on the consumer leads to a lack of organizational vision. Even though there is no doubt that there is some truth in the assumption that the brand exists in the mind of consumer, the marketer should also consider that the process of listening only to consumer associations is essentially backward-looking. Consumers relate to previous marketing initiatives and hence are not visionary. Hereby, the vision for the brand stemming from the brand corporation risks a lack of future perspective: 'Brand management is enacted as a tactical process of cyclical adaptation to consumers' representations of the focal brand whereby brand image gradually supplants brand identity' (Louro and Cunha 2003, p. 863).

Summary

Managing a brand according to the principles of the consumer-based approach requires acknowledging that the brand is something residing in the minds of consumers and that listening to consumers is a prerequisite for skilled brand management. Still, the marketer is seen as in charge of communications as an assumption of linear communication applies to the cognitive consumer perspective.

The marketer should start by making sure that consumers are sufficiently aware of the brand. Once an adequate level of brand awareness is obtained, brand image has to be communicated and the brand has to be positioned. The brand image should be built around the most relevant and congruent consumer associations.

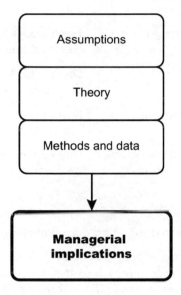

Figure 6.13 Managerial implications of the consumer-based approach

The elements should be tested for their cognitive suitability before application to brand image.

The brand should be positioned through consistency in communications. As memory is believed to be very durable in cognition, permanent memory codes can be obtained through remaining on the same course communications-wise.

The consumer-based approach also implies that the brand should be a strategic priority and all marketing actions should be seen as a long chain of events all influencing the brand image. The marketer might consider balancing the strong sides of the consumer-based approach with the strong sides of the identity approach as founding the brand solely on consumer associations might lead to a lack of vision for the brand.

Box 6.8 Do's and don'ts in the consumer-based approach

Do	Don't
Inquire consumer associations meticulously	Don't neglect the true owners of the brand (the consumers)
Use consumers' brand associations to determine the content of the brand	Don't believe you can formulate the brand strategy yourself
Find congruency in brand associations	Don't apply a scatter-gun technique

Communicate brand image consistently	Don't change brand communications too often
Think ahead in brand communications	Don't think that there are marketing actions that will not affect the brand
Identify your real competitors	Don't forget your brand's unique selling proposition
Consider if listening to customers drive your brand forwards in a visionary fashion	Don't forget that closeness to the market is your strongest asset.

Development of the consumer-based approach and later approaches

As mentioned in the introduction, the consumer-based approach has probably become the most dominant approach of the seven we present in this book. Therefore, we have chosen to round off this chapter with a few comments on the consumer-based approach, how it has developed since the 1990s, how we present it, and how other approaches define themselves against it.

As mentioned in the introduction, it is our goal to present the roots of each approach, the founding publications and main theories, methods and data, and its managerial implications. In each approach chapter we try to balance emphasis on the roots with the newest development of the approach.

Due to the fact that the consumer-based approach in many ways has developed into *the* textbook treatment of brand management, the development of the approach has moved in an all-encompassing direction. Therefore we have emphasized the roots of the approach and somewhat neglected its further development.

In this chapter we have spent the majority of our space introducing the reader to the quintessential cognitive brand and consumer perspective. It should, however, be noted that Keller has embraced the later approaches in his more recent publications. The consumer-based approach is concerned with brand knowledge, and when you think of it, there is nothing that cannot be seen as part of consumers' brand knowledge. In that way, all approaches of this book can be added to brand knowledge.

Keller and Lehmann (2003) claim that branding is all about understanding the customers' mindset. This mindset consists of five dimensions: awareness, associations, attitudes, attachments and activity. The first three dimensions can be recognized as components of the customer-based brand equity framework. The fourth dimension (attachment) is about loyalty and resistance to change. This dimension resembles the relational approach somewhat, while the latest dimension (that of activity) reminds us of the community approach, as it relates to consumer interaction.

In 2003 in *Journal of Consumer Research* Keller took stock of brand management theory. J. Aaker's work on brand personality (chapter 7), Fournier's brand relationship theory (chapter 8), and Muñiz and O'Guinn's conceptualization of brand communities (chapter 9) are mentioned as important contributions to the academic discipline. Still, they are added to the term 'brand knowledge'.

> These studies and others similar in spirit are noteworthy for their ability to use novel research methods to uncover overlooked or relatively neglected facets of consumer brand knowledge that have significant theoretical and managerial implications.
>
> (Keller 2003, p. 596)

Looking at brand management from the cognitive perspective implies that everything can be added to brand knowledge. Keller, however, recognizes that he looks at the brand from a specific angle:

> it should be recognized that this essay presented a representation of brand knowledge based largely on cognitive psychology. Important perspectives on branding and brand knowledge obviously can, and have been, gained from other disciplinary viewpoints, for example, anthropological or ethnographic approaches. Part of the challenge in developing mental maps for consumers that accurately reflect their brand knowledge is how best to incorporate multiple theoretical or methodological paradigms.
>
> (Keller 2003, p. 600)

The consumer-based approach can thus be hard to negotiate with as brand knowledge can be said to be all-encompassing. As Keller states in the two above-mentioned examples, the new approaches can be added to brand knowledge, and in that sense you can say that the consumer-based approach suffices.

One of the goals of this book is to deconstruct the field of brand management seen from a perspective rooted in the philosophy of science. And in this context, it is necessary to regard the latter approaches as something more than merely newer additions to brand knowledge. As we have mentioned in the section about the cognitive consumer perspective, the cognitive tradition deliberately neglects emotional and cultural factors in its search for explanations of human behaviour. Later approaches embrace the emotional and cultural factors that the cognitive tradition neglects in their search for explanations of human behaviour. Therefore, the purpose of fitting all kinds of brand knowledge into the same mould instead of understanding them separately can be questioned.

However, it would make a great student assignment (go to student questions below) to add the components of the personality, the relational, the community, and the cultural approach to the original map of consumer knowledge (figure 6.7).

The significant influence of the consumer-based approach is difficult to evaluate. The seven approaches of this book represent profoundly different brand and consumer perspectives, some more compatible than others. Still, it is unusual that one approach defines itself in opposition to another approach. But the consumer-based approach seems to be more deliberately challenged than the other approaches. The challenges come from two sides: the relational approach (of chapter 8) and the cultural approach (of chapter 10).

The relational approach does not explicitly define itself in opposition to the consumer-based approach. The relational approach, however, is influenced by phenomenology, which is a scientific and philosophical tradition stressing the 'inner reality' of consumers. In the world of brand management and consumer research the phenomenological view of the world defines itself in opposition to the information-processing view (see table 8.2). Thereby, the consumer-based and the relational approach represent very different points of departure when it comes to understanding the consumer and managing the brand.

The cultural approach (or its most important author, Douglas B. Holt) is much more explicit in his critique of the consumer-based approach. Holt defines four different branding models (see table 11.3) and stresses 'the mindshare model' (comparable to the consumer-based approach) as the dominant one. The cultural approach is then neatly formulated as a viable alternative to the consumer-based approach stressing its Achilles heel of emphasizing consistency in communication. In the cultural approach the brand is seen as a cultural artefact influenced by changes in time and culture (see a comparison between the two branding models/brand approaches in table 10.1).

Comments from the 'founding fathers' (2)

The value of consumer-based approaches to the study of branding and brand management

Kevin Lane Keller, Tuck School of Business, Dartmouth College

Without question, branding is a complex management area that deserves study from a variety of different perspectives and academic traditions. By providing a multidisciplinary approach, this book provides a welcome and invaluable resource for thoughtful students, scholars, and practitioners who want to fully understand branding and brand management.

This chapter introduced some of the key tenets of the consumer-based approach. As any good brand researcher will admit, any approach to the study of branding and brand management will have its advantages and disadvantages. Part of the power of a consumer-based approach is that it squarely focuses on the consumer as being at the heart of brand equity. Consumer-based approaches, if properly invoked and interpreted, are extremely versatile and can provide detailed insights as to how consumers make all kinds of brand-related choices.

Consumer-based approaches capitalize on the numerous research and industry advances in the study of consumer behaviour – how consumers think, feel, and act towards brands, products, services, companies, other consumers, and so on. Consumer-based approaches can provide the foundation for how and why consumers forge relationships with brands and form communities with others; how culture is manifested in consumer consumption behaviour; and how brands take on meaning that transcends physical products and services and strict service specifications.

As a note of caution, it is important to *not* narrowly view consumer-based approaches in terms of just information processing models. Although such models can be extremely useful to understand how consumers learn about brands and how that knowledge, in turn, affects how they respond to any aspect of marketing, researchers adopting a consumer-based approach to the study of branding and brand management have successfully introduced or adapted many other concepts related to non-cognitive issues and concerns.

The best consumer-based researchers recognize that branding and brand management are an art and science and that the strongest brands have achieved their success by being able to affect consumers both in their head and in their heart. Like the best marketing practitioners, consumer-based researchers adopt a broad view of how to think about consumers and strive to keep abreast of key cultural trends that suggest new areas of consumer behavior to study.

In my own research I have found that focusing on consumer brand knowledge structures provides a comprehensive, cohesive foundation for analysis and a common denominator by which many different topics and issues can be addressed. Fundamentally, the question becomes: how does any marketing action or any other event or trend that occurs in the marketplace affect how consumers think, feel and act about brands? Defining customer-based brand equity as the 'differential effect that brand knowledge has on how consumers respond to marketing activity' has allowed me to conceptualize sources and outcomes of brand equity in great detail and provide specific managerial guidelines based on this conceptualization.

With a consumer-based approach, concepts, theories and findings from diverse areas such as learning, memory, emotions, behavioural decision theory, and consumer decision making – to name just a few – can all be brought to bear to better understand how brands should be optimally built and managed. With such dramatic changes in the marketing environment due to increased globalization, technological advances, environmental concerns and many other factors, the power of the consumer-based approach to flexibly apply a variety of conceptual tools to address a variety of managerial concerns in brand management is truly invaluable.

Student questions

1 Which psychological tradition is associated with the consumer-based approach?
2 What is the most important metaphor for man in this tradition?
3 The brand 'ownership' can be said to be of an ambiguous nature. Describe the ambiguity.

4   How do we store information in memory?
5   Brand knowledge consists of two main categories. Name them.
6   In order for a brand to have high customer-based brand equity, the brand asso-
     ciations need to be .... [Add three adjectives]
7   Describe the idea behind process-tracing methods.
8   How come customer-based brand equity is associated with the idea of
     positioning?
9   *Student assignment.* Expand the brand knowledge model (figure 6.7) by
     adding knowledge from the personality, the relational, the community and the
     cultural approaches (See discussion in the last section.)

References and further reading

Key readings are in **bold type**.

Aaker, D. A. and Keller, K. L. (1990) 'Consumer evaluations of brand extensions', *Journal
    of Marketing*, 54 (January): 27–41
Aaker, J. L. (1997) 'Dimensions of brand personality, *Journal of Marketing Research*, 34
    (August): 347–56
Alba, J. W. and Hutchinson, J. W. (1987) 'Dimensions of consumer expertise', *Journal of
    Consumer Research*, 13 (March): 411–54
Allen, C. T., Fournier, S. and Miller, F. (2006) *'Brands and their Meaning Makers'*, in C. P.
    Haugtvedt, P. M. Herr and F. R. Kardes (eds) *Handbook of Consumer Psychology*,
    Mahwah NJ: Lawrence Erlbaum Associates
Anderson, J. R. (1983) *The Architecture of Cognition*, Cambridge MA: Harvard University
    Press
Bahn, K. D. (1986) 'How and when do brand perceptions and preferences first form? A
    cognitive developmental investigation', *Journal of Consumer Research*, 13 (December):
    382–93
Bettman, J. R. (1979) *An Information Processing Theory of Consumer Choice*, Reading
    MA: Addison-Wesley
Bettman, J. R. (1986) 'Consumer psychology', *Annual Review of Psychology*, 37: 257–89
Campbell, M. C. and Keller, K. L. (2003) 'Brand familiarity and advertising repetition
    effects', *Journal of Consumer Research*, 30 (September): 292–304
Fournier, S. (1998) 'Consumers and their brands: developing relationship theory in
    consumer research', *Journal of Consumer Research*, 24 (4): 343–73
Franzen, G. and Bouwman, M. (2001) *The Mental World of Brands: Mind, Memory, and
    Brand Success*, Henley on Thames: World Advertising Research Centre
Gade, A. (1997) *Hjerneprocesser. Kognition og neurovidenskab*, Copenhagen: Frydenlund
Gardner, H. (1985) *The Mind's New Science: A History of the Cognitive Revolution*, New
    York: Basic Books
Gross, R. and McIlveen, R. (1997) *Cognitive Psychology*, London: Hodder & Stoughton
Holt, D. B. (2005) 'How societies desire brands: using cultural theory to explain brand
    symbolism', in S. Ratneshwar and D. G. Mick (eds) *Inside Consumption: Consumer
    Motives, Goals, and Desires*, London: Routledge
Hoyer, W. D. and Brown, S. P. (1990) 'Effects of brand awareness on choice for a common,
    repeat-purchase product', *Journal of Consumer Research*, 17 (September): 141–8

Kardes, F. R. (1994) 'Consumer judgement and decision processes', in R. S. Wyer and T. K. Srull (eds) *Handbook of Social Cognition*, Mahwah NJ: Lawrence Erlbaum Associates

Keller, K. L. (1993) 'Conceptualizing, measuring, and managing customer-based brand equity', *Journal of Marketing*, 57 (January): 1–22

Keller, K. L. (2003) 'Brand synthesis: the multidimensionality of brand knowledge', *Journal of Consumer Research*, 20 (March): 595–600

Keller, K. L. (2005) 'Branding short cuts', *Marketing Management*, 14 (5): 18–23

Keller, K. L. and Lehmann, D. R. (2003) 'How do brands create value?' *Marketing Management*, 12 (3) (May/June): 26–31

Louro, M. J. and Cunha, P. V. (2001) 'Brand management paradigms', *Journal of Marketing Management*, 17: 849–75

Mitchell, A. A. (1982) 'Models of memory: implications for measuring knowledge structures', *Advances in Consumer Research*, 9 (1): 45–51

Muñiz, A. M. Jr, and O'Guinn, T. C. (2001) 'Brand community', *Journal of Consumer Research*, 27 (March): 412–31

Park, C. W., Jaworski, B. J. and MacInnis, D. J. (1986) 'Strategic brand concept–image management', *Journal of Marketing*, October: 135–45

Payne, J. W., Bettman, J. R. and Johnson, E. J. (1993) *The Adaptive Decision Maker*, Cambridge: Cambridge University Press

Ries, A. and Trout, J. (1983, 2001) *Positioning: the Battle for your Mind*, New York: McGraw-Hill

Robertson, T. S. and Kassarjian, H. H. (1991) *Handbook of Consumer Behavior*, Englewood Cliffs NJ: Prentice-Hall

7 The personality approach

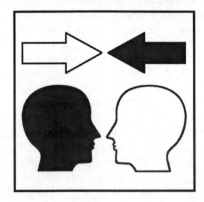

with a commentary by Adjunct Professor Joseph Plummer, Columbia Business School

---

Learning objectives

The purpose of this chapter is to:

Understand the assumptions of the personality approach
- The personality approach assumes that personality traits are important drivers of emotional bonding between brand and consumer

Understand the theoretical building blocks of the personality approach
- The personality approach has three supporting themes: personality, consumer self and brand–self congruence
- The personality approach draws on theory from psychology about the categorization of human personality
- The personality construct can, in interplay with consumer expression of self, be a driver of strong consumer–brand relationships

Gain insights into the methods of the personality approach
- Gain an overview of the mix of qualitative and quantitative methods that can be used to uncover brand personality
- Get an introduction to scaling techniques used in the personality approach

Understand the managerial implications
- Understand how a brand personality can be created and managed by using direct and indirect sources of brand personality

In 2006 Apple launched the first of three new television advertisements for Mac laptops. A young man dressed in casual clothes introduces himself as a Mac ('Hi, I am a Mac'). An older, more conservative-looking man enters the scene, introducing himself as PC. The two, clearly very different personalities, act out a brief vignette in which the capabilities and attributes of 'Mac' and 'PC' are compared. The PC is represented as a formal and stuffy person overly concerned with work – often being frustrated by the superior abilities of the more laid-back Mac. The two, the casual Mac and the more uptight PC, discuss some of the everyday difficulties of the PC and how the Mac does not have these problems. The Mac personality versus the PC personality is an example of a brand that takes the theoretical possibilities of the personality approach literally, using the brand personality to position and differentiate the brand against other brands in the same product category.

Consumers automatically ascribe personality to brands. This process is a central aspect of consumers' symbolic consumption and construction of self. The personality approach in brand management hence focuses on how and why people choose brands with certain personalities and how imbuing brands with personality thus can be a powerful tool to create and enhance brand equity. The assumptions, theories and methods of the personality approach borrow from the academic fields of human psychology, personality research and consumer behaviour. Understanding consumers' attraction to brand personalities has for long been an area of interest in consumer behaviour research, where research has focused on how brand personality enables consumers to express 'self' through the symbolic use of brand personality. In a brand management context, practitioners have viewed brand personality primarily as a way to differentiate the brand from other brands in the same product category; as a driver of consumer preference; and as a common denominator that can be used across different national cultures. Several interesting and groundbreaking research articles have been published, but one article in particular can be said to have stirred the pot and set new agendas: 'Dimensions of brand personality' (Jennifer Aaker 1997) presented a whole new theoretical framework and method for working with brand personality that has since been validated and expanded by several studies. This chapter offers an overview of the personality approach by providing insights into the assumptions, key theoretical elements and methodologies underlying the personality approach. Finally, this chapter describes and discusses the managerial guidelines that can be accumulated from the literature, supplemented with cases describing how companies can manage brand personality in practice.

Assumptions of the personality approach

Previous approaches in brand management have placed the Four Ps, the identity of the corporation, or the consumer at the heart of brand equity creation (respectively the economic approach in chapter 4, the identity approach in chapter 5, and the consumer-based approach in chapter 6). In the personality approach, it is assumed that consumers' need for identity and expression of self is a key driver of the consumption of a brand. This is why consumers, apart from the physical and functional characteristics of a brand, also consume brands due to the symbolic benefits they can provide.

> As a result, the symbolic nature of brands can be understood at the same level as the utilitarian nature of brands, which tends to be captured by models that are generalizable across product categories (e.g., multi-attribute model; Fishbein and Ajzen 1975). Therefore, like the multi-attribute model, which sheds insight into when and why consumers buy brands for utilitarian purposes, a cross-category framework and scale can provide theoretical insights into when and why consumers buy brands for self-expressive purposes.
>
> (Aaker 1997, p. 348)

Furthermore, it is assumed that if these symbolic benefits are expressed by imbuing the brand with a human-like character, then the brand will be strengthened significantly. A strong and attractive brand personality can, if well executed, serve as an important source of differentiation and brand power. Brand personality is an efficient driver of emotional bonding between brand and consumer because consumers bond with and act on brands with a brand personality to a greater extent than they do with brands that do not have a personality. The reason is that consumers 'see' themselves in the personality of the brand and can hence use the brand in their construction of identity and self. The more consumers perceive the brand personality as a reflection of own personality, the stronger the brand personality and brand. The function of a brand personality is, however, not limited to consumers' personal inward use as a source of construction of self. Brands with an attractive brand personality are also chosen and consumed due to their outward symbolic signalling value. The use of brand personality as a symbolic signal or source for self construction can be based on the brand personality itself or the personality of the ideal/actual users of a brand. The personality approach hence places the personality of the brand and the personality of its stereotypical or ideal user at the heart of brand management.

The basic assumptions regarding the brand in the personality approach are ones of a reciprocal and human-like exchange between brand and consumer. As depicted in figure 7.1, brands are endowed with human-like personalities, which are activated in a continuous reciprocal, dialogue-based exchange between brand and consumer.

In the personality approach, the emotional bond between the brand and the consumer is hence strengthened significantly if the brand has an attractive and relevant brand personality. For consumers, brands with a brand personality are hence appealing because they serve as a mean of construction of and expression of self. For companies brand personality can serve as an important source of differentiation, positioning, and a tool to build emotional bonds with consumers.

The personality perspective

The personality approach draws on theories and insights from, respectively, the fields of human psychology and consumer behaviour research. From human

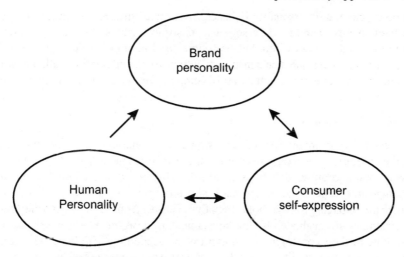

Figure 7.1 Brand personality construct

psychology the personality approach borrows theory about different categorizations of human character in theories about human personality dimensions and traits. From consumer behaviour research, it is knowledge about how consumers use brands in their construction and expression of self that is in play. The primary function of the brand is hence in this approach to express a personality that consumers can relate to and use for their own construction and expression of self. The subjects of analysis are respectively brand personality and consumer self, hence the brand relates to the individual consumers and is used by the individual – though also used to express social identity for others.

   In human psychology, personality is perceived as the pattern in which individuals can be divided according to how they fairly consistently react to different environmental situations. In a brand management context, the construct of brand personality refers to 'the set of human characteristics associated with a brand' (Aaker 1997, p. 347). The personality traits associated with a brand are assumed to be enduring, distinct and stable. The self-expressive value and the distinctiveness of the brand personality influence the attractiveness and the potential strength of the brand in general. In consumer behaviour research, it has long been acknowledged that consumers use brands for symbolic consumption and as means to express themselves by selecting brands with a particular brand personality. The extent to which consumers are able to use the specific brand as a point of reference for their own construction and signalling of identity lays the basis for differentiation of the brand from other brands in the same category. The level of consumers' identification with the personality of the brand determines the degree to which the consumers evaluate the brand as suitable or not for their own self-expression and construction of identity. Hence, a really powerful and differentiated brand (in the line of thinking behind this approach) is perceived by the consumer as a brand that contributes to the consumer's construction and expression of self. For the company, the brand personality is hence a source of differentiation as well as a driver of loyalty. The brand personality construct enables companies to imbue intangible symbolic cues into the 'behaviour' and communication of the brand. These symbolic cues enhance consumers' attraction to and relation with the brand and hence serve as an important driver of competitive advantage and brand loyalty.

The 'brand–consumer exchange'

The personality approach introduces a strong emotional bond between the brand and the consumer, based on consumers' use of the brand personality for the inward construction and outward expression of self. The nature of the brand–consumer exchange in the personality approach is interactive and dyadic, and revolves around the exchange of symbolic benefits. These symbolic benefits (the brand personalities) are evaluated by the consumer based on the extent to which they contribute to their construction and expression of identity. The brand–consumer exchange in the personality approach is perceived to take place between one brand and one consumer. The focus is hence like in the previous approaches individual and the nature of the relation is dyadic. It is this symbolically charged interaction between the brand and the consumer that motivates consumers to choose one brand over another. Because a brand personality sets off a process of social identification between the brand and the self of the consumer, it is assumed in the personality approach that the fulfilment and expression of self is one of the strongest basic driving forces that predispose consumers to act on and consume brands. The personality of the brand generates attention and interest from consumers, who feel that they can use the symbolic benefits of the brand in their construction and expression of self. In reverse, the stereotypical consumer of a personality-based brand also affects the evolution of the personality of the brand. The creation of brand personality is a dynamic cyclical process that sets off from the company and then in an interactive process between consumer and brand creates and enhances a certain brand personality. Consumers evaluate a brand personality based on their observations of the brand behaviour over time. These evaluations add up to a general assessment of the brand and of its role as a relationship partner. The logic is hence that the greater congruity there is between human personality characteristics and the consumers' actual or ideal self, the greater will be consumer preferences for that brand.

Summary

In the personality approach, human personality and consumers identity construction as well as expression is the pivotal point of brand equity creation. It is the symbolic benefits a brand can provide to consumers expressed through a certain brand personality that are assumed to be the key drivers of brand strength. The level of analysis is the individual consumer and the subject of analysis is consumer self and identity. The main function of the brand is not to provide utilitarian attributes and benefits as in the economic approach, but to enable consumers' construction

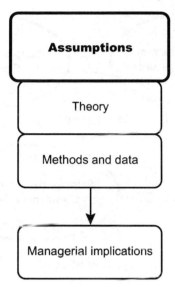

Figure 7.2 Assumptions of the personality approach

and expression of self by providing symbolic signal value. The strength of the brand is determined by the extent to which there is congruity between the brand personality and the personality or self of the consumer.

Theoretical building blocks of the personality approach

In this section the key constructs of the personality approach and their interrelation will be explained. The key constructs of brand personality provide the theoretical building blocks and draw on three supporting themes: personality, expression of self and congruence between brand personality and consumer self. The personality construct has its origin in theory from cognitive and social psychology about human personality. Consumers' construction and expression of self are widely studied in the field of consumer behaviour, but it also borrows from the field of psychology about the construction of identity. The last supporting theme, brand-self congruence, is derived from the field of social psychology and focuses on the social identification process consumers engage in with the brands they consume. The three supporting themes in the personality approach are all enhanced to fit into the context of brand management and provide theoretical input to the core theme – brand personality.

Supporting theme: personality

The concept of personality has its origin in the field of human psychology. The personality is one of the most significant manifestations of a human being's self-concept and has since the 1930s been an area of research in human psychology. The personality construct in human psychology focuses on the development of

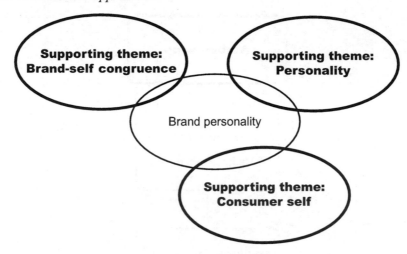

Figure 7.3 Supporting themes of the personality approach

frameworks for the categorization of human beings according to their personality. These frameworks define people according to different personality types defined by certain personality traits. It hence assumes that personality traits describe internal characteristics of human beings from which their behaviour in different situations can be predicted and explained. Personality traits can be described with adjectives like e.g. 'talkative', 'organized', 'imaginative' or 'responsible'. There are several theoretical frameworks used in the field of psychology for the categorization of personalities, but one of the more common is the framework of the 'Big Five'. This framework reduces the number of adjectives describing human personalities to five dimensions, representing the five overriding personalities according to which human beings can be categorized. If a brand is high on extroversion, then the brand behaviour, reflected in the personality traits, will be talkative, active, energetic and outgoing (see figure 7.4).

This framework hence presumes that the extent to which a person is extrovert or emotionally stable can determine or predict how that person will react to different situations. The Big Five framework hence provides a framework for classifying and categorizing human beings according to descriptors of human personality. The personality of human beings not only determines how they will react to different situations or behave in general, it also influences how humans are able to connect with other human beings and the role that people with different personalities play in relationships between two or more people.

Supporting theme: consumer self

Human beings attach meaning to possessions because we regard possessions as part of ourselves. The meaning consumers attach to possessions is key in the understanding of consumption patterns and the drivers that motivate consumers'

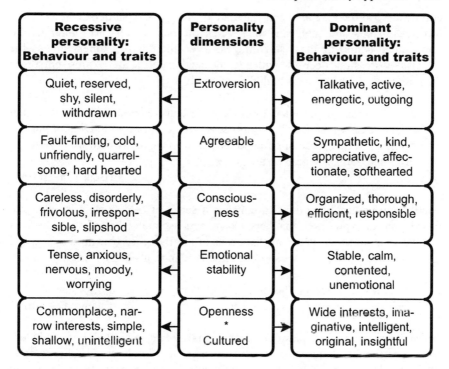

Recessive personality: Behaviour and traits	Personality dimensions	Dominant personality: Behaviour and traits
Quiet, reserved, shy, silent, withdrawn	Extroversion	Talkative, active, energetic, outgoing
Fault-finding, cold, unfriendly, quarrelsome, hard hearted	Agreeable	Sympathetic, kind, appreciative, affectionate, softhearted
Careless, disorderly, frivolous, irresponsible, slipshod	Consciousness	Organized, thorough, efficient, responsible
Tense, anxious, nervous, moody, worrying	Emotional stability	Stable, calm, contented, unemotional
Commonplace, narrow interests, simple, shallow, unintelligent	Openness * Cultured	Wide interests, imaginative, intelligent, original, insightful

Figure 7.4 Brand behaviour; from Smit, Van Den Berge and Franzen, 'Brands are just like real people' (2003), p. 24, © Copenhagen Business School Press 2003

symbolic consumption of brands. Consumer research and psychology have for long acknowledged that brands contribute significantly to consumers' sense of who they are or in other words their sense of self. Brands are considered important for consumers' construction and expression of self. Belk, who is a pioneer in the conceptualization of the self-concept, quotes William James (founder of the modern conceptions of self (1890, pp. 291–2)), in his quest for a conceptualization of how possessions affect the formation and expression of self:

> The sum total of all that he *can* call his, not only his body and his psychic powers, but his clothes and his house, his wife and children, his ancestors and friends, his reputation and works, his lands and yacht and bank-account.
>
> (Belk 1988, p. 139)

According to the modern conceptions of self, material possessions are thought to be an extension of our identity – and are defined as an important part of the so-called 'extended self'. The extended self is hence the extensions of self that humans produce through their relations with other people, our family, achievements and last – but in this context of brand management, certainly not least – our possessions. The nature and the importance of different possessions as contributors to the extended self fluctuate over time. Consumers hence neglect old possessions and seek new ones when the possessions no longer fit the consumers' actual or ideal self images. Even though consumers' needs for material possessions decrease with age, the need to define and express ourselves through possessions remains high throughout life.

> It seems an inescapable fact of modern life that we learn, define, and remind ourselves of who we are by our possessions.... Our accumulation of possessions provides a sense of past and tells us who we are, where we have come from, and perhaps where we are going.
>
> (Belk 1988, p. 160)

Apart from using possessions to enhance a sense of self, consumers also use possessions to express self to others. Consumers use brands to define themselves to others, demonstrate group affiliation or to tell the story of who they are and what they stand for. Consumers' self is structured in terms of two dimensions:

- *Attributes*. A person can be tall, lucky or can appreciate family values.
- *Narratives*. The attributes are linked to key events in life structured as stories.

Consumers use brands to play out their personal stories about their lives and identities, positioning themselves in relation to culture, society and other people. Objects or brands that people love are particularly important for the creation and maintenance and expression of self. 'Loved objects serve as indexical mementos of key events or relationships in the life narrative, help resolve identity conflicts, and tend to be tightly embedded in a rich symbolic network of associations' (Ahuvia 2005, p. 179).

Layers of consumer self

The consumer self construct (figure 7.5) is rather complex because the self refers to self on different levels. Objects can contribute to the construction of self on two levels. At the individual level, objects are consumed because they carry a symbolic significance for the consumer in relation to the creation and maintenance of self. Other consumption objects contribute to the social level of self – that is, the expression of self to others. Hence, the consumption of objects as a source of self can stem from consumers' need to create and maintain self at an individual level. This symbolic consumption of objects can also serve to express self to others at a more social group level. In the research literature, these levels are often referred to as the independent (individual) self and interdependent (social) self. The independent self consist of two categories of self, the actual and the desired self. The actual self is the objective representation of self – the way the self actually is. The desired self is a representation of something that the consumer would like to become, and finally the ideal self represents the consumer's perception of their own ideal self.

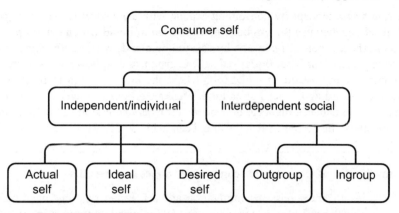

Figure 7.5 Consumer self construct

Brands contribute to the construction of self in various ways. They can help consumers achieve goals motivated by the desired self, meet needs for self-expression either socially or individually (the ideal self), or serve as a tool for connecting with the past; they can be symbols of personal achievement, an expression of individuality, or they can help people through life transitions. The self-expressive value and the distinctiveness of the brand personality have a significant effect on how attractive the brand personality is, as perceived by the consumer. But the self-expressive value is far more important than the distinctiveness. The self-expressive value of a brand personality depends on the level of consistency between the brand personality and the self-image of the consumer – the brand–self congruence. The third supporting theme of the personality approach is hence the construct of social identification between brand and consumer. In the academic literature this concept is often referred to as the brand–self congruence.

Brand–self congruence

When consuming a brand with a brand personality, consumers engage in a matching process to identify brands that are congruent with their own self images. This process is here referred to as brand–self congruence. The brand–self congruence construct has its origin in the concept of social identification from the field of psychology. This construct proposes that consumer behaviour is determined partly by the consumer's comparison of their own perception of self (either individual actual, ideal, or desired self, or their social out-group or in-group self as illustrated in figure 7.5) and the personality of the brand (because consumers tend to choose brands with a brand personality close to that of their own self). Self does not necessarily refer to the actual self; the brand personality can also be congruent with the ideal or desired self of the consumer. Depending on the function of the brand for either construction or expression of self, consumers use brand personalities in relation to self in two ways on an individual level. They either try to preserve their own self-concept by consuming brands with a personality matching their actual self, or they use the symbolic consumption of brand with a certain personality to enhance their self-concept, by consuming brands with a personality that is congruent with their ideal or desired self. Consumers can, however, also use the brands as an expression of social self, where the brand is used to position the consumer according to social or cultural reference groups in society. Using brand personality to enhance the ideal of desired self is an expression of the aspirations and dreams of the consumer that the brand can help them fulfil.

Box 7.1 Oil of Olay: female consumers' hopes and dreams

Deep insight into consumer motivation and self-brand relations is crucial when developing brand personality. In 1985 Joseph Plummer made an investigation of consumers' associations with the Oil of Olay brand that could be used to describe the brand personality of Oil of Olay. The result was rather surprising and illustrates well how brands can appeal not only to the actual self of consumers but also to the desired or ideal self of consumers. Consumers were asked to associate how they would describe Oil of Olay with other abstract descriptions, apart from it being a lotion. Consumers associated Oil of Olay with:

- An animal: a mink.
- Country: France.
- Occupation: secretary.
- Fabric: silk.
- Magazine: *Vogue*.

These associations brings to mind a French secretary wearing mink and silk reading *Vogue* while relaxing somewhere on the French Riviera. This elegant woman uses Oil of Olay every morning and evening to stay beautiful. The stereotypical user of Oil of Olay at the time had a personality far from the personality consumer associated with the Oil of Olay brand. She could be described as:

- Down-to-earth.
- Practical.

All in all, very different from the personality described as the personality of Oil of Olay, which was described as more up-scale, exclusive and sophisticated. These differences illustrate very well how some brands in their communication must address not necessarily the actual self of the stereotypical consumer but rather the desired or ideal self.

Adapted from Plummer (1985)

In brand management, the process of social identification is used to measure how well the brand personality matches the consumer's self image. Brand cues that evoke certain images of prestige and luxury activate a sensation and expression of high status. When consumers consume brands with a certain personality, a matching process takes place to determine whether the brand cues are consistent with the self images of the consumer. Or consumers adopt imaginary stereotypical users of a brand and then select the brands that match their own actual or desired self. The process of social identification depends on how the symbolic value of the brand is used by the consumer – what symbolic need the brand fulfils for the consumer. Consumers use brand personalities at a social or an individual level. As already mentioned, at the social level, brand personality serves to signal belonging to certain social groupings or subcultures. In that case, consumers reject brands and brand meaning that are not consistent with the references and images of the reference group the consumer is or would like to be a part of and use brands that are in accordance with their aspirations.[3] At the individual level, the brand can fulfil a need from the independent self to differentiate from groups of people and thereby demonstrate individual image and self.

The development of self congruence using brand personality is a dynamic two-way process. Consumers who prefer a particular brand because of its personality endow and influence the brand personality with their own self and symbolic signalling, strengthening or weakening the brand personality. To ensure that this process will strengthen and not weaken the brand personality, it is essential for the brand manager to ensure that the brand personality appeals to the right consumers and that their consumption of the brand underpins the existing personality of the brand. Getting this process right will consolidate and enhance the brand personality in the long run. Selecting and appealing to the right group of consumers can hence strengthen the brand, whereas attracting the 'wrong' group of consumers can devaluate the brand personality and undermine the credibility of the brand. The interaction between the brand and the consumer can hence be described as a cyclical process, either strengthening or weakening the brand.

Congruence between self and brand personality positively affects brand loyalty directly and indirectly through functional congruity, product involvement and brand relationship quality. This underpins the paramount importance of self–brand congruence, not only in the battle to attract and appeal to certain groups of consumers, but also for the long-term nurturing of brand–consumer relations, consumer-brand loyalty, and in the efforts to create the right brand personality.

Core theme: brand personality

Brand personality refers to both the personality endowed in the brand by the company and the brand personality perceived by consumers. One aspect of brand personality is hence what the company wants the consumer to think and feel about the brand, the other is what consumers perceive (and the two are not necessarily the same).

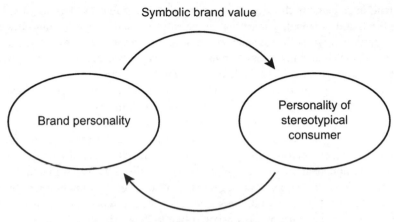

Symbolic brand value

Adds personality and symbolic value

Figure 7.6 The brand–self exchange of symbolic brand value in the market place

The personality statement (the communication goals the company has for the brand) must be reflected in the brand personality and serve as the guiding platform for the creation and enhancement of the brand in the long run. The personality statement delivers important input to the creative strategy.

The other side of the brand personality construct is what consumers actually feel about the brand. How much does the brand personality appeal to consumer self and motivate consumers to choose the specific brand because of the symbolic benefits they can derive from the brand personality? The three supporting themes of the personality approach cover, respectively:

- *Personality.* Theory from psychology provides a framework for endowing brands with a relevant personality.
- *Consumer self.* How consumers use brands to construct self and the different layers of self that the brand manager must be aware of.
- *Brand self congruence.* Describes how the congruity between the consumer's self and the brand determines how strong the brand personality can grow.

In 1997 Jennifer Aaker published the first research-based conceptualization of the personality construct in a brand management context. The outcome of her research was published in the article 'Dimensions of brand personality' (in *Journal of Marketing Research*). Her conceptualization of the personality construct builds on the theoretical and methodological frameworks from psychology, mentioned above, about the categorization of people according to the salience of different personality dimensions. It focuses on investigating if and how the categorization of human personalities from psychology also applies to brands. Aaker made an extensive investigation with the aim of identifying which personality traits people associate with a wide range of brands. Aaker came to the conclusion that it is

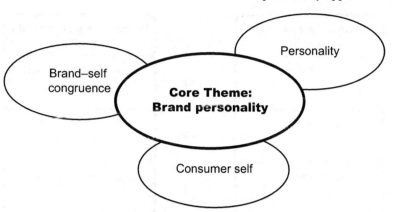

Figure 7.7 Core theme of the personality approach: brand personality

possible to transfer the idea of personality dimensions from human personality psychology to brands and brand management. The study resulted in the Big Five of brand management (the five dimensions of brand personality) (see figure 7.8). They describe the five major groupings of personalities consumers associate with brands and conclude that brands, in the same way humans have a unique personality, are perceived as having unique and distinct brand personalities. The five groupings of personalities have, in complementary research following the Aaker study, indicated that these five personalities apply, not only in the United States, where the study was originally made, but have also proved to be valid in other Western cultures. In Latin and Asian cultures, however, there seem to be some variations in how the different personality dimensions are rated (Aaker *et al.* 2001; Sung and Tinkham 2005)

The personality traits describe the characteristics that people associate with each brand personality dimension. These traits should ideally be reflected in the attributes of the brand or/and in the 'behaviour' of the brand. From the consumer perspective, the brand personality can be uncovered by exploring what consumers associate with the brand. From the company perspective, it can be uncovered by analysing the product-related attributes like brand name, logo, communication style, price, distribution, etc. All these elements add up to the brand personality. Apart from the more product-specific attributes, the brand personality is also reflected in the characteristics attributed to the brand and in the associations, symbolic values and emotional responses to the brand or the emotional relationship with the brand. For a brand personality to be successful, it must be consistent and durable.

A strong and consistent brand personality can lure people to consume that brand because they feel personally associated with the brand personality. If the attributes or behaviour of the brand (marketing activities) are not consistent with the brand personality, consumers are likely to abandon the brand because the personality loses credibility. From the marketing perspective, brand personality is closely

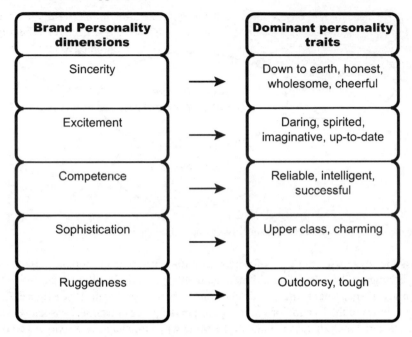

Brand Personality dimensions	Dominant personality traits
Sincerity	Down to earth, honest, wholesome, cheerful
Excitement	Daring, spirited, imaginative, up-to-date
Competence	Reliable, intelligent, successful
Sophistication	Upper class, charming
Ruggedness	Outdoorsy, tough

Figure 7.8 Dimensions of brand personality

related to and an important driver of brand identity and is a useful management tool that can be used to benchmark brand personality within or across product categories. The brand personality framework can be used to materialize abstract, intangible brand ideas and provide direction for the implementation of the brand idea in the user imagery, advertising and more product-related aspects like packaging. Succeeding in developing and implementing a strong, attractive and unique brand personality increases consumer preferences and evokes consumer emotions and bonding with the brand. This increases the level of trust and loyalty between brand and consumer. A key reason why brand personality can be such an effective tool for brand management is that consumers consume brands as a means in their identity construction projects – brands are important for consumers' construction and expression of self. The brand personality construct and consumers' expression of self are hence closely related. The framework of Aaker is the most up-to-date conceptualization of a personality framework for brand management, because it reflects the most recent insights into the mechanisms of human personality and brand personalities.

In practice, other theoretical frameworks and foundations for imbuing personality into brands have been widely used. The effectiveness of these tools and methods are, however, not supported by an extensive study like the Aaker framework. Theory about archetypes and narrative structures is an example of these alternative foundations for brand personality tools that have been widely used, especially by advertising agencies, to build a brand platform or personality.

Theory about archetypes represents a more deterministic and predetermined perspective on the drivers of human behaviour than the personality construct presented in this chapter because it bases the drivers of human consumption on universal predetermined behavioural patterns latent in all human beings.

Box 7.2 Archetypes and brand personality

Carl Gustav Jung was a Swiss psychiatrist. He pioneered the theory about archetypes based on extensive psychological studies in the early 1900s. Jung built the theoretical notions of archetypes on an idea that all human beings share a collective unconscious. This collective unconscious defines us at a psychological level like DNA codes define us at a microscopic physical level. The collective unconscious is the root of our communication and consists of psychological codes that transcend time. The collective unconscious is, according to Jung, '"identical in all men and thus constitutes a common psychic substrate of suprapersonal nature which is present in every one of us". This collective unconscious act as a communal well in the mind filled with psychic content that we all share' ('The archetypes and the collective unconscious', pp. 3–41 in K. Wertime, *Building Brands and Believers*, 2002, p. 60)

Archetypes are believed to be the basic mechanisms and source codes that enable people to communicate and connect at a rudimentary subconscious level. These codes are believed to be static, universal and deeply rooted in the human psyche. Jung further believed that the unconscious level of the human psyche is an active agent in people's lives and a significant factor that shapes everyday actions. Archetypes are expressions of the patterns of fundamental psychic content that we all share and are related to instinctively. They cover a range of basic elements in the human psyche like evil, happiness, heroic and maternal feelings. In religion and culture archetypical expressions have been used for millennia to express universal truths.

In brand management, archetypical patterns can, according to Mark and Pearson (2001), provide fundamental, timeless and universal reference points, by using symbols and images tapping into the unconscious. In that way brand managers can ensure brands achieve symbolic significance for all consumers because they address the archetypical level of unconscious patterns that we all share. Mark and Pearson's framework for working with archetypes in brand management consists of twelve archetypical personalities. These twelve archetypes are believed to be able to fulfil different, subconscious, archetypical needs for consumer:

Basic archetypical need
- Stability and control, and need to feel safe
- Belonging and enjoyment and a need to love and feel part af a community
- Risk and mastery and a need to achieve and perform well
- Independence and fulfilment and a need to find harmony and happiness

Archetypical personality

- Creator
- Caregiver
- Ruler
- Jester
- Regular girl/guy
- Lover

- Hero
- Outlaw
- Magician
- Innocent
- Explorer
- Sage

A brand imbued with archetypical meaning is believed to enhance the creation of emotional affinity, which makes way for the rational arguments for buying a product. In the personality approach archetypical symbols are the meaning used as the path opener between brands and consumers. Get a Donna Karan dress and feel like a queen or see the Christmas ads from Coca-cola and feel the innocence. Archetypes mediate between products and customer motivation by providing symbolic meaning. Archetypical meaning hence makes brands come to life and ensures that consumers can relate to the product or brand on an emotional level.

Source Mark and Pearson (2001)

Summary

The theoretical building blocks of the personality approach consist of the three supporting themes: personality, consumer self, and consumer–self congruence. Personality describes the basic concept of personality that the personality approach draws on from the field of human psychology, characterizing the main personalities that human beings can be categorized according to. The concept of self describes how consumers consume and choose brands based on their ability to contribute to their construction and expression of self. The construct of brand–self congruence describes the process of identification that takes place between the personality of a brand and the personality of the consumer and establishes that the greater the congruence between the personality of the brand and the personality of the consumer the more likely is that brand personality to succeed. The core theme of the personality approach is brand personality. The framework 'Dimensions of brand personality' developed by Aaker (1997) consists of five dimensions that brands can be divided according to and an explanation of how these dimensions can be expressed in the communication of a brand personality by emphasizing certain traits or behaviours.

Methods and data of the personality approach

The methods and data used in the personality approach vary, depending on what the focus of the study is. For the research of brand personality, the mainly quantitative method developed by Aaker (1997) has gained support and has been widely used to uncover dimensions of brand personality, also across different national cultures.

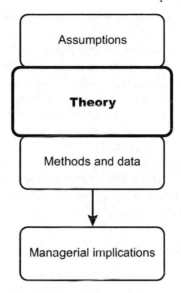

Figure 7.9 Theory of the personality approach

But research into the correlation between brand personality and consumers' expression of self and other more in-depth research dominates this approach. Research of brand personality and consumers' expression of self in the personality approach is conducted using a mix of qualitative and quantitative methods. Quantitative methods are used for categorizing and uncovering brand personality and for the study of consumers' self expression through brand personality; the focus is on rich and descriptive qualitative data. Qualitative data are necessary in order to gain understanding of the complex nature of consumer self and how it affects consumption patterns and ultimately how brand personality can be used to enhance consumers' expression of self. The methods in the personality approach hence vary from the very quantitative statistical studies of brand personality at one end of the scale to longitudinal field studies of brand personality and consumer expression of self at the other extreme.

Quantitative methods for researching brand personality

Investigating brand personality takes place in a cross-field between psychology and consumer research. In psychology, quantitative methods dominate, while consumer research methods are becoming increasingly qualitative. The aim of quantitative methods is, simply put, reducing ambiguity by transforming perceptions into structured quantifiable categories – or, as in the case of methods for studying brand personality, reducing consumers' perceptions of how a brand can be characterized, described and perceived as a personality into a structured set of brand personality dimensions. Until 1997 a variety of methods were used to explore and measure brand personality, but none of them had been validated by research extensive enough to deliver reliable, valid and generalizable results.

In the 1997 study conducted by Jennifer Aaker, an extensive primarily quantitative study of the dimensions of brand personality, the aim was to develop a framework that would be generalizable across brands and industries. The quantitative method used by Aaker for measuring brand personality has subsequently been validated by several studies and is widely used today. The aim was to identify a limited (manageable) number of dimensions that can be used to categorize all brands. For this purpose Aaker developed a method based on a structured quantitative measurement technique (scaling) combined with factor analysis of the large quantity of data generated in the study. To get a grip on what scaling techniques are all about, the most common scaling techniques used in marketing will be explained in the next section.

Questionnaires and scaling techniques

Questionnaires and scaling techniques are at the heart of methods for measuring brand personality. This short introduction will enable the reader to know the basics about scaling.

When using questionnaires and scaling techniques in practice, it is important to consider and develop customized research designs that fit the measurement objectives of the study. For this process knowledge of the mechanisms of statistics is essential. Scaling refers to the process of measuring or ordering entities according to the attributes or traits that characterize them. An example could be a scaling technique that could involve estimating individuals' levels of extroversion, or how consumers perceive the personality of a certain brand. There are different scaling methods that can provide different results suited for different objectives. Certain methods of scaling estimate magnitudes on a continuum, while other methods provide only the relative ordering of the entities. In brand management, and specifically in the personality approach, scaling techniques are used to determine the nature and strength of consumers' attitudes or opinions towards a specific brand personality. There are four types of scales: nominal, ordinal, interval and ratio. They have different properties suitable in different situations depending on the type of information needed.

- *Nominal scales* are the weakest form of scale. The numbers assigned to entities serves only to identify the subjects under consideration. Nominal scales are used only to categorize or label – the number has no mathematical properties. Examples are inventory codes or ISBN book codes.
- *Ordinal scales* seek to impose more structure on objects by rank-ordering them in terms of the subject's characteristics, such as weight or colour. As with nominal scales, identical objects are given the same number, but the ordinal scale has the added property that it can tell us something about the direction or relative standing of one object to another. An example is a preference ranking: to what extent does a consumer prefer one brand to another brand? In order to

be able to draw conclusions about differences between the numbers (reflecting how much a consumer prefers one brand over another), we must know something about the interval between the numbers. Since ordinal scales do not provide that, interval scales can be used.

Box 7.3 Ordinal scales applied

Ordinal scales express consumers' satisfaction or evaluation of one product or one brand, e.g. 'How satisfied are you with your current newspaper?'

	Question	**Score 1–5**
1	Not satisfied	
2	Neither satisfied nor dissatisfied	
3	Satisfied	
4	Very satisfied	
5	Extemely satisfied	

- *Interval scales* are grounded on the assumption of equal intervals between the numbers, i.e. the space between 5 and 10 is the same as the space between 45 and 50 and in both cases this distance is five times as great as that between 1 and 2 or 11 and 12, etc. Numbers indicate the magnitude of difference between items, but there is no absolute zero point. Examples are attitude scales and opinion scales – this scale would be able to measure how much a consumer prefers one brand to another.

Box 7.4 Interval scales applied

Interval scales express the standing of several brands in relation to each other, e.g. 'Assign the different beer brands according to the brand you prefer the most:' (assign the number 1 to the brand you prefer and assign the number 5 to the brand you least prefer)

Brand	**Score 1–5**
Miller's	
Coor's light	
Carlsberg	
Budweiser	
Heineken	

- *Ratio scales* are the most powerful and possess all the properties of nominal, ordinal and interval scales. In addition they permit absolute comparisons of the objects, e.g. 6 m is twice as high as 3 m and six times as high as 1 m. Numbers indicate magnitude of difference and there is a fixed zero point.

Ratios can be calculated. Examples include: age, income, price, costs, sales revenue, sales volume and market share.

The brand personality scale and the self concept

The Likert scale was adapted by Aaker to measure brand personality. This type of psychometric response scale is often used in questionnaires and in survey research. When responding to a Likert questionnaire item, respondents specify their level of agreement with a statement. In Aaker's brand personality study, a measurement scale for measuring brand personality was developed consisting of a five-point Likert scale measuring to what extent consumers agree that a personality dimension describes brand personality: from 1 (strongly agree) to 5 (strongly disagree). This scale was used to measure forty-two dimensions of brand personality based on more than 1,000 respondents. After generating data, analysis is needed to sort out the results of the study. Factor analysis is often used to analyse data in the personality approach, because it is particularly suitable when dealing with a large quantity of data, as is often the case in brand personality studies. Factor analysis is a statistical data reduction technique used to explain variability among observed random variables (also called factors).

Other methods

The methods used for studying self consist of either descriptive methodology, where consumers are asked to determine to what extent a word or a symbol is self-descriptive. After that, the congruence between self and brand personality can be measured. It consists of a two-step procedure, where the initial step uncovers the personality traits consumers attribute to a certain brand and the second step determines to what extent these personality traits are congruent with the personality traits identified in the descriptive exploration of self. Most studies of brand personality and self mix descriptive methods and the brand personality scaling method (as developed by Aaker 1997).

Apart from these rather quantitative methods, it can also be useful to include more qualitative methodologies like free association methodology, photo sorting or autobiographical methods, where consumers describe their autobiographical memory related to certain stimuli that have a relation to the brand in question. These methods can uncover self and the brand personality. After that the congruence between self and brand personality can be explored. This is often done by using a scale where consumers rate their perceptions of own self according to the personality characteristics of the brand. Quantitative regression analysis can then be used to measure the congruity between brand personality and the consumer's self-concept.

Critique of quantitative methods and scaling techniques

Quantitative scales tend to be developed under a laboratory setting and may not be the best survey tool for capturing the more unconscious aspects of people's consumption of brands for their symbolic benefits – often qualitative research is perceived to better capture the nature of consumption behaviour. This is why quantitative research methods are often used in combination with qualitative methods. Often qualitative methods are used to ensure a deep understanding of the phenomena before a quantitative research method with aim of generating generalizable results is developed. Aaker solved this problem by combining the quantitative study with qualitative methods in the exploratory phase – free association method was used to ensure that the personality trait list generated from the theoretical reviews of human personality theory was complete and accurate to explain brand personality. Free association methods, photo-sorting techniques or in-depth interviews are often combined with quantitative approaches in the personality approach to respond to the dilemma of commercial research into consumer behaviour and perceptions and the need to generate generalizable results.

Box 7.5 'Six steps' method of exploring and measuring brand personality

- Set up a qualitative study of the personality traits that people ascribe to the brand. Gather a complete list of all personality traits mentioned from all relevant shareholders.
- Reduce the number of relevant traits by narrowing down the field. This can be done by using a scaling technique where respondents are asked to judge how well a trait describes a brand on a seven-point scale ranging from 1 (not at all descriptive) to 7 (extremely descriptive). Select the traits with an average score of 6 or more.
- Further reduction of the trait number by using factor analysis for the aggregate database – to identify the final number of traits (in Aaker's case five brand personality dimensions).
- For every factor (personality dimension) a new factor analysis is done to identify traits that accurately describe each dimension in greater detail (to ensure rich description of each dimension and a more full description of personality).
- Confirm the test results with a new sample of respondents to ensure validity of both brand personality dimensions and the accuracy of how well the traits describe each dimension.
- If necessary test the results across national cultures to ensure that the strategies developed based on the results are applicable internationally, or define possible adjustments due the differences in national culture.

Summary

Quantitative studies and questionnaires are at the heart of the data and methods used in the personality approach. The methods used to uncover brand personality are derived from psychology and involve measuring what personality consumers

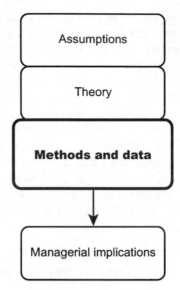

Figure 7.10 Methods and data of the personality approach

attribute to brands, by applying different scaling techniques. To gain insights into the self concept and its relation to brand personality, quantitative methods are, however, not suitable. This is why the quantitative methods that have dominated the personality approach in the recent years have been accompanied by more qualitative and loosely structured research methods to uncover the unconscious aspects of consumer self.

Managerial implications

We have learned how the personality approach assumes that consumers consume brands because they contribute to their construction and expression of identity. The managerial focus of the personality approach can be derived from that assumption. The primary and most important task for the brand manager in the personality approach is namely, to understand the mechanisms of identity construction that consumers use the brand for and be able to translate them into a brand personality that delivers value and relevance for the consumer. This is why theory in the personality approach focuses on how imbuing a personality into a brand can enhance consumer bonding and the interaction between consumers' self and brand personality. The effectiveness and success of a brand personality hence depends on the extent to which management is able to imbue the brands with a personality that is attractive, relevant and enhances consumers' creation and/or expression of self. To master this process is not easy because it requires deep insight into consumers' identity construction and how this process lays the grounds for consumers' motivation for the consumption of brand personalities that will assist them in their construction and expression of self. This insight must be used to create a coherent personality through the wide array of brand activities, ensuring that the brand personality statement is expressed in all the behaviour and communication of the brand. It also requires that close attention is paid to pioneer brand users and target consumers, because, as pointed out in the sections on assumptions and theoretical building blocks, a brand personality is created through a cyclical interaction between the brand and the consumer. But the efforts to create a strong personality are worth while. Several comparisons and studies point to the fact that brands with strong personalities outperform brands without. Furthermore, once created, a brand personality usually has a long 'life' and serves as an effective tool to build consumer loyalty.

Self and brand personality management

The basis of a strong brand personality is insight into how the symbolic benefits of the brand personality contribute to consumers' construction and expression of self. The focus is hence on individual consumers and the psychological processes that lay the grounds for consumers' inward individual and outward social use of brands. The human self is a complex concept and must be researched properly, using the right methods, as described in the methods and data section, to uncover how consumers use the symbolic benefits of the brand before the brand personality can be constructed to match these symbolic consumption demands. Effective use of brand personality depends on the brand's ability to enhance consumer self-expression. Before that can be achieved research must uncover what parts of the self construct are in play in the specific brand. Does the bonding between the consumer and the brand personality happen because the brand appeals to the individual self and is used mainly for the inward construction of identity or is the primary task for the brand to contribute the expression of the consumer's social self, where it is the outward signal of the values of the brand that are in play? These are important steps in understanding how the brand relates to the consumer self that the brand managers must uncover. The steps relate to the consumer self construct (table 7.1).

Exact knowledge about the mechanisms and focus of self for the particular brand in question is a prerequisite for the ability to develop a brand personality that is relevant and attractive to consumers. After having uncovered at what level the brand personality relates to the consumer by contributing to consumers' self construct, the brand personality can be developed.

Sources of brand personality

Once the consumer self has been uncovered steps must be undertaken to construct or maintain the brand personality. As explained in the theoretical building blocks of the personality approach, consumers automatically attribute human personality traits to brands. According to the brand personality framework developed by Aaker (1997), the personalities that consumers attribute to brands can be divided along five main personality dimensions. These five dimensions

Table 7.1 Creating brand personality in accordance with the consumer self construct

Step 1 – Uncover internal potential	Uncover internally what brand personality is viable for the company to create. The brand personality must be authentic, meaning that the personality must be in line with what the company is able to deliver and live up to
Step 2 – Uncover the social and individual level of consumer self	Uncover if the brand personality primarily helps consumers express the individual or social self
Step 3 – Elaborate the understanding of how the brand personality interacts with consumer self	Uncover if the brand is used to express the individual self, explore if it is the actual, ideal or desired self the brand appeals to
Step 4 – Create and alter the brand personality	Once the right brand personality appealing to the wanted group and type of consumer self has been created the brand must be continuously monitored. Brand personalities evolve and can be altered or diminished with the personality profiles of stereotypical consumers. This cyclical process of how the brand evolves in interaction with the personality of different consumer target groups must be closely monitored and adjusted to make the best of the brand

can serve as the basic template for creating a suitable brand personality. The personality traits are a more nuanced description of the behavioural character traits that must be built into the brand personality and expressed through all the different sources and modes of communication that the brand uses to express personality. The brand personality dimensions are long-term and a strategic tool. The brand personality statement is more short-term and contains the more nuanced personality traits that can be altered over time and can serve as a guide for how the brand should appear and behave more specifically. An example of how a brand personality can be constructed using the brand personality framework (figure 7.11).

Consumer perceptions of a brand personality are formed and influenced by all the direct and indirect contacts the consumer has with the brand or other users of the brand, also named the sources of brand personality. The direct sources of brand personality are: the set of human characteristics associated with the typical user of the brand, the employees of the company producing the brand; the CEO, or endorsers of the brand also affect how the consumers ultimately will perceive the brand personality. In that way, personality traits of the people associated with that brand are transferred directly and unfiltered to the brand personality itself. Personality can also be transferred indirectly to the brand through the product-related attributes and product category associations, but also brand communication like the brand name, logo, style, price and distribution channel affect how the brand personality will be perceived by consumers.

Box 7.6 Brand personalities in practice

Sincere

Ford, Hallmark, Coca-cola are all examples of sincere personalities that attempt to establish a warm and caring character. Sincere personalities are good at establishing long-term relationships with consumers built on trust. Sincere personalities inherently consist of traits such as warmth, family-oriented and traditional. With these traits the brand is expected by the consumer to display trustworthy and dependable behaviour, which is good for building strong and long-lasting relationships.

Exciting

The exciting brand personality type is associated with traits like youthfulness and energy. Examples of exciting brand personalities are Virgin, MTV and Pepsi. They usually target younger consumer demographics and seek differentiation against an established market leader. The exciting personality is good at generating attention and appears attractive and cool. But the exciting personalities are seldom perceived as viable candidates for long-term relationships.

The goals and vision of the brand should hence be reflected in the brand personality. And the organization must make sure that they have the right capabilities to deliver the traits and behaviour that consumers expect from the brand personality chosen.

When developing a brand personality, brand managers have direct and indirect sources of brand personality at their disposal to create and shape the desired brand personality. The direct and indirect sources of brand personality shape in interplay the full picture of the brand personality and it is important that the behaviour, signal value and symbolic clues expressed through both the direct and indirect sources of brand personality are coherent to ensure that the consumers experience, perceive and evaluate the brand personality as authentic and true to its own nature.

- *Direct sources of brand personality.* The set of human characteristics associated with the stereotypical brand user, company employees, the CEO, brand endorsers. These human characteristics can be of both a symbolic nature, like sophistication, or they can have a demographic nature, like age, social class, etc. The direct sources of brand personality are always 'person-based'. The founder of Virgin, Richard Branson, advocates new thinking and doing things differently through all the products inherent in the Virgin brand. His personality traits are transferred directly to the Virgin brand. Richard Branson is very visible as a CEO and his personality helps promote a certain Virgin brand personality to consumers.
- *Indirect sources of brand personality.* All the decisions made about the physical, functional and tangible aspects that can be experienced by the

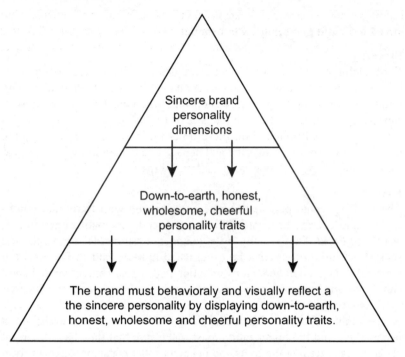

Figure 7.11 Brand personality dimensions, traits and brand behaviour

consumer, like the price, shape, distribution and promotion, are the indirect sources of brand personality. They contribute to the brand personality indirectly by giving the consumer clues about the brand personality. A company with a strong brand personality does not need to have a very visible CEO advocating a certain brand personality, as is the case with the direct sources of brand personality. Brand personality can also be transferred indirectly from management to the brand, by choosing different vehicles of communication. For example, MTV is expressing an exciting brand personality through its events, sponsorships, website and advertising; the sources of brand personality are indirect, since a vehicle of communication is used.

Having uncovered the sources of brand personality and how these sources can be used actively to shape the personality of the brand, it is important to establish an efficient communication platform that can launch the brand personality as distinctive and attractive, but also underpin the personality traits of the brand. The communication platform should not consist only of traditional marketing tools like ads, website, etc. A distinctive brand personality cannot be built through communication only. The behaviour of the brand is also a necessary and important part of a brand personality. To create an authentic and believable brand personality, the brand manager must engage in a wide range of branding activities that express personality and create an emotional bond with the consumer. Activities like sponsorships, events or add-on consumer services matching the personality of the brand are essential to complete the picture. Too often companies fail on this because they emphasize short-term goals focused on reaching sales targets or they end up responding *ad hoc* or emulating competitors' strategies.

The creation of brand personality

The goal of brand personality is to describe a mix of perceptual reality from the consumer perception – they should reflect the way consumers feel about the brand rather than just expressing how the company would like the consumer to feel. The creation of brand personality consists of the following steps:

- *Identification of personality.* Identify personality dimensions and personality traits to be communicated and built into the 'behaviour' of the brand. By narrowing down the relevant traits as described in the methods and data of the personality approach, it is possible to finally to end up with the brand personality profile describing the traits and facets characterizing the brand personality.
- *Make sure it is appealing.* Make sure that the personality appeals to the consumer, by analysing the consumer self–brand exchange. Should adjustments be made to the brand personality based on an analysis of how consumers are to use the symbolic attributes of the brand?
- *Understand target groups.* Make sure that the right consumer groups are targeted and the right brand endorsers are chosen. The typical consumer of a brand can have an enormous impact on how the brand personality is perceived by the other future consumers. This is why getting the target group right (early adopters) from the beginning can be crucial for the success of the brand personality. See more in the section about early adopters and brand–self congruence.
- *Align the personality of the brand and the consumer.* Analyse the extent to which the brand is congruent with consumers' self and align the personality accordingly.
- *Develop the communication platform.* Having identified the personality dimensions that should characterize the brand, it is important to develop an efficient communication platform that underpins that personality.

Early adopters and brand–self congruence

Early adopters of a brand are critical for the alignment of brand personality, because they are the group of consumers that other consumers will identify with and use as a measure for the authenticity of the brand personality. This process takes place because, as explained in the sections on theoretical building blocks, consumers' self expression has not only an individual but also a social dimension, where consumers seek inspiration from reference groups for brand consumption and use brands to demonstrate belonging to certain reference groups. The brand can hence be reinforced in a cyclical process if the right target group picks it up because it will serve as inspiration for other consumers who identify with or aspire to identify with the reference group that this target group represents. Early adopters can be used, as a control group, to make sure that the brand actually expresses desired personally traits. If early adopters display personality traits that are similar to or in line with the personality of the brand the brand personality will be reinforced and strengthened. If the group of early adopters on the other hand do not share personality characteristics with the brand personality communicated – then the brand personality will be weakened.

The greater the brand congruity between the personality of the ideal target consumer and the personality of the brand the stronger will the brand personality grow. Early adopters are hence critical for aligning the brand personality and can be a useful tool when measuring and aligning brand–self congruence and they can potentially reinforce the personality of the brand and can be used actively in the advertising campaigns and management of the brand. The brand–self congruence can be used as a measure for evaluation of how the brand personality interacts with the self of consumers. To what extent is there brand–self congruence? And how does this fit or lack of fit affect the brand personality? The results can lay the basis for continuous alignment of the brand personality and its appeal to the target consumer and use of personality endorsement.

Brand personality and consumer–brand relationships

The two constructs of brand personality and brand–consumer relationships are closely related. Generally, how a relationship evolves and the level of intimacy that can be achieved depend on the personalities of the partners involved in that relationship. In brand management the brand personality influences the behaviour and how the brand interacts with the consumer – the brand relationship. Different brand personality types have different effects on the strength of the brand–consumer relationship. Brands with

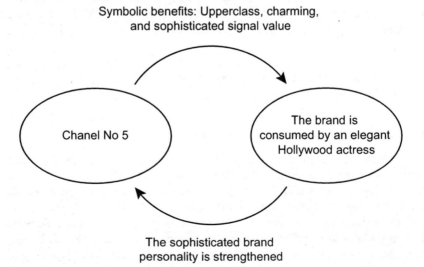

Symbolic benefits: Upperclass, charming,
and sophisticated signal value

Chanel No 5

The brand is
consumed by an elegant
Hollywood actress

The sophisticated brand
personality is strengthened

Figure 7.12 Brand–self congruence of Chanel No. 5

sincere personality traits encourage progressively stronger relationships compared with exciting brands. This is why sincere personalities are often valued as a more stable and better choice for a long-term relationship as opposed to exciting brand personalities. In practice, considering and managing a brand personality is closely related to the management of the relationship that brands have with consumers. But it is not only in practice that these two concepts are becoming more and more inter-twined. Some of the more prominent researchers of respectively the personality approach (Jennifer Aaker) and the relational approach (Susan Fournier) along with Adam Brasel have joined forces and conducted an interesting study exploring how different personalities affect the interaction between the brand and the consumer as the relationship evolves. The study also indicates the boundaries of and can provide guidelines for appropriate behaviour of different personality types. A conclusion of the study is hence that a sincere brand personality poses much higher demands for accuracy and infallibility. Consumers are much less forgiving if a sincere brand personality makes a mistake than if an exciting brand personality commits that same mistake. This can have serious consequences on how the relation between the brand and the consumer can evolve.

Box 7.7 When good brands do bad

The article 'When good brands do bad' explores the correlation between brand personality and consumer–brand relationships. For this purpose Aaker *et al.* (2004) set up a field study: two online film processing companies, one with a sincere brand personality (expressed through pre-tested graphic element, tonality, font, content, and links to other sites), the other more exciting. The idea was to expose the customers of the two different brand personalities to the same transgression, followed by attempts to recover and excuse the transgression. Since transgressions according to theory are almost inevitable in long relationships, it is of major importance how consumers respond to them and the damage can be limited. The evolution of the relationship would hence consist of comparable trans-gressions and attempts to resolve the situation. It turned out that the consumers were much more reluctant to forgive the online film processing company with the sincere brand personality than the exciting brand person-ality. The sincere brand showed no sign of recovery after reparation attempts, whereas the exciting brand character shows signs of a strengthened relationship after a transgression if recovery activities were attempted immediately after the transgression had occurred.

Aaker *et al.* (2004) concludes that the evolution and boundaries of consumer-brand relationships are to a great extent affected by what person-ality type the brand possesses. The study illustrates how transgressions brands commit are perceived differently depending on what personality types that brand has. The study hence demonstrates the interrelation between brand personality and consumer–brand relationship. The study suggest that instead of interpreting and managing brand personality as a static construct, it could be valuable to have a more dynamic approach to brand personality that also includes the roles that different personalities are able to play in consumer–brand relationships. Brands with sincere personality traits encourage progressively stronger relationships than exciting brands. But sincere brand personalities are much more vulnerable to transgressions than exciting brands. Hence, depending on the personality of the brand, research indicates that if recovery attempts are initiated by the marketer after a transgression, then these can dilute the negative effects of failures (transgressions) and sometimes even drive the relationship to a satisfaction level beyond the level prior to the transgression incident.

Box 7. 8 Do's and don'ts of the personality approach

Do	Don't
Remember to uncover the complex ways the brand contributes to consumers self construction and expression	Develop a brand personality without knowing exactly what kind of self the brand addresses
Make a thorough personality statement that can guide brand-building activities	Limit the brand personality to being described by one personality dimension
Consider how the brand personality sets the standard and boundaries for how the brand can behave	Make sure to have the right plan for how to cope with transgressions that matches the brand personality type
Make sure that the organization is able to deliver on the promise and expectations linked to the chosen brand personality.	Limit the question of brand personality solely to marketing
Choose and focus on the right target group	Forget that the stereotypical user of the brand affects the brand personality.
Take a dynamic approach to brand personality, analyse how the brand personality affects the relationship with your consumer	Ignore consumers' relations with the brand and the effect these relations have on the brand personality.

The dynamic of how a brand personality and the actions of a brand affect the consumer–brand relationship is essential to include in any brand management consideration. What personality is suitable for the brand in question and is the organization as such able to deliver on the promise/expectations that, for example, a sincere brand personality sets out? Hence the personality traits and the relationship roles that different personalities can play in a consumer–brand relationship ought to be a pivotal in the management of brand personalities. Relationships with sincere brands deepen over time, and relationships with exciting brands have the evolutionary character of a short-lived fling. Research findings suggest that dynamic construal of brand personality is more accurate and useful for management in describing the potential of a brand personality. The interrupt events and relationship contracts between brand and consumer formed on the basis of the consumer–brand interaction can reveal much more about the strength of a brand personality than a more static perception of brand personality. In practice this is also why recently much research into brand personality overlaps research into the consumer–brand relationship.

Summary

The primary focus for the brand manager in the personality approach is to build an attractive and relevant brand personality that can serve as a strategic tool to ensure a deep and long-lasting connection with consumers. The prerequisites for creating the right brand personality are insights into how consumers use the specific brand in their construction and expression of self. Understanding these mechanisms can ensure that right perpetual personality mix is created for the brand personality and

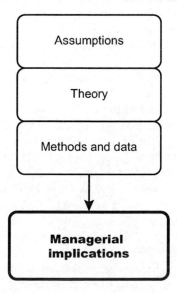

Figure 7.13 Managerial implications of the personality approach

that the right means of communication for that personality is used. The right platform for the brand personality requires that both the direct and indirect sources of brand personality are considered. Target group users and early adopters can be used as control groups and a measure for the evaluation of whether the brand is on the right track and ensure a continuous alignment of the brand–self congruence. Adopting a dynamic approach to brand personality including analysis of the relationship role different personalities are able to act out in the brand–consumer relationship is essential to gain the complete and full picture of how the brand personality and the consumers interact.

Comments from the 'founding fathers' (3)

Brands and personality: the origin

Joseph Plummer, Columbia Business School

As mass media evolved from print to electronic media in the 1940s, 1950s and 1960s, the battle for brand name recall and recognition became intense. Some agencies and advertisers created special ways to generate brand recall beyond simply spending more money – Leo Burnett in particular, with their ability to bring a brand name to life through memorable characters like Tony the Tiger, the Marlboro cowboy and the Jolly Green Giant. I was lucky to be a part of that period at Leo Burnett in the late 1960s and 1970s when these and other advertising icons were born.

One of my favourites that I worked on was Morris the Cat for Nine Lives cat food. Morris had an attitude, like most cats, and wouldn't accept any old brand – he liked Nine Lives and could 'persuade' his owners to serve it. The magic of this idea was that cat owners tend to 'humanize' their cats. They give them personalities, human feelings and ascribe a great sense of independence to them.

In 1979 I joined Young & Rubicam, where I was blessed to work with Frazier Purdy. In 1980 he and I were reviewing new campaigns for Dr Pepper, a challenger brand in the United States to Coca-cola and Pepsi. Frazier rejected the three campaigns because he said they didn't 'capture the attitude of the brand'. That brilliant observation triggered my past experience with Morris and Nine Lives. If they could 'humanize' a cat, was it possible that consumers could 'humanize' a brand? Could a brand have attitudes – maybe even a personality? We undertook some very innovative research with the help of Howard Leonard of the Y&R research department to see if Dr Pepper had a personality, one that was perceptually different from Coca-cola and Pepsi. The results were astonishing! Consumers could imagine and express different personalities of the three brands through choices of personality characteristics like fun-loving, masculine and energetic, and a selection of symbols like certain animals.

We were so encouraged by the initial results that we studied other agency brands like Oil of Olay, Jell-o, Kentucky Fried Chicken and Merrill Lynch. All the brands had clear and measurable personalities. The journey then began to share this news with clients and integrate brand personality into the Y&R strategy process. Twenty-five years have passed since Frazier and I stumbled on to brand personality. It is used throughout the advertising industry worldwide today and the phenomenon has been studied carefully by leading academics such as Jennifer Aaker and Kevin Keller in the United States.

Source Edited version of the preface to Marco Lombardi (ed.) *La marca, una come noi. La personalità di marca nell'era post spot*
Milan: Franco Angeli (2007)

Student questions

1 What scientific field does the personality approach draw inspiration from?
2 How does the personality approach perceive the exchange between brand and consumer?
3 Why is self important in the personality approach?
4 What is the difference between personality dimensions and personality traits?
5 What would you use if conducting a study of brand personality, and why?
6 What are the indirect and the direct sources of brand personality?
7 How can early adopters affect the brand personality?
8 What is the relation between brand personality and brand relationship?
9 What kind of relationship should a company aiming at creating a sincere brand personality expect to be able to achieve with its consumers, and why?

References and further reading

Key readings are in **bold type**.

Aaker, J. (1997) 'Dimensions of brand personality', *Journal of Marketing Research,* **34 (August): 347–56**

Aaker, J., Benet-Martinez, V. and Garolera, J. (2001) 'Consumption symbols as carriers of culture: a study of Japanese and Spanish brand personality constructs', *Journal of Personality and Social Psychology,* 8 (3): 492–508

Aaker, J., Fournier, S. and Brasel, A. S. (2004) 'When good brands do bad', *Journal of Consumer Research,* 31 (June): 1–16

Ahuvia, A. C. (2005) 'Beyond the extended self: loved objects and consumers' identity narratives', *Journal of Consumer Research,* 32 (June): 171–84

Azoulay, A. and Kapferer, J-N. (2003) 'Do brand personality scales really measure brand personality?' *Brand Management,* 11 (2): 143–155

Belk, R. W. (1988) 'Possessions and the extended self', *Journal of Consumer Research,* 15 (2): 139–68

Chaplin, L. N. and John, D. R. (2005) 'The development of self-brand connections on children and adolescent', *Journal of Consumer Research,* 32: 119–29

Chung, K. K., Dongchul, H. and Seung-Bae, P. (2001) 'The effect of brand personality and identification on brand loyalty: applying the theory of social identification', *Japanese Psychological Research*, 43 (4): 195–206

Durgee, J. F. (1988) 'Understanding brand personality', *Journal of Consumer Marketing*, 5 (3): 21–6

Escalas, J. E. and Bettman, J. R. (2005) 'Self-construal, reference groups and brand meaning', *Journal of Consumer Research*, 32 (3): 378–89

Diamantopoulos, A., Smith, G. and Grime, I. (2005) 'The impact of brand extensions on brand personality: experimental evidence', *European Journal of Marketing*, 39: 129–49

Govers, R. C. M. and Schoormans, J. P. L. (2005) 'Product personality and its influence on consumer preference', *Journal of Consumer Marketing*, 22 (4): 189–97

Helgeson, J. G. and Supphellen, M. (2004) 'A conceptual and measurement comparison of self-congruity and brand personality: the impact of socially desirable responding', *International Journal of Market Research*, 46 (2): 205–33

James, W. (1890) *Principles of Psychology*, Vol. I: New York: Holt

Johar, G. V., Sengupta J. and Aaker, J. (2005) 'Two roads to updating brand personality impressions: traits versus evaluative inferencing', *Journal of Marketing Research*, 42: 458–69

Kleine, R. E., III, Kernan, J. B. (1988) 'Measuring the meaning of consumption objects: an empirical investigation', *Advances in Consumer Research*, 15 (1): 498–504

Mark, M. and Pearson, C. S. (2001) *The Hero and the Outlaw: Building Extraordinary Brands through the Power of Archetypes*, New York: McGraw-Hill

Monga, B. A. and Lau-Gesk, L. (2007) 'Blending co-brand personalities: an examination of the complex self', *Journal of Marketing Research*, 44 (3): 389–400

Phau, I. and Lau, K. C. (2001) 'Brand personality and consumer self-expression: single or dual carriageway?' *Journal of Brand Management*, 8 (6): 428–44

Plummer, J. (1985) 'How personality makes a difference', *Journal of Advertising Research*, 24 (6): 27–31

Sirgy, M. J. (1982) 'Self-concept in consumer behavior: a critical review', *Journal of Consumer Research*, 9 (3): 287–300

Smith E. G. Van den Berge, E. and Franzen, G. (2003) 'Brands are just like real people', in F. Hansen and L. B. Christensen (eds) *Branding and Advertising*, Copenhagen: Copenhagen Business School Press: 22–43

Sung, Y. and Tinkham, S. F. (2005) 'Brand personalty structures in the United States and Korea: common and culture-specific factors', *Journal of Consumer Psychology*, 15 (4): 334–50

Swaminathan, V., Oage, K. L. and Gürhan-Canli, Z. (2007) '"My" brand or "our" brand: the effects of brand relationship dimensions and self-construal on brand evaluations', *Journal of Consumer Research*, 34 (2): 248–59

Thomas, T. T. W. (2004) 'Extending human personality to brands: the stability factor', *Brand Management*, 11 (4): 317–29

Wertime, K. (2002) *Building Brands and Believers: How to Connect with Consumers using Archetypes*, Singapore: Wiley

8 The relational approach

with a commentary by Associate Professor Susan Fournier, Boston University School of Management

---

Learning objectives

The purpose of this chapter is to:

Understand the assumptions of the relational approach
- The brand is perceived as a viable relationship partner and a 'dyadic' brand perspective is hence introduced in brand management
- a view of the consumer as an existential being

Understand the main theoretical building blocks and how they are connected
- Animism
- Human relationships
- The brand relationship theory

Provide insights into the variety of methods used to research relationships
- Depth interviews and life story method

Understand the managerial implications
- The brand has to act as a true friend

Understand the academic implications
- A paradigm shift
- inspiring new ways in brand management

Relationships are a fundamental part of the way we live our lives. We use relationships for many different things and their importance to us differs significantly. We have lifelong relationships to our siblings that might be characterized by a profound feeling of sharing the same important values stemming from the same family background. You might have a best friend from your kindergarten days. But you also have relationships to fellow students and colleagues knowing that you will only uphold the majority of these relationships in the period of time where you share the same working or university sphere. Long or short, deep or shallow – relationships are instrumental parts of everyone's lives, structuring meaning and adding life content.

Research has proved that consumers experience relationships with brands (Fournier 1998), and just like human relationships, consumer–brand relationships are of a very diverse nature. Brand relationship theory reached a wide brand management audience when 'Consumers and their brands: developing relationship theory in consumer research' by Susan Fournier was published in *Journal of Consumer Research* (March of 1998).[4] Drawing on theories about human relationships and the idea of brand personality, the study went on to investigate the marketing 'buzz word' at the time; relationships.

Box 8.1 Customer relationship management and brand relationship theory

The term 'relationship marketing' was first introduced in the literature on services and then became an important notion in business-to-business markets, where the business relationships often are longer than in business-to-consumer markets. In the literature on services and relationships a service encounter is defined as; 'the dyadic interaction between a customer and service provider' (Bitner *et al.* 1990, p. 72).

Fournier's aim was to establish a thorough framework for the use of this metaphor and apply it to consumers' brand relations; 'In a sense, the field has leapt ahead to application of relationship ideas and the assumption of relationship benefits without proper development of the core construct involved' (Fournier 1998, p. 343).

Customer relationship management and brand relationship theory are hence not necessarily the same. Customer relationship management offers different tools to manage a customer relationship on a long-term basis instead of focusing on the singular transaction while brand relationship theory goes to the root of the relationship metaphor.

Sources Bitner *et al.* (1990) and Fournier (1998)

Brand relationship theory is also a continuation of theory about brand loyalty. Loyalty is often closely linked with the sensation of a relationship. Loyal consumers are valuable consumers. Creating brand loyalty is all about managing the brand–consumer exchange long-term instead of a short-term exchange focusing on the transaction. But while brand loyalty is an expression of *if* a consumer chooses the brand on a continuous basis, applying the brand relationship theory offers explanations of *how* and *why* brands are consumed by loyal consumers.

In real life people relate to one another in many different ways. The same is true as to how they relate to the brands they buy. To reduce it simply to a matter of loyalty or lack of loyalty is like saying that you either marry everybody you meet or they will never be a meaningful part of your life.

(Fournier 1998b)

Brand relationship theory builds on a comprehensive phenomenological study. Thereby, the scientific and philosophical tradition of phenomenology is added to the context of brand management. This addition implies a significant shift in the way brands and consumers are perceived and investigated.

The other six approach chapters of this book feature the same structure, ending with the managerial implications of the approach. This chapter deviates from that structure.

Brand relationship theory has become very influential and the brand relationship metaphor has in many ways become the equivalent of the interpretive branding paradigm that has been dominant since the mid-1990s. The idea of the brand relationship provides great insights and is yet very elusive and difficult to translate into concrete managerial implications. Therefore, the concluding section of this chapter is renamed 'Implications of the relational approach'. In this section we will only touch briefly upon the managerial implications and also allow space for explaining the tremendous academic impact of this approach. This concluding section will describe how and why it can be identified as a paradigm shift fuelling the forthcoming approaches by entering the life-worlds of consumers, applying an entirely qualitative research design, and focusing on meaning instead of information.

Assumptions of the relational approach

In the previous approaches, we have seen quite a development in the assumed brand and consumer perspectives. In the economic approach (chapter 4) and the identity approach (chapter 5), the point of departure for understanding brand value creation is the organization from which the brand stems. In the consumer-based approach of chapter 6 the brand was presumed to be a cognitive construal in the mind of the (cognitive man) consumer. In the personality approach (chapter 7), a dialogue-based brand–consumer exchange was introduced to the field of brand management. The relational approach of this chapter also implies a dialogue-based take on brand management and does, in several ways, resemble the personality approach.

However, we have chosen to present the personality and the relational approach as two different approaches because they stem from very different scientific and philosophical traditions and thereby imply very different consumer perspectives and the use of very different methodologies.

The relational approach is grounded in phenomenology. Phenomenology is a qualitative, constructionist research tradition emphasizing the accessing of an 'inner reality' and, as a consequence, the validity of 'lived experience'. The relational approach is the first approach relying on purely qualitative research. Brand consumption is understood only through a deep and holistic understanding of the personal context in which the brand is consumed.

The 'brand–consumer exchange'

The brand relationship theory is based on a 'dyadic' brand–consumer relationship, implying an equal exchange between brand and consumer. Both parties contribute to brand value creation, which takes place in an ongoing meaning-based exchange. The fact that the arrows in Figure 8.1 form a circular motion reflects that the development of the brand–consumer relationship is a never-ending process, influenced by the same parameter changes as human relationships.

Even though the focus of the relational approach is the ongoing exchange (or relationship) between brand and consumer, it is important to stress that relationships are phenomena influenced by contextual changes. The brand relationship theory also aims at understanding the lives of consumers in a holistic manner; implying that the environment of the consumer is not delimited from analysis. But it is important to understand that the approach focuses on the exchange between brand and consumer, while the understanding of the consumer's social context is the pivotal point of the community approach (chapter 9) and the impact of the consumer's cultural environment is conceptualized in the cultural approach (chapter 10).

In the broader context of brand management, the relational approach implies a major shift in assumptions. Considering the methodologies and scientific and philosophical traditions of the previous approaches, this shift is a significant step towards a new conceptualization of the brand as something 'owned' by the consumer.

The 'ownership' by the consumer is at the heart of the consumer-based approach (chapter 6), but the consumer perspective of this approach rests upon an if–then logic (if you are faced with stimulus X, your reaction will be Y) highlighting the similarities among consumers and the consumer as an information-processing 'computer'. Thereby, the view of man behind the consumer-based approach is more related to a machine metaphor and consumers are more seen as manipulable objects. Therefore, the 'ownership' by the consumer in the consumer-based approach can be questioned. Sure, the brand is perceived as linked with the associations in the mind of the consumer, but the brand manager can also be seen as a 'computer programmer' programming consumers by applying the exact right cues and triggers to marketing communications. Even though the relational

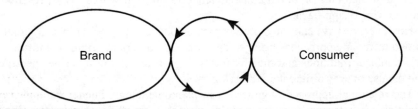

Figure 8.1 'Dyadic' brand–consumer relationship

approach features the dyadic brand–consumer relationship, the consumer seems to be more the 'owner' of the brand than in the previous approaches.

The phenomenological perspective

Phenomenology is a penetrating research style that accesses an 'inner reality' through researching what is felt, perceived and thought. Phenomenology is closely linked with the existentialism branch of philosophy. Here, the human experience of key existential topics such as life, death and time is the basis for understanding man.

Phenomenological research assumes a socially constructed reality as opposed to the assumed external and objective reality of the positivist tradition. This is why phenomenological research emphasizes 'lived' or 'felt' experience, which is also a recurrent notion of the brand relationship theory.

In the relational approach, consumers are investigated as individuals and their inner and idiosyncratic realities are considered valid. The relational approach is meaning-based. Meaning is created in the interaction between sender and receiver and is opposed to the concept of information which implies a notion of linear communication from sender to receiver:

> What matters in the construction of brand relationships is not simply what managers intend for them, or what brand images 'contain' in the culture, but what consumers do with brands to add meaning in their lives. The abstracted, goal-derived, and experiential categories that consumers create for brands are not necessarily the same as the categories imposed by the marketers in charge of brand management…. This reality that consumers' experiences with brands are often phenomenologically distinct from those assumed by the managers who tend them – commands a different conception of brand at the level of lived experience, and new, more complex approaches to the social classification of branded goods.
>
> (Fournier 1998, p. 367)

The relational approach is concerned with understanding the identity projects of consumers. It is important to notice that it is the *individual* identity projects that are investigated in this approach. The cultural approach (chapter 10) is concerned with *collective* identity projects. So the relational approach beats the drum for integrating knowledge of individual identity projects in the management of a brand, while the cultural approach does the same in favour of our collective identity projects.

Summary

The relational approach rests upon assumptions regarding the brand–consumer exchange as a 'dyadic' and cyclical process resembling a human relationship. Brand meaning is constituted through this process to which both parties contribute equally. The relational approach is linked to the tradition of phenomenology

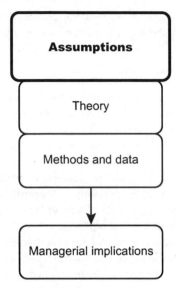

Figure 8.2 Assumptions of the relational approach

implying an existential view of man. 'The inner reality' of the consumer becomes both valid and valuable data material by the application of this perspective. The phenomenological perspective emphasizes a holistic view of the consumer and thereby takes an interest in many aspects that are not directly related to the actual consumption choice or behaviour.

Theoretical building blocks of the relational approach

It goes without saying that the brand relationship theory is the core theme of the relational approach. Applying the relationship metaphor to a brand–consumer construct requires an abstraction towards regarding the brand as something human. The human propensity to endow inanimate objects or mental constructs with human characteristics is called *animism*. A prerequisite for the relationship theory is the literature dealing with brand personality and therefore animism is the first supporting theme. Animism will be reviewed very briefly; the inquiring reader should refer to chapter 7: the personality approach. Human relationship theory serves as the second supporting theme of the relational approach to brand management.

Supporting theme: animism

Human beings have a tendency to endow objects and even abstract ideas with human personality characteristics. Brands can be animated, humanized and personalized. A prerequisite for applying knowledge from the relational approach to the management of a brand is that that brand is perceived as a personality as this furthers the consumer–brand relationship. As illustrated in figure 7.1, human

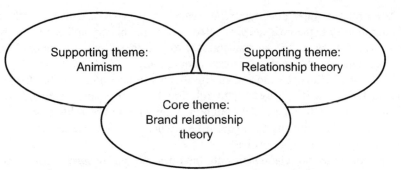

Figure 8.3 Supporting themes and core theme of the relational approach

personalities are 'transformed' into brand personalities (the modified Big five) and consumers interact with brands that suit their self-expressive benefits best.

When working with brand personality, archetype theories from psychology are also very popular. Simplified versions of what Jung called archetypes are widely used as the basis of brand development and advertising. Empirical studies show a connection between profits and having a brand more or less consciously connected with a personality or archetype.

Supporting theme: relationship theory

As described in the introduction, relationships are fundamental in the development of the human psyche. It is difficult to imagine life without any relations with other people. Relationships are in many ways how we embed ourselves in the world.

Relationships are constituted of our continuous reciprocal exchanges between interdependent relationship partners. For a relationship to exist, active inter-changes between relationship partners are required. Relationships can be described as purposive because they add and structure meaning in people's lives. The meaning added and structured by relationships is of a *psychological,* a *socio-cultural* and a *relational* nature:

- *Psychological meaning* is linked with the identity of the participants in the relationships. In a consumption context, important research has highlighted the link between consumers and their consumption choices, establishing the central concept of possessions as part of the extended self. The way relation-ships correspond to the formation of identity is through the way they help solve life themes (central to the core identity and the personal history), important life projects (key life roles) and current concerns (related to daily tasks).

It is important to understand the way psychological meaning refers to life themes, life projects, and current concerns. These different 'levels' of psychological meaning work as pivotal points in several important brand management and consumer research studies (e.g. Mick and Buhl 1992; Fournier and Yao 1997; Fournier 1998).

A few relationships reflect your *life theme,* which is the core theme (or themes) of your life. A life theme is deeply rooted in personal history and is often difficult to verbalize because it is so fundamental to you that it is often 'buried' in the subconscious (e.g. being free versus not being free).

Life projects fluctuate more than life themes in accordance with changes in circumstances, and life cycle and relationships are also influenced by the construction, maintenance and dissolution of key roles in life. A life project relates to the most significant choices in our lives – what do we choose as our education, profession – and family priorities.

The most practical relationships are the ones spurred by *current concerns* and they are directed toward completion of tasks in everyday life. An example could be your hairdresser, the employees at your child's daycare facility and so on.[5]

Besides providing psychological meaning, relationships apply socio-cultural as well as relational meaning to the ones engaged in them.

- *Socio-cultural meaning* is linked with changes in our life conditions. Socio-cultural meaning can be divided into five broad socio-cultural contexts (age/cohort, life cycle, gender, family/social network, and culture) which all influence how participants approach relationships. Relationships change as life does – think about college graduation, becoming a parent, getting ready for retirement, and so on. Life falls into different eras and so do relationships.
- *Relational meaning* of relationships deals with the fact that all relationships are part of a network of other relationships. The nature of one individual relationship is thereby influenced by the fact that it is part of a jigsaw puzzle of other relationships fitting the requirements of the person having the relationship.

Any relationship is further affected by *contextual* influences. In that sense, relationships grow with us, adjust to our changing lives and influence the changes in our lives as well. In other words, relationships develop over the course of time and are constituted of a series of repeated exchanges between the relationship partners. In that sense, relationships are *process phenomena*, constantly changing.

In sum, relationships add and structure meaning in our lives. Remember that the meaning is of a psychological, socio-cultural and relational nature. Furthermore, relationships never stand still and are influenced by an infinite number of contextual factors.

Relationships take place between human beings. But since people tend to endow brands with human-like personalities, the characteristics of a relationship can be applied to brands as well. How this complex notion is conceptualized in the world of brand management will be explained in the next section.

Core theme: the brand relationship theory

Through extensive research into three female informants' lived experiences with brands Fournier was able to prove that brands can and do serve as viable relationship partners in the sense that they are endowed with human personality characteristics and are used for solving *life themes, life projects* and *current concerns* (as well as matching the other characteristics of a relationship).

Box 8.2 Background of the brand relationship theory

The study behind the brand relationship theory involves three female informants; Jean, Karen and Vicki.

Jean is fifty-nine years old, has been married to Henry for most of her life, and tends a bar in her small blue-collar home town. She is the mother of three grown-up daughters and of Italian descent. Her Catholic faith and family traditions are important to her. When it comes to life themes, affiliation and stability are important in Jean's life. Jean displays brand relationship depicting these life themes as she enjoys using a portfolio of brands for many years. Having been a housekeeper, a mother and a waitress all her adult life, Jean sees herself as a consumer expert, knowing exactly which brands are 'the best'.

Karen's life situation is very different. She is a recently divorced thirty-nine year-old mother of two girls and works full-time as an office manager. She finds herself in a dilemma, on the one hand wanting to pursue new paths in her life, and on the other to create a stable home for her two young children. Karen's life themes are influenced by the transition phase she is experiencing. Karen does not display emotional attachment to brands to the same degree as the other two women. Due to the financial reality of being a single parent she has adopted a very practical approach to brand purchases, going for coupons and other promotions. However, she displays emotional attachment to a few selected brands that are central for upholding her sense of identity in her transitional phase. Karen also displays an experiential approach to brand consumption, reflecting her life situation, where she feels an urge to start over again.

Vicki is the youngest of the three respondents. She is twenty-three years old and in her final year of studying for her master's degree. Vicki is in a transition period between being a dependent child and an independent adult. She uses brands as means in a meaning-based communication system, trying out the potential identities and possible selves typical of the transition phase she is in.

The way the different life situations and life themes of the three women interact with the way they consume is the background of the brand relationship theory. Despite the different nature of their brand consumption, they all relate to brands in a way that is comparable to the way we relate to each other in human relationships. Examples of the three women's brand relationships can be found in table 8.1.

Source Fournier (1998)

The characteristics of the human relationships and the way these are connected with the identity of the participants' lives are hence transferred to the consumer–brand relationships and the concept of brand relationships between brands and consumers is verified; 'Whether one adopts a psychological or socio-historical interpretation of the data, the conclusion suggested in the analysis is the same: brand relationships are valid at the level of consumers' lived experiences' (Fournier 1998, p. 360).

As explained in the above section, human relationships take on very different forms and so do brand relationships. In the study behind the brand relationship theory fifteen brand relationships are identified.

The relationship forms resemble human relationships in the way they help fulfil goals and desires at the different life 'levels' of life themes, life projects and current concerns. Some brand relationships last all life and express some of its users' core values and ideas; others mean a lot (the consumer displays brand loyal behaviour) but the consumption of them changes as life progresses while others deliver on current concerns without being a fundamental part of the consumer's consumption pattern. The system of fifteen brand relationships:

> illustrates how the projects, concerns, and themes that people use to define themselves can be played out in the cultivation of brand relationships and how those relationships, in turn, can affect the cultivation of one's concept of self. For each woman interviewed, the author was able to identify an interconnected web of brands that contributed to the enactment, exploration, or resolution of centrally held identity issues.
>
> (Fournier 1998, p. 359)

The pattern of brand relationships resembles the pattern of human relationships in the cases of the three women serving as objects of research. This suggests that the role played by brands in the life of the individual consumer is deeply linked to the overall identity and the way the identity is reflected in their human relationships. A person with few but deep and lasting human relationships will also typically display loyalty to a few preferred brands, while a person who prefers to experiment more in the people department will also have a tendency to be rather experiential, when it comes to brand choice. Human relationships deliver on life themes, life projects and current concerns, and so do brand relationships.

Relationships are, however, also process phenomena and as such volatile and intangible. The same goes for brand relationships. The goal of a brand manager applying this theory to his or her work is to make the brand relationship as meaningful, stable and lasting as possible. The brand relationship needs to be of a high quality. Fournier advances the brand relationship theory by putting forward the *Brand Relation Quality* construct. The BRQ construct focuses on the quality, depth and strength of the consumer–brand relationship. Six important relationship factors (love/passion, self-connection, interdependence, commitment, intimacy and brand partner quality) are identified as influencing the durability and quality of the relationship. The relationship is basically meaning-based, reflecting the reciprocal nature of a relationship (read more about the consequences of managing meaning in the section on managerial implications).

Table 8.1 Relationship forms

Relationship form	Definition	Examples
Arranged marriages	Non-voluntary union imposed by preferences of third party. Intended for long-term, exclusive commitment, although at low levels of affective attachment	When married, Karen adopted her husband's favourite brands
Casual friends/ buddies	Friendship low in affect and intimacy, characterized by infrequent or sporadic engagement, and few exceptions for reciprocity or reward	Karen switches between five different detergent brands, buying whatever is on sale
Marriages of convenience	Long-term, committed relationship precipitated by environmental influence versus deliberate choice, and governed by satisfying rules	After a move of residence Vicki cannot buy her favourite brand of baked beans, which makes her reluctantly switch to a competing brand
Committed partnerships	Long-term, voluntarily imposed, socially supported union high in love, intimacy, trust and commitment to stay together despite adverse circumstances. Adherence to exclusivity rules expected	This is the relationship form Jean has with the majority of brands she uses for cleaning and cooking
Best friendships	Voluntary union based on a principle of reciprocity, the endurance of which is ensured through continued provision of positive rewards. Characterized by revelation of true self, honesty and intimacy. Congruity in partner images and personal interests common	In Karen's phase of finding her feet after a divorce, running every morning means a lot to her and has become a symbol of her new self. In this connection Reebok has become a brand that is 'a best friend' to Karen
Compartmentalized friendships	Highly specialized, situationally confined, enduring friendships characterized by lower intimacy than other friendship forms but higher socio-emotional rewards and interdependence. Easy entry and exit	Vicki uses a variety of different perfume brands to display different sides of herself in different situations
Kinships	Non-voluntary union with lineage ties	Vicki and Karen have 'inherited' some brand preferences from their mothers
Rebounds/ avoidance-driven relationships	Union precipitated by desire to move away from prior or available partner, as opposed to attraction to chosen partner *per se*	At work Karen could choose between a Gateway and an Apple computer. She chose the prior because she does not define herself as an Apple person

Childhood friendships	Infrequently engaged, affectively laden relation reminiscent of earlier times. Yields comfort and security of past self	To Jean the Estée Lauder brand evokes strong memories of her mother
Courtships	Interim relationships on the road to committed partnership contract	Wanting to find the 'right' scent, Vicki and her mother tried out several musk perfumes before settling for the Intimate Musk brand
Dependences	Obsessive, highly emotional, selfish attractions cemented by feeling that the other is irreplaceable. Separation from others yields anxiety. High tolerance of other's transgressions results	Appearance is important to Karen and she thanks Mary Kay and her running routine for her youthful looks. As this aspect of appearance is crucial for Karen's identity in her transitional phase as recently divorced, she is highly emotional and truly loyal to the Mary Kay brand
Flings	Short-term, time-bounded engagements of high emotional reward but devoid of commitment and reciprocity demands	Vicki tries out several trial-size shampoos and conditioners
Enmities	Intensely involving relationships characterized by negative affect and desire to avoid or inflict pain on the other	Karen has negative feelings towards Diet Coke, as she, taking great pride in not having any weight problems, enjoys being able to drink Classic Coke
Secret affairs	Highly emotive, privately held relationship considered risky if exposed to others	Karen has Tootsie Pops in her office desk and eats them in secret
Enslavements	Non-voluntary union governed entirely by desires of the relationship partner. Involves negative feelings but persists because of circumstances	Karen uses Southern Bell and Cable Vision, as she has no other choice

Source Fournier (1998).

The six most important facets, when upholding an important relationship are reflected in the Brand Relationship Quality part of the figure: love/passion, self-connection, commitment, interdependence, intimacy and brand partner quality. These are important factors when one evaluates a brand relationship and the sum of these factors reflects the perceived quality of the relationship.

The relationship quality is, however, also subject to an ongoing interplay between actions by the brand and the consumer of the relationship. Relationships

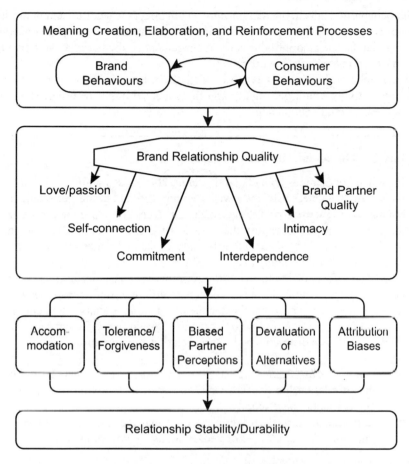

Figure 8.4 Preliminary model of brand relationship quality and its effects on relationship stability; from Fournier, 'Consumers and their brands', *Journal of Consumer Research*, 24 (1998), © 1998 by Journal of Consumer Research Inc. All rights reserved. 0093–5301/98/2404–0001503.00. Reprinted by permission of the University of Chicago Press

are in a constant state of flux as the process phenomena they are. Contextual changes as well as changes in the relationship *per se* determine the stability and durability of the brand–consumer relationship.

The way the brand relationship quality is constantly influenced by the brand actions as well as the consumer actions reflects very well the basic idea of the brand relationship theory: that of a dynamic and dyadic exchange between brand and consumer. The BRQ construct conceptualizes the many and complicated layers of the consumer–brand relationship, outlaying the meaning-based interaction, the six most important facets of an important relationship. These are the most important aspects of the establishment of the relationship, but Fournier adds the understanding of the frailty of any relation as she points towards all the actions from both participants in the relationship, which affect the stability and durability of the relationship. Hence, she not only introduces a whole new way of conceptualizing brands, she also introduces the management of the brand as an ongoing, complex and indeed unstable process.

Brand relationship theory has subsequently been extended by research into the way respectively brand personality and the expected brand relationship norms influence the brand relationship.

Box 8.3 The complexity of a relationship

In 'When good brands do bad', (Aaker *et al.* 2004) research illustrates how brands are evaluated differently when having different brand personalities but making the same mistake. The consumers were more forgiving towards the exciting brand personality than towards the sincere brand. The brand relationship was thus influenced differently when the brands were different (Read more about this study in chapter 7.)

In 'The effects of brand relationship norms on consumer attitudes and behavior' (Aggarwal 2004) it is studied how different fundamental perceptions of relationship norms influence the evaluations of marketing actions. In social psychology a distinction is made between two different kinds of relationships with distinctively different relationship norms:

- *Exchange relationships* are based on economic factors. People in this kind of relationship expect money in return for a favour or expect a comparable favour promptly.
- *Communal relationships* are based on social factors. Here, money in return for a favour is not expected. Benefits are not compared.

The line of thinking behind this research is that a brand is evaluated as a potential relationship partner in – more or less – the same manner as a human member of society. Certain norms for a relationship are identified in a brand relationship as they would be in a human relationship. After having tested how these norms work in the exchange between a brand and a consumer in situations of asking for help, the researcher is able to state that it is very important not to mix the behaviour of the two types of relationships. When a relationship is established, relationship norms (exchange-based and communal) are taken for granted, and violations of these norms are evaluated negatively.

This line of research extends on the idea that a relationship is a complex and volatile entity. And in the management of a brand relationship it is beneficial to consider both the brand personality and the implied relationship norms and make all marketing actions consistent accordingly.

Sources Aaker *et al.* (2004), Aggarwal (2004)

Summary

Traditionally, we speak of relationships between people. Expanding the notion to brands and consumers implies that consumers have the ability to endow brands with human personality traits. Therefore, animism – or the human propensity to endow dead objects or abstract concepts with human personalities – is the first supporting theme in this chapter. Theory on human relationships serves as the second supporting theme. Human relationships are important factors in all lives and deliver on life themes, life projects and current concerns. They are also process phenomena under influence from many different sources.

The brand relationship theory originates from a study into how consumers experience relationships with brands. This study provides us with a framework consisting of fifteen different brand relationship forms, resembling human relationships. But knowing what kind of relationship consumers experience with brands is not enough. The theory also provides us with the Brand Relationship Quality construct. It is a model that depicts how relationships are volatile process phenomena constantly under influence of other factors. The brand relationship theory is supplemented by research into how brand personality and relationship norms influence consumers' brand evaluations.

Methods and data in the relational approach

The most important methodologies of this approach are based on the scientific tradition of phenomenology. The relational approach takes brand management theory into the domains of experiential consumption. Here, the inner reality of the consumer is investigated and a holistic take on the way the life of the consumer

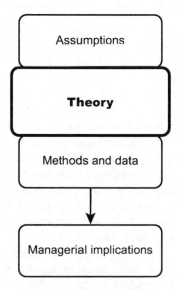

Figure 8.5 Theoretical building blocks of the relational approach

influences consumption is a prerequisite. Accessing the inner reality and thereby understanding the *whole* life of the consumer is primarily done by means of depth interviews and life story methods.

Depth interviews and life stories

One of the most widely used methods of accessing the inner realities of respondents is depth interviews. Often, depth interviews are combined with life story methods, where the respondent's own statements on life transitions and so on are recorded and intertwined with other statements in order to deepen the holistic understanding of the consumer's life world.

The 1998 publication by Fournier which introduced the phenomenological tradition to the discipline of brand management, constituting the relational approach, used depth interviews in combination with life story method. The phenomenological interview allows for 'the understanding of the subjective meanings of consumers' lived experiences with brands ... establishing consumer validity of the brand proposition as a whole' (Fournier 1998, p. 347).

The life-story case study makes it possible to link the statements put forward in the depth interviews with the stages and themes of the informant's life story, hence linking the consumer experiences with the central themes of consumer identity:

> Identity is reflected in one's life narrative, or life story, capturing various roles including past, present, and anticipated future selves. My life narrative describes the path of my identity development; it defines who I am, who I have been, who I am becoming, and/or who I am no longer.
>
> (Kleine *et al.* 1995, p. 328)

The life-story method is not, as such, separable from the depth interview: 'Phenomenological interviewing can be particularly powerful in chronicling personal transformation and change' (Hackley 2003, p. 122). But being aware of the fact that people structure their understanding of themselves in a narrative linked with the life story enables the researcher to draw more insightful and powerful conclusions based on the analysis of the interview.

The depth interview method involves a turning back to experiencing. Going back to individual and felt experiences supports a reflexive structured analysis that portrays the essence of an experience. By interpreting the retrospective and evident explanations of the respondent's experience with the phenomenon, this approach may reveal underlying structures and concepts. Uncovering these underlying structures opens up a deep understanding of what the experiences really have meant for the respondent. By understanding the experience at the individual level, it is possible to draw more general conclusions.

A depth interview takes several hours and can eventually be conducted in sequence meaning that you return to the same respondent several times in order to go still deeper into understanding his or her life world. Depth is definitely preferred to breadth when collecting data in this tradition.

Box 8.4 Depth is preferred to breadth

As described in box 8.2, only three informants served as basis of the original brand relationship research in order to secure depth: 'Size restrictions on the informant pool ensured the depth concerning life worlds and brand relationship portfolios necessary for thick description' (p. 347). Each respondent was interviewed for twelve to fifteen hours and the interviews were designed to complement the first-person descriptions of the brand use with the contextual details of the informants' life worlds: 'To stimulate discussion, kitchen cabinets were opened and informants were instructed to 'tell the story' behind any brand in the inventory' (Fournier 1998, p. 347). **The life-story information is gathered at a closing interview**. The research design had two purposes: 'Interviews were designed to yield two complementary types of information: (1) a first-person description of the informant's brand usage history and (2) contextual details concerning the informant's life world' (p. 347).

Source Fournier (1998)

Life stories often reveal themselves as undercurrents in phenomenological depth interviews. Allowing the respondent to talk for hours will hence often disclose important and recurring themes and values linked with their life history (often the life themes, life projects and current concerns of relationship theory are relevant, when understanding the nature of relationships). Linking these themes with statements about other subjects can deepen the understanding of the *whole* life of the respondent.

Box 8.5 Stories can be helped along

Consumers' unstructured stories about brand consumption can be helped along by the use of images. In a phenomenological study of coffee consumption 'informant-generated' images were used to stimulate stories of brand use. Ten days before the interviews were to take place the respondents were asked to collect a set of images describing 'how they felt about coffee' (coffee category images) and another set of images capturing their feelings towards their favourite coffee brand.

The interviews (of two to three or five hours) were then structured in three parts:

- Part one centred on the coffee category images. (How do respondents feel about coffee in general?) Central images were identified and laddering techniques were applied, meaning that the interviewee kept asking questions regarding the meaning of the pictures in order to capture the full context of category meaning.

- In part two of the interviews, insight into the use of coffee was obtained. Especially, how coffee consumption has changed over the course of time in the lives of the respondents was highlighted.
- The final part of the interviews focused on the consumers' brand relationships with their favourite coffee brands. The images identified by respondents to depict how they felt about their favourite coffee brands were used to help the stories along.

Deep insight into coffee consumption in general, category use in different stages of life, and relationships with favourite brands was obtained through this method. Comparing stage one and stage three of the interviews highlighted the difference between coffee consumption in general and perceived brand relationships specifically.

Source Fournier and Yao (1997)

Conducting a long interview, the interviewer can apply the techniques of box 8.6. A depth interview requires a prior agreement and a set time, date, and place in order to be successful (remember that a depth interview takes hours and that foreseeable disturbances should be eliminated). It is important that the interviewee is well aware of the magnitude of the task prior to the interview.

The interviewer should be well prepared for the interview, meaning that he or she should be well informed about the topic for the interview, but should still keep an open mind remembering that it is the respondent's *experiences* that are of interest and considered valid in this kind of interview. Below you will find guidelines for the conduction of depth interviews. First, we will explain some of the key terms.

Biographical questions are asked in order to record who the person is, as well as to get the talk going. Grand-tour opening questions are very broad questions opening up for the interview; these will guide the interviewer as to where the interview might be going. Especially in the beginning of the interview, prompting techniques can be applied in order to help the interview along. Prompting techniques are techniques to express interest to help the interviewee along and make them elaborate on the topic. It can be done by raising your eyebrows or repeating the last word of a sentence in an interested way in order to encourage the respondent to explain more. The interviewer is also encouraged to 'play dumb'. It is important not to intimidate the respondent by appearing too clever or superior in other ways. Playing decidedly dumb might not prove necessary but is preferable to the opposite. Remember that you are allowed access into the life world of the respondent and he or she should feel as comfortable as possible about letting you in. A successful depth interview is very much a matter of trust.

Box 8.6 Conduct a long interview yourself

- Start out by asking biographical questions. (Ask about age, occupation, family background, etc.)
- Ask 'grand-tour opening questions', e.g. if you investigate consumption of sports goods, start out by asking broad questions regarding your respondent's interest in sport before going into the more detailed questions about their preferred brands.
- Apply prompting techniques for the grand-tour opening questions, e.g. repeat the last word of a sentence, and raise your eyebrows in order to make your respondent comfortable about telling his or her stories.
- Listen for key terms, topic avoidance, and minor misunderstandings.
- Allow minor changes of subject – they might lead to further insight.
- If not, gently get the interview back on track.
- Eventually 'play dumb'.
- Do not disturb the process by taking notes.
- Record the interview on tape or video.
- Get a verbatim transcript of the interview for analysis.

Source McCracken (1988)

The task is not to test some predefined 'truths' but to discover the idiosyncratic truth of your respondent: 'People ascribe meaning to the objects that present themselves in consciousness. The task of the researcher is to explore events or processes by gathering first-hand descriptions of these feelings, thoughts and perceptions' (Hackley 2003, p. 114). And remember that the respondent is always the expert!

Data analysis

The recorded and transcribed depth interviews contain huge amounts of unstructured data. This kind of data is difficult to categorize but should open up completely new insights. Therefore, the data analysis is a complicated and important part of the process. It requires an 'insider perspective' of the researcher. Since the lived or felt experiences of respondents are considered valid data, the researcher strives for proximity to these experiences. (In positivist research traditions the researcher strives for distance to the objects of study.)

Repeated analysis is required in order to detect central quotations that can be beneficial in order to pinpoint important themes and metaphors. Repeated analysis also implies the possibility of 'auto-correcting loops', a process of detecting new and central patterns in the interview by going through it repeatedly. These loops ensure the integration of the researcher's and the respondent's perspectives as well as a holistic approach to the investigation.

Preferably, data collection and analysis should be conducted by the same person to further ensure the holistic perspective.

Summary

The relational approach is founded on the scientific tradition of phenomenology. Phenomenology implies that focus is on the 'inner world' of people, and not the 'outer world' that can be subject to other kinds of study.

Respondents' perceptions of their own experiences are considered valid data as well as the topic of interest in this research tradition. Depth interviews combined with life story methods are the most suitable methods for gaining insight into the life-worlds of respondents.

Conducting a phenomenological study, the researcher should strive for proximity to the research process and should ideally collect data as well as analyse them. Data analysis should contain auto-correcting loops in order to detect central themes and metaphors to structure the large and unstructured amounts of data.

Implications of the relational approach

By now it should be clear that the relational approach introduces a dyadic brand perspective, an existential view of the consumer, phenomenological methods, and a precise conceptualization of key brand relationship concepts (brand relationship forms and the brand relationship quality construct). All these elements draw an accurate and coherent picture of the radical shift in brand management that is the consequence of the relational approach.

The big challenge is, however, to transform the above described characteristics of the relational approach into managerial implications that are actually adaptable to real-life situations. Talking about the appropriateness of conceiving the brand as

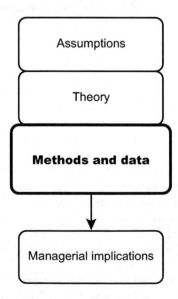

Figure 8.6 Methods and data of the relational approach

a meaning-based construct created in a dynamic and dyadic process between brand and consumer is much easier than adapting these thoughts to actual branding strategies! The literature behind the relational approach is very accurate and detailed when it comes to methods and scientific background. The same literature does not, however, give much advice when it comes to managing the brand, nor does it provide insight into best practice case examples: 'Relationship marketing is powerful in theory but troubled in practice' (Fournier *et al.* 1998, p. 44).

As mentioned in chapter 1, the analysis behind this book rests upon the Kuhnian notions of paradigms and scientific revolutions. And the relational approach seems to be the indicator of a major paradigm shift in brand management. Therefore, we have chosen to touch only briefly upon the managerial implications of the relational approach and thereby also leave space to focus on its academic implications. There should be no doubt of the importance of the relational approach; it seems almost impossible to find a brand management publication from 1998 and onwards that does not quote Fournier's brand relationship theory.

Managerial implications

From the literature we can deduce the following implications: the management has to be founded on meaning; the marketer is offered the opportunity to go far beyond the concept of brand loyalty; a relationship is a volatile entity; and the amount of information can be overwhelming. The same literature, however, provides some overall guidelines on how to manage a 'relational' brand success-fully. The brand has to act as a true friend.

The fact that the process is dynamic implies that the management of the brand is an ongoing process in which meaning is negotiated on a continuous basis. The marketer should be able and willing to continuously adapt the strategy to fluctua-tions on the meaning negotiation. Managing meaning thereby requires insight into the lives of the brand's customers as well as a continuous integration of the lived experiences of consumers into the execution of the brand strategy. This condition leads to one of the factors that make the management of the relational brand difficult: the risk of information overload.

Wanting to manage your brand by means of the brand relationship theory, you need real and deep insight into your consumer base: 'True customer intimacy – the backbone of a successful, rewarding relationship – requires a deep understanding of the context in which our products and services are used in the course of our customers' day-to-day lives' (Fournier *et al.* 1998, p. 49). As explained in the methods and data section of this chapter, the methods for acquiring the right kind of data in the relational approach supply the marketer with a vast amount of unstructured data. This data and information complexity in the relational process contains the risk of a standstill.

By entering the 'life-worlds' of your consumers you have the opportunity to gain true insight into how the brand in question fits into the lives of customers. A 'rela-tional' marketer collecting and analysing knowledge about his or her customers runs the risk of having to integrate incompatible knowledge in the branding strategy. The trick is to find some common factors in the meaning negotiation between the brand and key customers and integrate them in the branding strategy.

Hence, it is difficult not to get lost in the potential information overload of the relational approach. The deep, and potentially insightful, knowledge of consumers and their lives offers the marketer the main advantage of the relational approach: the opportunity of going beyond brand loyalty.

Understanding brand consumption in the light of the relational approach offers the marketer the opportunity to answer questions not answered by measurements of brand loyalty (*if* the brand is consumed on a continuous base versus *how* and *why*).

Wanting to reap the benefits from deepening the loyalty concept through use of the brand relationship theory should be weighed up against the difficulties of managing a consumer–brand relationship. Getting the management of the relations-based brand right should start by the implementation of the assumptions behind the theory. The brand is perceived as being endowed with a personality, the brand–consumer exchange is assumed to be dyadic, and 'dialogue' and 'friendship' seem to be appropriate metaphors. The personality of the brand as well as the norms and values of the consumer strongly influence the evaluation of the brand's actions. These assumptions should serve as guidelines when managing the brand in question. The brand should act as a true friend.

The marketer needs to be open to a truly equal and dyadic relationship. In all aspects, there should be a balance between 'giving' and 'getting'. If over-exploited (for instance by an excessive gathering of data in any encounter with the marketer) the consumer might see the marketer engaged in relationship marketing as an enemy rather than a friend. A friendly marketer respects the basic rules of friendship (to provide emotional support, to respect privacy, to preserve confidences and to be tolerant of other friendships among others) and should apply them to the management of the brand: 'For the brand to serve as legitimate relationship partner, it must surpass the personification qualification and actually behave as an active, contributing member of the dyad' (Fournier 1998, p. 345).

Furthermore, the marketer should be open and honest about the motivation for approaching the consumer and in return offer the consumer benefits corresponding to the inconvenience.

The marketer should be very aware not to exploit the consumer's confidence and be aware to return any favour in one way or the other. A consumer willing to 'share secrets' should receive some benefits and in all be treated as a friend in order for the brand relationship to develop and grow. *Quid pro quo* is a fundamental principle in the relational approach.

Academic implications

The relational approach implies a major paradigmatic shift in brand management and can be identified as the one approach leading brand management into the twenty-first century. As described in chapter 3, the period of analysis (1985–2006) can be divided into three periods, the first focusing on the sending end of brand communication, the second with a focus on the receiving end and the third emphasizing the context of brand consumption. The relational approach belongs to the second period of time where the consumer is the pivotal point. The relational approach is, however, very different from the other two approaches emphasizing the consumer (the consumer-based approach and the personality approach).

We have three reasons for identifying the relational approach as an important indicator of a paradigm shift. First, it is the first approach applying solely qualitative methods. Second, the approach is meaning-based. Third, it takes brand research into the domain of the consumer, emphasizing a holistic view of the consumer. The interest in consumers' life worlds is associated with a phenomenological research tradition. For these three reasons, we see the relational approach as a trailblazer for the two forthcoming approaches, namely the community approach and the cultural approach.

The concept of meaning is often opposed to the concept of information. Information is considered external stimuli to the consumer, while meaning stems from the inner reality, life and identity of the consumer: 'Phenomenology can conceive consumption not merely as behavioural response to external stimuli but as a meaning-directed behaviour driven by emotions, feelings and fantasies' (Hackley 2003, p. 112).

A phenomenological approach adapts a psychological view of the individual. Thereby, the relational approach is based on an idiosyncratic view of meaning creation, based on a basic idea that reality construction takes place in the mind. The notion of meaning is also central to the community approach and the cultural approach, but in these approaches meaning is found in the social interaction with others and in the surrounding culture and society, respectively. In that sense, the relational approach is the first meaning-based approach of three.

Psychological phenomenology is about investigating how an individual interacts with external objects to learn about the structures that make up the individual's construction of reality. Phenomenology has special capabilities for uncovering non-rational aspects of consumption.

The phenomenological tradition features a distinctive take on the question of validity. The positivist research traditions assume an outer reality, a reality that can be touched, studied and measured. In this tradition, validity means that different studies performed by different researchers should end up with exactly the same result.

In the phenomenological tradition, 'lived' or 'felt' experience is considered valid, which depicts clearly how different the phenomenological tradition is from the positivist research ideal. Reality is not 'out there' to be touched and measured but is rather constituted within the individual respondents. How we perceive and feel about a phenomenon constitutes the phenomenon – the world is inseparable from the subject, and vice versa. Phenomenological perspectives will thereby be subjectivist and the first person perspective is an important prerequisite in phenomenology for generating knowledge. It is assumed that no underlying world exists which is raised over perception and conceptualizing. In other words, the way phenomena are perceived by the individual constitutes the true world: 'Phenomenological social research takes the embodied, experiencing agent as a starting point and explores the mutually constructed 'life-world' of participants, the world of lived experience from which all others derive' (Hackley 2003, p. 112). To exemplify: if a consumer experiences a shopping experience as hurtful, then the shopping experience *is* hurtful, no matter if videotapes or witnesses contest that no harm was done to the customer.

In consumer research the contrasting views of consumer behaviour in the dominant information-processing perspective (reflected in the consumer-based approach, chapter 6) and a phenomenological perspective is identified. In table 8.2 some of the main differences are highlighted. Going through these differences should make it easier to understand why – and how – the relational approach implies such a significant shift in the way brands and consumers are perceived.

By adding the phenomenological (experiential) consumer behaviour perspective to the discipline of brand management, the brand is taken into a whole new era,

Table 8.2 Differences between the information-processing and the experiential consumer perspective

	Information processing	*Experiential/phenomenological*
Products	Objective features Tangible benefits	Subjective features Symbolic benefits
Stimulus properties	Verbal	Non-verbal
Resources	Money	Time
Task definition	Problem-solving	Hedonic response
Type of involvement	Cognitive responses Left-brain	Reaction, arousal Right-brain
Search activity	Information acquisition	Exploratory behaviour
Individual differences	Demographics Socio-economics	Creativity Religion
Cognition	Memory Knowledge structure Beliefs Thought generation	Subconscious Imagery Fantasies/daydreams Free association
Affect	Attitudes Preferences	Emotions Feelings
Behaviour	Buying Purchase decision Choices	Usage Consumption experience Activities
Criteria	Utilitarian Work Mentality: economic	Aesthetic Play Mentality: psychosocial
Output consequences	Function Results Purpose	Fun Enjoyment Pleasure

Source Hirschman and Holbrook (1992)

where brand consumption and brand loyalty are to be understood as closely inter-twined with consumers' 'inner realities'. The focus is not on the mere transaction or the exact moment of choice but on all that lies behind consumption choices. The consumer's whole identity (as perceived by the consumer himself) is to be under-stood if one wants to gain insight into brand consumption.

Thereby, the emphasis moves away from the domain of the marketer and into the 'chaotic' domain of consumers. Even though the managerial implications of the relational approach are not very concrete, the approach leads the way towards new horizons where the role of consumers' social interaction (the community approach) and their cultural context (the cultural approach) are being conceptu-alized and translated to managerial implications. These approaches also feature a variety of qualitative methods that have become acceptable by the launch – and immense success – of the relational approach.

It seems that brand management in a way 'lets go' of the brand via this approach. The brand is suddenly 'out there' in a chaotic and ever-changing context. In the previous approaches, the concrete interaction between brand and consumer is being investigated from different angles and there is a focus on defining what a brand is. In the relational, the community and the cultural approaches brand management research seems to expand focus to different scenarios (consumers' individual life worlds, social interaction with other consumers, and cultural context, respectively) where the brand is not the 'main character' or the starting point of the research, but merely a factor like many others in complex individual, social and cultural networks.

Summary

The management of a brand relationship is a dynamic process, leaving room for the negotiation of both similar and conflicting views and many different players. It goes without saying that it is difficult to manage in practice. The approach is meaning-based, implying brand value is co-created in an ongoing process between brand and consumer. This means that the marketer has to let go of total control of the brand and incorporate the meaning created by consumers in the management of the brand. Furthermore, the management is considered a very dynamic process where the meaning is constantly negotiated under the influence of the many factors influencing both human and brand relationships.

In truly understanding the consumers lies a risk of information overload, leaving the marketer with too much knowledge to incorporate it in the brand communication. The approach, however, also contains the opportunity to go far beyond the notion of brand loyalty and understand *how* and *why* the brand is being consumed on a continuous basis in addition to *if* it is being consumed.

If one wants to reap the benefits of this understanding, it is pivotal to treat customers as true friends. The real-life brand relationship should reflect the prerequisites of the relational approach in the sense that the brand–consumer exchange is seen as a dyadic and dynamic process. The consumer should accord-ingly be treated as an equal partner and not just sources of information.

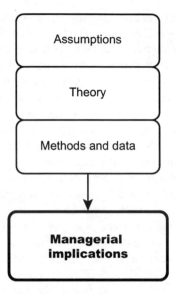

Figure 8.7 Managerial implications of the relational approach

The relational approach has some very profound consequences for the future development of the scientific discipline of brand management. It is a clear indicator of a paradigmatic shift for three reasons: it implies a shift towards qualitative methods, it is meaning-based, and it emphasizes understanding of the life worlds of consumers rather than measuring the mere brand–consumer transactions. In that way it opens the way to the further development of the discipline embodied in the two approaches to come: the community approach and the cultural approach.

Comments from the 'founding fathers' (4)

The value of the relationship approach to the study and management of brands

Susan Fournier, Boston University School of Management

Nearly twenty years ago I was promoted to Vice-president of Consumer–Brand Relationships at Young & Rubicam, an advertising agency in New York. The position was my idea: a translation of the revolutionary B2B relationship marketing paradigm into the B2C world. I quit two weeks later on the heels of a stark realization that the frameworks and concepts I would need to execute my position had yet to be created. So off I went to the University of Florida to pursue the development of consumer–brand relationship theory in consumer research.

The case was not an easy sell to a faculty comprised largely of dyed-in-the-wool experimental cognitive psychologists who thought of brands as economic sources of information. People have relationships with inanimate brands, do they? Do tell! The methods I brought to bear to illuminate my phenomenon were equally troubling. My thesis rested largely on phenomenological interviews among three—yes, three—women. The addition of scale development work and some LISREL modelling surely helped. But, in the end, the brand relationship ideas I generated seemed to sell themselves. My thesis set forth several essential relationship tenets that helped academics and practitioners think about their brands in new and powerful ways.

The first tenet stated that the provision of meaning lay at the core of all consumer–brand relationships. Consumer–brand relationships were purposeful; they were engaged as meaning-laden resources to help people to live their lives. Consumers played active roles as meaning makers in the brand relationship, mutating and adapting brand meanings to fit their life projects and tasks. Significant brand relationships were based not on low or high category involvement levels, but on the significance of the brand's meanings in the person's life. Even mundane goods could foster strong relationships provided their meanings resonated in the personal and cultural world.

A second tenet emphasized the variability of brand relationship types and forms. The relationship perspective forced us to acknowledge that highly committed and emotive brand loyal relationships were not the only meaningful consumer–brand engagements. A broadened view of relationship space included flings, secret affairs, committed partnerships, and friendships, not to mention adversaries, enmities, and master–slaves. Each of these relationships was governed by a unique set of contract rules: 'do's' and 'don'ts' concerning behaviours in the relationship. Friends should not reveal secrets to others, for example, and marital spouses should not cheat. Brand relationships could be distinguished as strong versus weak, hierarchical versus egalitarian, formal versus informal, positive versus negative. Strong relationships could be qualified beyond loyalty and affect using the brand relationship quality (BRQ) scale and its added facets of self connection, sociocultural connection, interdependence, partner role quality, and intimacy. The astute relationship manager recognized that consumer–brand relationships were complex, and managed relationships according to their operative dimensions and rules.

A third tenet supported that relationships were dynamic and reciprocating phenomena that evolved and changed over time. Relationships unfolded through stages, including Initiation, Growth, Maintenance, and Decline. They manifested characteristic development trajectories: Biological Life Cycle, Passing Fad, Cyclical Resurgence, and Approach Avoidance Curve. Importantly, everything the brand did had the potential to affect the relationship. Brand behaviours—from packaging and logo choices to the salutations on customer service letters—sent 'signals' regarding the type of relationship contract that was in place. These signals controlled inferences and relationship strength levels. Sometimes the consumers' received view of the relationship was not what the managers thought they had in play.

The relationship perspective was powerful in that it forced marketing researchers and practitioners to acknowledge important principles governing consumers' engagements with brands. Co-creation. Personal and Cultural Resonance. Implicit Contracts. Relationship Norms. Brand Relationship Quality and Strength. Consumer Relationship Management. These constructs and essential tenets have helped us to better understand, measure, and manage our brands. Recent research continues to build upon basic relationship fundamentals, exploring, for example, the rules and biases associated with communal versus exchange relationship templates, accommodation and tolerance processes in relationship development, relationship transgressions, relationship dissolution processes, personal relationship styles and their influence in the brand relationship space, sociopolitical brand relationships, ethnic and cultural differences in brand relationship behaviours, methods for relationship strength measurement, and the functions and provisions of relationships with brands. I am honoured to have participated in this paradigm shift in marketing thought.

Student questions

1 Which scientific tradition is associated with the relational approach?
2 Which philosophical tradition is associated with the scientific tradition?
3 Describe the difference between life themes, life projects and current concerns.
4 What is animism?
5 Which factors influence brand relationship quality?
6 Which are the most important methods in the scientific tradition of the relational approach?
7 How does the perception of validity in this approach differ from a positivist validity perception?
8 Should you as a researcher attempt to base your study on as many respondents as possible?
9 How should you avoid becoming the enemy in the eyes of the consumer?
10 Explain why the relational approach indicates a paradigm shift.

References and further reading

Key readings are in **bold type**.

Aaker, J. L. (1997) 'Dimensions of brand personality', *Journal of Marketing Research*, 34 (August): 347–56
Aaker, J. and Fournier, S. (1995) 'A brand as a character, a partner and a person: three perspectives on the question of brand personality', *Advances in Consumer Research*, 22: 391–5

Aaker, J., Fournier, S. and Brasel, S. A. (2004) 'When good brands do bad', *Journal of Consumer Research*, 31 (June): 1–16

Aggarwal, P. (2004) 'The effects of brand relationship norms on consumer attitudes and behavior', *Journal of Consumer Research*, 31 (June): 87–101

Allen, C., Fournier, S., and Miller, F. (2008) 'Brands and their meaning makers', in C. Haugtvedt, P. Herr and F. Kardes (eds) *Handbook of Consumer Psychology*, Mahwah NJ: Lawrence Erlbaum Associates, 781–822.

Bitner, M. J., Booms, B. H. and Tetreault, M. S. (1990) 'The service encounter: diagnosing favorable incidents', *Journal of Marketing*, 54 (January): 71–84

Fournier, S. (1991) 'A meaning-based framework for the study of consumer–object relations', *Advances in Consumer Research*, 18 (1): 736–42

Fournier, S. (1994) 'A Person–Brand Relationship Framework for Strategic Brand Management', Ph.D. dissertation, University of Florida

Fournier, S. (1995) 'Toward the development of relationship theory at the level of the product and brand', *Advances in Consumer Research*, 22: 661–2

Fournier, S. (1998a) 'Consumers and their brands: developing relationship theory in consumer research', *Journal of Consumer Research*, 24 (4): 343–73

Fournier, S. (1998b) 'More than a name: the role of brands in people's lives', *Working Knowledge: A Report on Research at Harvard Business School*, 2 (1): (interview)

Fournier, S. and Yao, J. L. (1997) 'Reviving brand loyalty: a reconceptualization within the framework of consumer–brand relationships', *International Journal of Research in Marketing*, 14 (5): 451–72

Fournier, S., Allen, C. and Miller, F. (2008) 'Mapping Consumers' Relationships with Brands', working paper, Boston University.

Fournier, S., Avery, J. and Wojnicki, A. (2008) 'Contracting for Relationships', working paper, Boston University.

Fournier, S., Solomon, M. and Englis, B. (2008, forthcoming) 'When brands resonate', in B. H. Schmitt (ed.) *Handbook of Brand and Experience Management*, Boston MA: Elgar Publishing.

Fournier, S., Tietje, B. and Brunel, F. (2008) 'Measuring Relationship Strength with the Brand Relationship Quality (BRQ) Scale', working paper, Boston University.

Fournier, S., Dobscha, S. and Mick, D. G. (1998) 'Preventing the premature death of relationship marketing', *Harvard Business Review*, January–February: 42–51

Gürhan-Canli, Z. and Ahluwalia, R. (1999) 'Cognitive and relational perspectives on brand equity', *Advances in Consumer Research*, 26 (1): 343–5

Hackley, C. (2003) *Doing Research Projects in Marketing, Management and Consumer Research,* London: Routledge

Hirschman, E. C. and Holbrook, M. B. (1992) *Postmodern Consumer Research: the Study of Consumption as Text*, Newbury Park CA: Sage

Holbrook, M. B. and Hirschman, E. C. (1982) 'The experiental aspects of consumption: consumer fantasies, feelings, and fun', *Journal of Consumer Research*, 9 (September): 132–40

Kleine, S. S., Kleine R. E. III, and Allen, C. T. (1995) 'How is a possession "me" or "not me"? Characterizing types and an antecedent of material possession attachment', *Journal of Consumer Research*, 22 (December): 327–43

McCracken, G. (1987) 'Advertising: meaning or information', *Advances in Consumer Research*, 14 (1): 121–5

McCracken, G. (1988) *The Long Interview*, Newbury Park CA: Sage Publications

Mick, D. G. and Buhl, C. (1992) 'A meaning-based model of advertising experiences', *Journal of Consumer Research*, 19: 317–38

Paulssen, M. and Fournier, S. (2008) 'Attachment Security and the Strength of Commercial Relationships', working paper, Boston University.

Stern, B. B., Thompson, C. J. and Arnould, E. J. (1998) 'Narrative analysis of a marketing relationship: the consumer's perspective', *Psychology and Marketing*, 15 (3): 195–214

Thompson, C. J., Locander, W. B. and Pollio, H. R. (1989) 'Putting consumer experience back into consumer research: the philosophy and method of existential phenomenology, *Journal of Consumer Research*, 16 (September): 133–46

Zahavi, D. (2003) *Fænomenologi*, Frederiksberg: Roskilde Universitetsforlag/ Samfundslitteratur

9   The community approach

with a commentary by Associate Professor of Marketing, Albert M. Muniz Jr, De Paul University, and Professor of Marketing Thomas C. O'Guinn, Wisconsin School of Business

---

Learning objectives

The purpose of this chapter is to:

Understand the assumptions of the community approach
- The idea of a 'triadic' brand relationship is central to the community approach
- A social brand perspective is introduced to brand management

Understand the main theoretical building blocks and how they are connected
- Community theory
- Subcultures of consumption
- Brand community

Provide insights into the variety of methods used to research brand communities
- Ethnographic methods
- 'Netnography'

Understand the managerial implications
- The marketer as observer
- The marketer as facilitator

The Sacramento Jaguar Club is introduced as:

> We are a group of people who enjoy the company of other JAGUAR enthusiasts. We enjoy dining together, driving our cars together and attending various events together. Whether you now own a JAGUAR, would like to own a JAGUAR, or you once owned a JAGUAR you are welcome to join us for fun, feasting, and general merriment.
>
> (Jaguar Clubs of North America, www.jcna.com)

Googling 'Apple user groups' results in more than 16 million hits, indicating the enormous interest consumers have in the sharing of their Apple consumption experiences with other Apple users.

Consumers form communities around brands. In brand communities, a brand is the focal point of social interaction among passionate consumers. These consumers use the community to share their brand experiences and brand stories. Brand communities may rest entirely on consumer interaction, while others are more or less facilitated by a marketer, but they tend to evolve and thrive around old brands with an interesting history and high involvement products such as cars, motor cycles and computers. Brand communities can be a very powerful force affecting brand value, because the meaning found in the social engagement – the 'dining', 'fun' and 'feasting' of the Sacramento Jaguar Club or the exchange of user tips in Apple user groups – in brand communities adds significantly to brand loyalty. Brand communities have existed for long in practice. The 'breakthrough' research article on the subject was 'Brand community' by Muñiz and O'Guinn (published in 2001 in *Journal of Consumer of Research*). This publication constituted the conceptualization of the brand community in the context of brand management.

This chapter offers insights into the assumptions, key theoretical elements and methods of the community approach and finishes off by providing the managerial guidelines.

Assumptions of the community approach

The brand approaches of the 1990s (the consumer-based approach, the personality approach and the relational approach) dealt with the exchange between one marketer and one consumer. All three approaches fundamentally changed the traditional notion of brand equity as something created entirely in the domain of the marketer. The personality approach and the relational approach further constituted brand value as something co-created in a dialogue between marketer and consumer (the 'dyadic' brand relationship). The community approach adds meaning found in the social interaction *among* dedicated brand consumers (the 'triadic' brand relationship) to the theories of how brand value can be created: 'The brand communities are social entities that reflect the situated embeddedness of brands in the day-to-day lives of consumers and the ways in which brands connect consumer to brand, and consumer to consumer' (Muñiz and O'Guinn 2001, p. 418). In other words, the existence of a brand community *also* requires interaction between consumers.

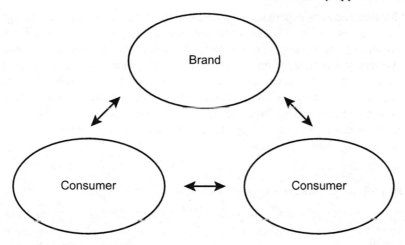

Figure 9.1 The 'brand triad': a brand community exists *only* when there is interaction between at least two consumers

The assumptions of the community approach fall into two categories. First, the 'brand triad' notion implies changes in the way the 'brand–consumer exchange' is perceived. Second, the community approach adds a social brand perspective to brand management. The methods used to research brand communities borrow from the scientific tradition of ethnography. These methods reflect the new assumptions in the context of brand management, since the ethnographic research tradition builds on a socio-cultural rather than individualistic perception of man (or in brand management, the consumer).

The 'brand–consumer exchange'

[brands] are social entities experienced, shaped, and changed in communities. Therefore, although brand meaning might be ascribed and communicated to consumers by marketers, consumers in turn uncover and activate their own brand meanings, which is communicated back to the marketers and the associated brand community.

(Brown *et al*. 2003, p. 31)

The community approach adds *groups* of consumers to the picture, which changes the basic premises of the 'brand–consumer exchange'. In the continuous brand–consumer dialogue shaping the brand, the marketer no longer finds himself having a dialogue with only one consumer, but with potentially millions of consumers. These consumers are likely to continue the brand dialogue long after the marketer believes the meeting is over. New rules of the game apply to the management of a brand, when countless consumers are able to share good and bad experiences, their roaring enthusiasm, and incredible rumours in face-to-face settings as well as on the internet.

The social benefits experienced by consumers in brand communities add significantly to brand loyalty. Community consumers are extremely loyal and enthusiastic consumers, but at the same time, communities of consumers are also autonomous consumers capable of *collectively* rejecting marketing actions. Many of the advantages associated with consuming the brand are created or enhanced *among* the community members, leaving the marketer with limited options of influencing brand meaning. This shift in negotiation power influences the creation of brand meaning and brand equity as the negotiation of brand meaning primarily takes place on consumers' terms.

Box 9.1 Who owns the Apple brand now?

Apple introduced a handheld personal computer – the Apple Newton – in 1993. In 1998 Apple chose to discontinue the Newton and take the Apple brand in new directions with, among other things, the iMac and the iPod.

Even though Apple chose to manage the brand differently, 'autonomous' consumers keep the Apple Newton brand alive in a vibrant grass-roots brand community. Dedicated Newton users have taken over the responsibilities of the marketer and are now running a web-based brand community that has at least 22,000 daily users. Offering technical support, software development and the cultivation of brand meaning, the brand community keeps the abandoned product and brand alive and kicking. Mythical and supernatural narratives are part of the Newton brand community ethos and are used for telling tales of miraculous performance and the survival of the brand, investing the brand with powerful brand meaning.

Source Muñiz and Schau (2005)

Due to the shift in negotiation power, communities are difficult to manage. Consumers are able to 'hijack' a brand (Wipperfürth 2005) and endow it with brand meaning very far from that intended by the marketer or choose to overrule management decisions as in the case of the Apple Newton brand.

Besides providing social benefits to consumers, brand communities serve as important information sources. The sharing of brand information can benefit both consumers and marketers.

Brand management from the community approach perspective is complex, and the autonomous groups of consumers can be hard to deal with. But the levels of brand loyalty and the depths of brand meaning found in communities can be priceless, making it worth while knowing the basic mechanisms ruling this approach.

The socio-cultural perspective

The social brand perspective put forward in the community approach draws on the scientific tradition of ethnography. This tradition represents an intellectual framework as well as a set of methodologies. As an intellectual framework, it focuses on the concept of culture and its influence on (consumer) behaviour. The methodological orientation emphasizes a 'real world' approach, which means that researchers participate in the real world of the subjects of investigation. Ethnography stems from the tradition of cultural anthropology.

The publication of the brand community theory in 2001 set off a wave of research. This wave of research introduced the ethnographic perspective in brand management focusing on the consumer as a cultural player in a social setting using the consumption experience as the source of important personal social experiences.

Summary

This new research 'cluster' acknowledges the social nature of brands and the inter-active involvement of *groups* of consumers in the creation of brand value and brand meaning.

Core to the community approach is the 'triadic' brand–consumer relationship and the social brand perspective. The triadic relationship implies consumers must interact, not only with the brand, but also with each other. The marketer is outnumbered in the brand–consumer exchange, making management of the brand difficult. At the same time, the existence of a brand community represents great advantages such as unforeseen levels of consumer loyalty and the possibility to cultivate deep consumer-driven brand meaning.

The community approach hence represents a social brand perspective and is associated with the scientific tradition of ethnography.

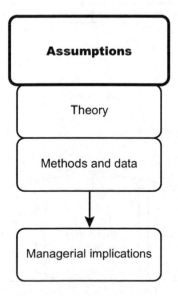

Figure 9.2 Assumptions of the community approach

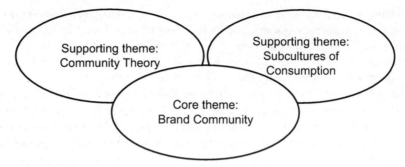

Figure 9.3 Supporting themes of brand community

Theoretical building blocks of the community approach

The key constructs of the brand community theory will be presented in this section. They are the three markers of community: the question of geography, the interconnectedness with subcultures of consumptions, and different variations of the brand community (the brandfest, the brand community and the community brand). But in order to understand the origin of the brand community concept, it is essential to know the origin of these concepts. The two supporting themes are hence initially presented before the core construct.

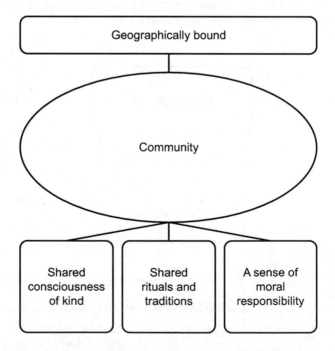

Figure 9.4 Conceptualization of the community in the sociological tradition

The brand community theory draws mainly on two supporting themes: theories about *communities* and *subcultures of consumption*.

Supporting theme: community theory

The word 'community' is comprehensible to everybody, but how it is to be understood in the context of brand community requires a more accurate definition. Community is a key concept in sociology characterized by having three markers – three basic characteristics – transcending the countless shapes and forms of a community. The three markers of a community are: consciousness of kind, shared rituals and traditions, and a sense of moral responsibility.

If these characteristics are present, a community does exist in theory. In the traditional sense of the word, a community is a geographically bound entity. A community may be geographically bound in a neighbourhood or at the premises of a tennis club. In the same sense it can be formal (the tennis club requiring a membership) or informal (the neighbourhood community feeling is simply there).

Supporting theme: subcultures of consumption

The brand community theory is also inspired and influenced by research into *subcultures of consumptions*. Subcultures of consumption were first conceptualized in 1995 by researchers Schouten and McAlexander after a three-year ethnographic study of groups of Harley-Davidson bikers. The level of identification between the Harley-Davidson bikes and their consumers facilitated the emergence of subcultures. These findings added social interaction to concepts like consumer loyalty, brand meaning, etc , and have inspired a whole new stream of research into the social aspects of consumption. The difference between a subculture of consumption and a brand community will be depicted at the end of this section.

Core theme: the brand community

Researchers Muñiz and O'Guinn pinpointed the existence of brand communities, when they observed: 'active and meaningful negotiation of the brand between consumer collectives and market institutions' (Muñiz and O'Guinn 2005, p. 252). During the course of a two-year study of consumers and their social interaction around three brands (Saab, Ford Bronco and Macintosh). Muñiz and O'Guinn found proof of the existence of brand communities and defined them as 'a specialized, non-geographically bound community, based on a structured set of social relationships among users of a brand' (2001, p. 421).

The research took place in both face-to-face settings and on websites relating to the three brands of study. The three markers of community were displayed in both kinds of environment. Muñiz and O'Guinn were hence able to introduce the brand community notion to the academic world of brand management. Since the three markers of community were displayed in both environments, the brand community notion led to a dissolution of the geographical aspect of the original community definition. Brand communities exist in face-to-face clubs as well as in virtual environments facilitated where 'imagined others' share their passion for a certain brand. A brand community is therefore not restricted by geography, unlike the traditional perception of the community being a geographically bound entity. The community in a brand context relates to a common understanding of a shared identity. The internet is of course an important vehicle in the formation of communities based on the sense of a shared identity with 'imagined others'.

As regards the first marker of a community: 'consciousness of kind' findings in the research suggest that 'Members feel an important connection to the brand, but more importantly, they feel a stronger connection toward one another. Members feel that they 'sort of know each other' at some level, even if they have never met' (Muñiz and O'Guinn 2001, p. 418).

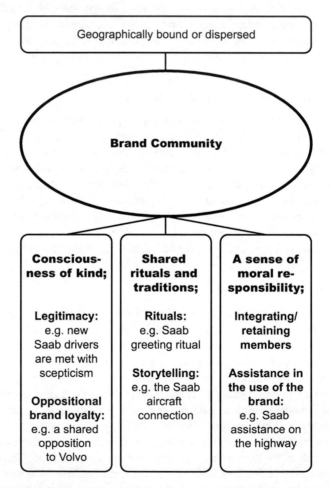

Figure 9.5 Brand community construct (with examples from the Saab community) as conceptualized by Muñiz and O'Guinn, 'Brand community', *Journal of Consumer Research*, 27 (2001), pp. 412–31

This feeling of 'sort of knowing each other' is characterized by and enhanced by two aspects: 'legitimacy' and 'oppositional brand loyalty'. 'Legitimacy' is based on observations indicating that members have a feeling of other members either being members for the right or the wrong reasons. As expressed by one community member: 'We' are the members 'really knowing' how and why the brand should be consumed, while 'they' consume the brand for the 'wrong reasons'. 'Oppositional brand loyalty' is the other characteristic that can enhance members' 'consciousness of kind'. Brand community members underpin this sense of belonging by sharing a dislike for competing brands. Macintosh community members tend to criticize PCs and Microsoft, while in the Saab brand community, for instance, there is a general tendency to put down the competing Swedish car brand, Volvo.

The second marker of community, 'Shared rituals and traditions' 'typically focus on shared consumption experiences with the brand. All the brand communities encountered in this project have some form of rituals or traditions that function to maintain the culture of the community' (ibid., p. 421). These rituals include special greetings, a celebration of the history of the brand, and sharing stories of the brand; 'Storytelling is an important means of creating and maintaining community' (ibid., p. 423). The storytelling aspect of the brand community can be very powerful. In the case of the Apple Newton brand community 'Supernatural, religious, and magical motifs are common ... There are strong elements of survival, the miraculous, and the return of the creator' (Muñiz and Schau 2005, p. 739).

The third marker of a brand community; 'sense of moral responsibility', 'is a sense of duty to the community as a whole, and to the individual members of the community, and it 'is what produces collective action and contributes to group cohesion' (ibid., p. 424); these characteristics were also displayed in the social interaction around the three brands in question. The communities display moral systems, but not in a very high-flown sense of the word – they do not relate to life-and-death matters: 'Moral systems can be subtle, and are highly contextualized. Such is the case with brand communities' (ibid.). These moral systems serve two major purposes: the integration and retention of members and the assistance of members in the proper use of the brand.

Brandfests, brand communities and community brands

The quintessential brand community pivots around an already existing brand and is usually established and run by enthusiastic volunteers. However, the three markers of community can also be observed at so-called brandfests, where a proactive marketer establishes consumer interaction that can facilitate the evolvement of a brand community. McAlexander *et al.*'s (2002) study of the intentional building of brand communities offers insight into the possibilities of a proactive marketer. If the marketer understands and respects the dynamics of a brand community it is possible to proactively create a platform that facilitates a brand community to evolve: 'Even owners who came to events dwelling on how different they felt from others often left after two or three days believing they belonged to a broader community that understands and supports them in realizing their consumption goals' (ibid. 2002, p. 42).

Corporate-sponsored brandfests are often used for recruitment of new members, while the existing communities typically consist of diehard brand enthusiasts.

Brands like Napster and Linux add a new category to the approach. The internet-based sharing of, respectively, MP3 files and an operating system for computers that can be downloaded free of charge is in fact *created* by a community. They are both not only powerful brands but also masters of completely changing the premises of their businesses. MySpace and YouTube are also interesting cases to consider if one wants to gain insight into how the premises of the community approach have in fact changed whole industries by fundamentally changing how consumers interact. These community brands display the same characteristics as the brand communities and brandfests but add another dimension to the scope of the approach, since no marketer (in the traditional sense of the word) exists. Still, it is the principles of the community approach that apply.

Brand communities and subcultures of consumption

As explained above, the formulation of a brand community theory is very much influenced by subcultures of consumption. The two concepts, however, differ significantly and should not be confused. 'A subculture of consumption [is] a distinctive subgroup of society that self-selects on the basis of a shared commitment to a particular product class, brand, or consumption activity' (Schouten and McAlexander 1995, p. 43).

Apart from this self-selection, different markers from the three markers characterizing a brand community are used to characterize a subculture: The markers of a subculture of consumption are:

- A hierarchical social structure.
- Ethos is manifested in shared beliefs and values.
- Unique jargons and rituals.
- Unique modes of symbolic expressions.

These characteristics are more far-reaching than the 'consciousness of kind', 'rituals and traditions' and 'sense of moral responsibility' that characterize a brand community. In this regard it is important to notice that the membership of a

Table 9.1 Variations of brand community

	Brandfests	*Brand communities*	*Community brands*
Marketer's role	An endorsing marketer	An existing marketer	The community *is* the marketer
Consumers' role	Open to share brand meaning	Co-creators of brand meaning	Creators of brand meaning
Examples	Camp Jeep Harley Davidson rallies	Car clubs Apple user pages	Napster Linux

consumption subculture (being formal or informal) is more demanding than the membership of a brand community. A subculture tends to define itself in opposition to the broader culture, which is not the case with brand communities. 'Brand communities do not typically reject aspects of the surrounding culture's ideology. They embrace them' (Muñiz and O'Guinn 2001, p. 414).

In the subculture the brand has a socially fixed meaning. In brand communities, brand meaning is socially negotiated rather than delivered unaltered from consumer to consumer. The subculture study is more individually focused on the transformation of self where the brand community approach departs in a social constructionist perspective.

Summary

The brand community concept is rooted in the sociological notion of community and the idea of subcultures of consumption. Three markers characterize a brand community: 'consciousness of kind', 'rituals and traditions' and a 'sense of moral responsibility'. Brand communities can be geographically bound as well as dispersed. The brand community concept expands into different variations; marketer-facilitated brandfests, typical brand communities run by enthusiasts, and community brands where the community becomes the marketer. A brand community does not define itself in opposition to the surrounding society, as opposed to a subculture of consumption.

Having described the key theoretical building blocks of the community approach, the next section provides guidelines for how one can build a research design to explore a brand community. This research is necessary if the aim is to

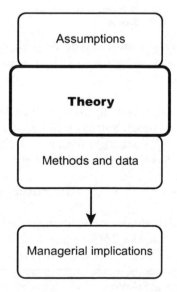

Figure 9.6 Theoretical building blocks of the community approach

analyse the potential to either facilitate or benefit from a brand community by observing and extracting brand meaning to be used actively in a brand strategy.

Methods and data of the community approach

Research in the community approach borrows from the scientific tradition of ethnography. Ethnography was developed around the turn of the twentieth century as a new approach to the study of cultural and sociological research phenomena. The pioneers of this new scientific approach sought 'fundamental truths about human nature, social affiliation, and the conduct of daily life' (Mariampolski, 2006, p. 4). Ethnography has (very roughly) evolved from a methodology used for the study of 'exotic' and 'primitive' people in the early twentieth century to being used increasingly for studies of cultural issues in all kinds of societies, to being applied to the arena of marketing research in the mid-1980s.

Uncovering the socio-cultural interaction of a community cannot be done in a laboratory setting or by the use of questionnaires. Research into how meaning is created requires participation and an open mind. Academic ethnographic research designs often span several years, requiring full immersion into the community of interest. Conducting a marketing-based study of a brand community is different from conducting an academic study. The marketing study often needs to be conducted over a much shorter period and with a less explorative aim. But the principles of the ethnographic research tradition can still deliver valuable insights even though the study has to adapt to limited resources and a tight time frame. In this section, these principles will be outlined along with an introduction to funda-mentals of ethnography's twenty-first-century younger sister, 'netnography'.

The ethnographic research tradition

Ethnographic research is also known as field research, observational research or participant observation and is characterized by researcher participation and a variety of data:

> In its most characteristic form [it] involves the ethnographer participating, overtly or covertly, in people's daily lives for an extended period of time, watching what happens, listening to what is said, asking questions – in fact, collecting whatever data are available to throw light on the issues that are the focus of the research.
>
> (Hammersley and Atkinson 1994, p. 1)

The ethnographic research tradition sets no limits on data collection. A participant researcher is free to collect any kind of data that is believed to add to the study of the subject or phenomena of interest. Common data types are interviews (more or less structured), depth interviews, visual impressions, print, video-recording, and photographs. Taking notes and photographs/video of all relevant observations also helps memory of minor details that might prove important. A deep understanding of a small sample of data is preferrable to the opposite. The participant researcher may collect data incognito or may identify himself as he sees fit.

Understanding people in the ethnographic research tradition means understanding them in their own environment and from the perspective of the participants. In practice, this means that gaining a deep insight into the consumption experiences in a supermarket requires the researcher to be present – in the actual supermarket. If the researcher is subjected to the same consumption experience as the consumer, this sharing of the consumption experience will enable a deeper and more real understanding from the perspective of the subject investigated. The focus on everyday behaviour therefore requires a presence in the natural setting of the research participants.

Box 9.2 Getting too close?

In a three-year ethnographic study by Schouten and McAlexander (1995) of the Harley Davidson subculture of consumption, the researchers started out their fieldwork without any specific interest in the biker lifestyle. Their immersion into the biker lifestyle had the consequence that they ended up being motorcycle owners as well as enthusiasts living the lifestyle to the fullest. Getting so fully immersed into the subcultural environment made them ponder one of the classic dilemmas of ethnography: that of the insider/outsider dilemma. Involvement in the social interaction in question – 'going native' – is a prerequisite for understanding the social processes taking place, but over-involvement brings the researcher too close to the phenomena of study to observe and transmit the facts of the research accurately.

Source Schouten and McAlexander (1995)

The researcher needs to get close to the subjects of research. 'Going native' is a term covering the ethnographic research ideal: to live in a certain environment long enough to truly understand the social and cultural phenomena from an 'insider perspective'. One way to solve the insider/outsider dilemma is to team up in pairs, where one researcher adopts an insider role while the other remains an outsider.

Box 9.3 Solving the insider/outsider dilemma

Researchers Muñiz and Schau solved this dilemma quite easily when researching the Apple Newton brand community. One researcher bought a Newton and used it for writing the research article. He became the insider participant, dependent on the Newton brand community for support in the use of the abandoned (by the marketer) handheld assistant. The other researcher took the outside position, ensuring objectivity in the study.

Source Muñiz and Schau (2005)

In the ethnographic tradition, it is more appropriate to talk about a research draft than a research design. The researcher must to go with the flow of the research process. During the exploration of the brand community unexpected observations or information that was not thought to be relevant before colleting data may guide the researcher's attention in new directions. This unstructured collection of data is often characterized by a combination of formal and informal methods. An example could be an interview in a private home, the interview being the formal method. During the course of the interview it becomes clear that the respondent becomes uncomfortable when the interview touches upon certain subjects. Observations of blushing cheeks and a shifty glance might also count as data if they serve the aim of the research (even though these observations are informal and not planned ahead).

Even though the ethnographic research tradition hails qualitative data it does not reject the use of quantitative data. Qualitative data may be triangulated with quantitative measures if it furthers the deeper understanding of the object of research.

Box 9.4 Quantitative triangulation of qualitative data

Algesheimer *et al.* (2005) conducted ethnographic research in 'The social influence of brand community: evidence from European car clubs', attempting to 'develop and estimate a conceptual model of how different aspects of customers' relationships with the brand community influence their intentions and behaviors' (p. 19). Algesheimer *et al.* identify five central hypotheses in the body of academic literature. During the development of a quantitative research design for studying these hypotheses, the authors conducted exploratory qualitative research through in-depth interviews with car club presidents and focus groups with car club members, experts and graduate marketing students to evaluate and secure the best possible research design. The survey was developed, 282 car clubs were contacted and a potential of 2,440 members were reached with the survey. The survey was made available on line and all participants were contacted via e-mail with additional questions. Through a mathematically based analysis the five hypotheses were assigned different weights, which made the managerial implications very precise. Including quantitative methods and broadening the range of data to include a large number of members from many different car clubs ensured that it was possible to derive generally applicable conclusions based on the results of the inquiry.

Source Algesheimer *et al.* (2005)

Ethnography allows for creative interpretations. The deep analysis of the sample of data should manifest itself in rich, insightful ('thick') description uncovering as many details as possible in order to provide understanding of as many layers of meaning as possible.

The tradition is suited to the exploration of new themes. As an ethnographic researcher should attempt to be open-minded in his work, unintended knowledge and issues may occur in the process and should not be ignored.

Netnography

> [N]etnography involves the transplantation of ethnography, one of the most venerable marketing research procedures, to cyberspace, the latest marketing milieu.
>
> (Brown *et al.* 2003)

The internet-based methodology of netnography plays an important role in several of the community research studies. Applying the principles of ethnography to internet-related fieldwork, it is an obvious information source to collect knowledge of the geographically dispersed brand communities. Netnographic methods are used for gaining insight into internet-shared brand meaning on community websites and can also be used in combination with a more traditional ethnographic research design. Community members can be contacted and recruited for interviews and/or observation, or e-mail questionnaires can be circulated with the help of the community.

Box 9.5 How to do an ethnographic study of a brand community yourself

- Pair up and let one be an inside observer while the other remains outside the community. This will enable you to gain insight into the deeper structures of the brand community while still being able to analyse the information properly.
- Start with an exploratory phase uncovering all expressions of community. Be creative; everything counts as data (photos, video, etc.).
- Observe – go to the everyday environment of the consumer; watch, listen and learn. Let respondents take the lead, do not interfere and ensure a lot of data. Join a community, go to community face-to-face meetings, sign up as an online user, join discussion forums.
- Be objective, try not to assume anything and put all prejudices aside.
- Be loving – respect your respondents, they are opening their hearts to you! Do not mistreat the information. Start slowly and build confidence.
- Make sure that your presence does not make the respondents change their routine – you need an accurate picture of the true nature of the brand community.
- Start out by being very open and ask questions in an unstructured fashion. Go with the flow and encourage respondents to elaborate and explain statements further.

- Base the more in-depth investigation on the data from the exploratory phase. What seems strange or interesting can in that way be elaborated.
- Rich description and analysis with a variety of media is to be preferred. Consider both verbal and non-verbal sources of data and ways of describing the community and the brand meaning and experiences, traditions and rituals shared in the brand community.

Summary

The community approach represents a social brand perspective and the community concept is a key concept in sociology. Acquiring new knowledge in this perspective requires methods facilitating the understanding of socio-cultural interaction and meaning creation. Hence, the methods used to explore brand communities are rooted in the ethnographic tradition departing in a socio-cultural perspective on man. Getting close to subjects of interest by participating in their natural environment is key in the brand community approach. The data collection is versatile as all kinds of data shedding light on the phenomena count. Rich and deep analysis with a variety of different expressions in a small sample is preferable to a big sample with little variation. Getting close to the virtual brand communities requires the adaptation of netnography – the ethnographic principles applied to web-based research.

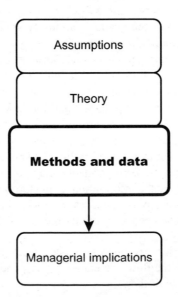

Figure 9.7 Methods and data of the community approach

Managerial implications

> a brand with a powerful sense of community would generally have greater value
> to a marketer than a brand with a weak sense of community. However, it should
> also be recognized that a strong brand community can be a threat to a marketer
> should a community collectively reject marketing efforts or product change, and
> then use communal communications channels to disseminate this rejection.
>
> (Muñiz and O'Guinn 2001, p. 427)

Community consumers can be a source of immense brand loyalty: they tend to serve
as brand missionaries, they are forgiving, extremely loyal and less apt to switch brand
than others. Brand community members provide important feedback to the corporation about the brand; even 'grass-roots R&D' can be one of the benefits of having
engaged consumers in a brand community. The emotional bond between the brand
and community members makes consumers eager to contribute to the success of the
brand. Brand loyalty (to a product brand) tends to 'spill over' (to the corporate brand).
In the case of cars, many sponsored brand communities represent the corporate brand
(such as Volkswagen or Ford clubs) while the majority of consumers seem to identify
with their particular car model, e.g. a Volkswagen Passat or a Ford Bronco. The
membership of the corporate-level brand community seems to activate a sense of
belonging to the corporate brand, building grounds for future repeat purchases.

However, there are also downsides to an active brand community. Besides the
collective rejection mentioned in the quotation above, rumour control in
computer-mediated environments is another potentially serious problem.
Consumers may also 'hijack' the brand and collectively take the brand in other
directions than the marketer had in mind (as in the case of the Apple Newton).

There are basically two ways of managing a brand community: one is as an
observer, the other is as a facilitator. In the latter sections we have introduced how
the assumption of a social brand is reflected in the theoretical constructs and how
these constructs imply the use of ethnographic research methods for the gathering
of information about brand communities. Now the managerial implications of
these three layers are provided along with managerial guidelines on how to act as
a marketer when observing or facilitating a brand community.

Observing brand communities

Community members are diehard fans. They choose to spend leisure time on a
brand, cultivating profound brand meaning. A marketer can gain a deep insight
into these layers of meaning simply by observing the community. This insight can
be valuable in the marketing of the brand to more mainstream consumers.

Observations can take place in the face-to-face venues as well as in the virtual
communities. A brand manager may enrol in clubs, join rallies or subscribe to user
groups, to name a few possibilities. The social interaction in the brand community
should be observed applying the appropriate ethnographic (and 'nethnographic')
data collection techniques in order to deduct brand meaning.

Box 9.6 Insights from the Volkswagen 'Beetle' community

In 1998 Volkswagen re-launched the legendary 'Beetle'. The original Beetle was launched in 1934. The idea was to produce a car for the people, which at the time was a revolutionary concept. Hugely popular over many generations, the inexpensive VW Beetle surpassed all production records, with more than 20 million cars leaving the VW assembly lines.

In a marketing study on 'retro-branding', researchers Brown *et al.* dived into the brand meaning shared on Beetle-related community websites. By means of a netnographic method, they gained insight into the negotiation and exchange of brand meaning among community members. Adopting a holistic perspective on the community-based brand–consumer exchange, valuable information regarding the delicate matter of re-launching a cult brand was retrieved. Examples are: Beetle fans seem divided on the issue of the technology of the new car. They tend to celebrate an innocent approach to the 'hippie' era of the 1960s and 1970s, with which the Beetle is very much associated. The Beetle is closely linked with family heritage and childhood memories in many cases. Memorable advertising campaigns from the 1960s are still fondly associated with the Beetle.

Sources www.volkswagen.com; Brown *et al.* (2003)

Brand mystique can be uncovered and used as a source of inspiration for marketing campaigns aimed at the mainstream users of the brand. Brand meaning attached to existing products can be applied to the marketing of new products. User experiences and 'grass-roots R&D' are shared in brand communities and can be applied to the intended marketing of the brand.

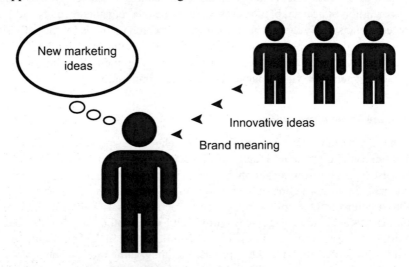

Figure 9.8 The marketer as observer of a brand community

However, any marketer acting as an observer in a brand community should tread extremely cautiously. Community consumers do not like intentional marketing and they do not like anyone looking over their shoulder. Community members prefer to feel autonomous and in charge of the brand, and would most likely resent being spied on. Another potential danger is the dilution of brand mystique, which ultimately can lead to the brand losing its appeal.

The marketer should be aware that a competitor can just as easily 'snoop' into shared brand meaning and hence attempt to steal potential unreleased brand meaning. Therefore, it is essential to be well informed and up-to-date about what happens in both formal and informal brand communities.

A brand community is an important information source, as consumers share user experiences and brand meaning. Any marketer should pay attention to this valuable source of information in order to obtain true consumer intimacy. But be aware that the information source is equally accessible to competing marketers.

Facilitating brand communities

The marketer facilitating a brand community should be just as cautious as the observing marketer. A brand community is a powerful force and, in order for a community to thrive, the facilitating marketer is advised to adopt a 'behind the scenes' approach.

An internet-based user group, a face-to-face club or a well orchestrated brandfest can proactively facilitate valuable consumer interaction. Facilitating a brand community can be a great retention tool, but caution and very discreet marketer presence is essential. It is important to note that it is, in fact, the social interaction around the consumption of the brand that spurs brand loyalty and contributes to the building of brand meaning. A marketer must hence engage members, not only with the brand, but also with each other. A photo or design contest is not enough, no matter the number of participants. In order for a community to exist, the marketer should for example engage the consumers as interactive judges in the photo contest. There are countless examples of brands setting up websites or other kinds of interaction platforms, where it is not interaction between consumers but interaction between the marketer and many consumers that is mistakenly labelled a community. The interaction between consumers is what makes the brand community unique and beneficial for brands. This interaction between consumers must not be confused with dialogue merely between the marketer and consumer, even though there might be a dialogue with many consumers.

Building a brand community the size of a club/community must be considered, depending on what the aim is with brand community. Research indicates that smaller clubs engender higher levels of member identification. Enthusiasm and involvement of community members tend to be greater in small communities outside the active control of a corporation and this involvement and identification is key for enhancing brand loyalty. The dilemma is, however, that the marketer seems to have a greater opportunity for influencing members in larger communities. Interpersonal relations dominate in the smaller clubs while the direct influence of the marketer on key member behaviour is greater in the larger communities.

The community approach is more suitable for the retention than the acquisition of members. Findings prove that the active engagement of consumers in a brand community is more efficient when targeting consumers who already have an affirmative relationship with the brand instead of newcomers to the brand.

No selling should be attempted in the community setting. If the marketer manages to facilitate a successful brand community, the increased brand loyalty will pay off when the consumers are ready. Trying to push a sale in a community context would turn off members' community spirit and could ultimately make them leave the community and the brand.

This overriding dilemma in the community approach is reflected in all aspects of the managerial implications. On the one hand, community members are so enthusiastic about a specific brand that it plays a role in their social life; on the other hand, they do not like intentional marketing. Community members prefer to feel on their own and in charge of brand meaning and the interaction in the community.

Box 9.7 Do's and don'ts in the community approach

Do	Don't
Acknowledge the power of the consumer in the creation of brand meaning and equity	Don't ignore community member feedback and prevent collective rejection of marketing activities
Use the feedback from community members for grass-roots innovation	Don't involve your customers too much, as it can result in resentment
Purposely select, initiate, manage and control the interactions among consumers	Don't be too present as a marketer – adopt a 'behind the scenes' presence
Build brand communities that enhance shared customer experiences	Be aware that competitors can 'snoop' easily through the community
Use brand communities mainly as a retention tool	Don't use communities to recruit new consumers
Use brand communities to tap into brand meaning	Don't attempt selling within the context of the community
Use community ethos to develop and vitalize the brand	Don't overuse the unique ethos of the community and thereby dilute brand mystique

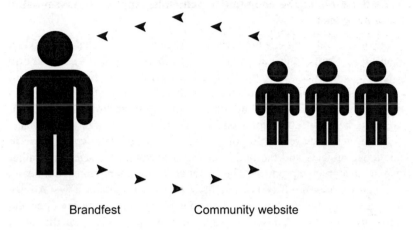

Figure 9.9 The marketer as facilitator of a brand community

Can all brands attract communities?

Brand communities tend to evolve around brands with a long and interesting history, high-involvement products, brands threatened by competition, expensive brands or brands with considerable maintenance costs. There is also the 'nerd' factor; very technical and complicated products also have the potential for attracting communities.

Cars and motor cycle brands often attract communities. Especially iconic brands, representing a certain lifestyle (Harley-Davidson, Chrysler Jeeps) have the potential for very strong communities and these brands can use the communities as an important part of brand ethos. Computers and gadgets also seem to attract communities. 'Helping each other out' is a big part of community building and is a very good reason for joining both a car/motorcycle as well as a computer brand community. The threatening competition factor is important for the many Apple Macintosh enthusiasts. Here, the brand community has an almost idealistic tone as its identity is in many ways defined in opposition to Microsoft. The 'nerd' factor is evident in the case of some of the community brands, as for example Linux.

Cultural brands[6] also attract communities. Movies like *Star Wars* and popular television shows also have brand community appeal. It is, however, important not to delimit oneself from the benefits of a vibrant brand community if your brand does not match these characteristics. More and more fast-moving consumer goods (FMCGs) have proved to be very successful in engaging their consumers in vibrant brand communities.

Box 9.8 Libresse: the community principles applied to fast-moving consumer goods

A line of feminine hygiene products is marketed by Swedish paper product giant SCA. The products are marketed as Libresse (globally), BodyForm (UK), Nana (France), Nuvenia (Italy), Libra (Australia), Nosotras (Spain) and Saba (Mexico and Central America). SCA has successfully managed to apply the principles of the community approach to an FMCG in an innovative marketing effort customized for the youngest of their target audience.

These web sites resemble youth magazines and are devoted more to emotional subjects and the bodily changes of young teenage girls rather than to the marketed products. They offer space for interaction about health and beauty issues, boyfriends, sexuality and puberty, to name a few. Advice about love, bodily issues and self-esteem is given, chat rooms are open and horoscopes are provided. Great insight into the psychology of the target audience has facilitated an innovative platform for brand loyalty. The Australian website is one of the most innovative ones, encouraging the user to be a 'Libra girl', get a 'Libra nickname' and thereby access to an otherwise restricted area of chat rooms, e-diaries and horoscopes.

Sources www.libresse.com; www.libragirl.com.au

Brand communities can successfully be facilitated around low-involvement products. In the case of these not-so-obvious brands, a community should be based on a deep understanding of the consumption context rather than the brand itself (the consumption context meaning the psychological and social concerns of young girls in the Libresse case). Active selling like in other communities, should not be attempted here, but providing a platform for social interaction may work well both as a retention tool and also as a way for new users of the product to become familiar with and trust that specific brand. The brand community platform helps the consumer discuss and solve some of the more emotional issues linked with the consumption of the product, which works as very good trust creating mechanism.

Summary

Marketers can benefit from a brand community in many ways. The marketer can reap benefits either by observing brand communities and extracting brand meaning or by facilitating consumer interaction through a brand community. Both roads to obtaining the benefits of a brand community require the discretion of the marketer who should adopt a 'behind the scenes' presence. Neither selling nor the recruitment of new consumers should be attempted. Managerial discretion is key in the community approach. The focus should be on facilitating the sharing of consumption experiences between consumers. High-involvement brands with a

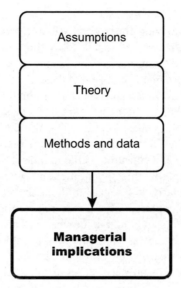

Figure 9.10 Managerial implications of the community approach

long history or technically complicated brands are the more obvious ones to attract a brand community, but the facilitation of a brand community is also possible for an FMCG brand.

Comments from the 'founding fathers' (5)

Brands and communities

Albert M. Muniz, Jr, De Paul University, and Thomas C. O'Guinn,
University of Wisconsin School of Business

Like many successful collaborations, this one began over food and drink. We had both been talking for some time about the lack of sociological thought in mainstream consumer behaviour. We had both used brands in debates and discussions with our psychologist friends. Brands seemed such as an obvious product of social forces and constructs. If brands could have personalities (actually, we don't think they do), could they not be the centre of a meaningful social aggregation, a community? Meaning, objects, and meaningful objects are often at the centre of communities. Brands were the perfect extension of contemporary social thought. So went our academic argument.

So over food and wine more than a decade ago we coined the term 'brand community'.

In truth, we were also both drawn to this topic by our own personal brand community experiences. We both had (somewhat) vintage Saabs in the early 1990s. While driving these cars, we were frequently stopped by complete strangers who wanted to talk to us about our Saabs, the brand's history, where we had them serviced, and our advice on very Saab-centric problems. We quickly came to realize that these weren't complete strangers stopping us; they were fellow members in a community of Saab enthusiasts. When we looked at the behaviours of these self-proclaimed Saabists, we realized that they were a lot like the Apple Macintosh enthusiasts that we had encountered at various points of our lives. We also realized that the fields of branding and consumer behaviour, as they existed then, could not adequately explain this phenomenon. The social aspects of consumption, particularly with regard to the consumption of brands, were almost completely unexplored. Thus a research calling was revealed.

Brand research had been bound up in what was a sometimes useful, but very limited, idea of brands as summations of attitudes. To be clear: it was an unarguably impoverished view of brands. It was worse than incomplete. It did not and could not properly capture the social nature of brands. Brands are about meaning: meaning clearly left open by summations of attitude. Further, brand meaning derives from society, its forces, agents, and institutions, among them marketers and consumers. It is an essentially communal process.

What we saw among users of brands reminded us of what we saw in cohesive neighbourhoods: a sense of community. We began to think that community might be a useful way to think about the relationships between users or admirers of brands. As we thought about it more, and collected more data, and read more of the classical sociological literature on community, we became convinced that we were on to something. Human beings living in consumer cultures aggregate around brands in a manner similar to those occurring in traditional face-to-face communities. It was a novel idea that made perfect sense.

Obvious cases came first. In our earliest work we studied mostly small-share brands. We initially gave some the impression that brand communities occurred only with a small fraction of consumers and represented marginal populations. More than a decade later we are delighted to observe that the brand community construct and its application have proven to be quite mainstream in both theory and application. Social network marketing, often through brand communities, is now commonplace. Large-share multinational brands (as well as start-ups) now use the construct, the essential dynamics we revealed (e.g. desired marginality, communal legitimacy, oppositional brand loyalty, the communication structures of communities, essential communal metaphors, communal co-creation, community-generated content, narratives and language). We are honoured through our modest connection to canonic social thought.

Student questions

1 Under which circumstances does a relationship between a marketer and multiple consumers exist?
2 Under which circumstances would a brand community exist in the same case?
3 Name some of the appealing qualities of the Apple Newton brand in a brand community context.
4 How can the Apple Newton brand community affect the Apple brand?
5 What does it take for a brand community to turn into a subculture of consumption?
6 Which brand perspective does the ethnographic tradition add to brand management?
7 Which research design would you create for tapping into the shared brand meaning of an Internet based community?
8 Which research design would you apply to the study of a car club?
9 How does the Libresse marketer manage to create a brand community around an FMCG?

References and further reading

Key readings are in **bold type**.

Algesheimer, R., Dholakia, U. M. and Herrmann, A. (2005) 'The social influence of brand community: evidence from European car clubs', *Journal of Marketing*, 69 (July): 19–34
Brown, S., Kozinets, R. V. and Sherry, J. F., Jr (2003) 'Teaching old brands new tricks: retro branding and the revival of brand meaning', *Journal of Marketing*, 67 (July): 19–33
Hackley, C. (2003) *Doing Research Projects in Marketing, Management and Consumer Research*, London: Routledge
Hammersley, M. and Atkinson, P. (1994) *Ethnography: Principles in Practice*, 2nd edn, London: Routledge
Kozinets, R. V. (1997) '"I want to believe": a netnography of the X-philes' subcultures of consumption', *Advances in Consumer Research*, 24: 470–5
Kozinets, R. V. (2002) 'The field behind the screen: using netnography for marketing research in online communities', *Journal of Marketing Research*, 39 (February): 61–72
McAlexander, J. H. and Schouten, J. W. (1998) 'Brandfests: servicescapes for the cultivation of brand equity', in J. Sherry, Jr (ed.), *ServiceScapes*, Chicago: NTC Business Books
McAlexander, J. H., Schouten, J. W. and Koenig, H. F. (2002) 'Building brand community', *Journal of Marketing*, 66 (January): 38–55
Mariampolski, H. (2006) *Ethnography for Marketers: a Guide to Consumer Immersion*, Thousand Oaks CA: Sage Publications
Muñiz, A. M., Jr, and O'Guinn, T. C. (1995) 'Brand Community and the Sociology of Brands', paper presented to the 1995 Association for Consumer Research annual conference. Minneapolis MN
Muñiz, A. M. Jr, and O'Guinn, T. C. (2001) 'Brand community', *Journal of Consumer Research*, 27 (March): 412–31
O'Guinn, T. C. and Muñiz, A. M., Jr. (2005) 'Communal consumption and the brand', in S. Ratneshwar and D. G. Mick (eds) *Inside Consumption: Consumer Motives, Goals, and Desires*, London: Routledge

Muñiz, A. M., Jr and Schau, H. J. (2005) 'Religiosity in the abandoned Apple Newton brand community', *Journal of Consumer Research*, 31 (March): 737–47

Muñiz, A. M., Jr, and Schau, H. J. (2007) 'Vigilante marketing and consumer-created communications', *Journal of Advertising*, 36 (3): 35–50

Schouten, J. W. and McAlexander, J. (1995) 'Subcultures of consumption: an ethnography of the new bikers', *Journal of Consumer Research*, 22 (June): 43–61

Wipperfürth, A. (2005) *Brand Hijack: Marketing without Marketing*, New York: Portfolio

Websites

www.jcna.com
www.libragirl.com.au
www.libresse.com
www.volkswagen.com

10 The cultural approach

with a commentary by L'Oréal Professor of Marketing, Douglas B. Holt, Saïd Business School, Oxford University

Learning objectives

The purpose of this chapter is to:

Understand the assumptions of the cultural approach
- The brand is perceived as a cultural artefact and a cultural brand perspective is hence introduced in brand management

Understand the main theoretical building blocks and how they are connected
- The theory of cultural branding – a study into how brands become icons
- The No Logo movement and its resistance to branding
- The citizen-artist brand prospect – a viable brand scenario for the future of cultural branding

Provide insights into the variety of methods used to research cultural consumption
- In order to understand cultural consumption, macro-level analysis is applied to micro-level data

Understand the managerial implications
- The management of an iconic brand requires the ability to think and act like a cultural activist
- The management of all brands requires consideration of corporate social responsibility

The last approach of this book is called the cultural approach because it is based on analysis of brands and branding in the light of cultural influences. The approach emphasizes the cultural forces in society and how these can be used to build iconic brands as well as the impact of branding practices on the globalized culture and marketplace.

Starbucks is often referred to as a cultural icon or a brand icon. In 1971, Starbucks was founded as one single coffee shop in Seattle; by the end of 2006 the American corporation owned around 12,440 coffee shops and stores around the world. Starbucks initiated what subsequently has been referred to as the 'Starbucks Revolution' as an expression of how much Starbucks has changed the way coffee is consumed all around the world. The financial success is substantial and Starbucks is one of the global 'brand icons' serving as a common frame of reference. All in all, Starbucks is a tremendous marketing success.

Starbucks is, however, also subjected to criticism for acting as a cultural imperialist and for not taking interest and paying enough attention to fair trade, etc. Its success hence goes hand in hand with being one of the brands that is most fiercely criticized by the anti-brand movement: 'Starbucks has become a cultural icon for all the rapacious excesses, predatory intentions, and cultural homogenizations that social critics attribute to globalizing corporate capitalism' (Thompson and Arsel 2004, p. 631).

This dualism – the tremendous success of the Starbucks brand and the concerns it spurs – is characteristic of the cultural approach. The literature of the approach focuses, on the one hand, on the building of iconic brands, and on the other, the concerns of the anti-brand movement. Increasingly, the most successful brands attract counter-cultural forces.

Seemingly contradictory, the common ground in the approach is the cultural brand perspective, in which the brand is regarded as an important part of and contributor to mainstream culture. Both parties (the literature concerned with the building of iconic brands and the anti-branding movement) are mostly concerned with the brands representing corporate America. These hugely successful brands are the ones that are pointed out as examples of best practice; meanwhile these brands are also the ones that attract the majority of critical voices from socially and culturally concerned citizen movements.

The cluster of literature dealing with this dual cultural perspective on brand management emerged around the millennium. A key reading is 'Why do brands cause trouble? A dialectical theory of consumer culture and branding' by Holt (published in *Journal of Consumer Research* in 2002). This article relates to both sides of the cultural brand perspective, and even proposes a future brand scenario based on the tensions in the cultural approach. The opposing viewpoints and the glimpse towards the future will be reviewed as theoretical building blocks of the cultural approach. Prior to that, the assumptions of the approach will be reviewed and the chapter will be rounded off with an insight into the methods and managerial implications of the approach.

Assumptions of the cultural approach

The individual brand perspectives introduced in the 1990s (the consumer-based approach, the personality approach and the relational approach) had different takes on understanding the exchange between a marketer and a consumer. The consumer-based approach turned the spotlight on the consumer, while the personality approach and the relational approach further constituted brand value as something co-created in a dialogue between marketer and consumer (the 'dyadic' brand relationship). The community approach added meaning found in the social interaction *among* dedicated brand consumers (the 'triadic' brand relationship) to the main theories of brand value creation. Inspired by cultural studies, the cultural brand perspective adds the exchange between macro-level culture and brands to the picture. The literature deals with the way marketers can use cultural forces to build strong brands (ultimately brand icons) and what brands and branding do to culture.

It is consumer culture rather than the individual consumer that is researched in the cultural approach. One could argue that the pivotal point is still the brand meaning found in groups of consumers just as in the community approach, but the focus of analysis is completely different:

> In contrast [to research in communities], this article focuses on brand cocreation in a context where brands are not the central focus; thus, it is necessary to unpack the meanings and sociocultural processes that continually problematize and ensure a brand's legitimacy to its various consumer groupings.
>
> (Kates 2004, p. 455)

Box 10.1 Macro-level culture defined

The identity approach (chapter 5) is also concerned with cultural aspects of branding. In the identity approach, culture is defined as culture at a micro-level – specifically organizational culture. The cultural approach focuses on culture in a macro perspective, applying findings from the culture surrounding us all to branding practices.

In this approach, macro-level culture is defined as the *social* definition of culture. In this definition, culture is closely intertwined with meaning and communication. In specific cultures, specific meanings and values are shared (as collective representations) and it is through this common ground of understanding that a culture can be said to exist. Cultural studies departing from this definition of culture hence attempt to clarify the explicit and implicit meanings of the culture in question, as well as understanding how meaning is produced and circulated.

Source du Gay *et al.* (1997)

What can culture do to brand value creation?

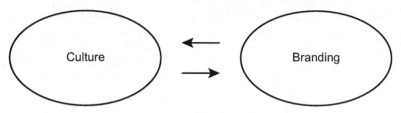

How does branding affect culture?

Figure 10.1 Scope of the cultural approach

The 'brand–consumer exchange'

In the cultural approach, the brand is analysed as a 'cultural artifact moving through history' (Holt 2004, p. 215) and is as such comparable to e.g. a Hollywood movie, a Pulitzer Prize-winning novel or a music festival concert. The brand is a storyteller, endowed with cultural meaning and an important factor in the intricate web of cultural meanings used in the collective identity projects of consumers. In that sense, the brand is a vessel of meaning and myth making, successful only if it resonates with consumers' collective identity projects of the time. Understanding the brand–consumer exchange in the relational approach also requires an understanding of the identity projects of consumers. It is, however, important to note that the understanding and focus of consumers' identity projects is different in the two approaches. In the cultural approach consumers' identity projects are analysed at a (macro) collective level. The relational approach is concerned with the understanding of individual identity projects as important contributors to brand meaning.

In the macro-level focus of culture the brand is also a significant political and financial power and is at the centre of debate when it comes to issues and discussion surrounding globalization issues:

> With the growing impact of market institutions on almost all aspects of our lives, it does not take much imagination to see 'brands' and 'branding' as part of an increasingly dominant market economic and commercial ideoscape, carried by organizations such as WTO, by marketing and management practices and by the contemporary sovereign status of the liberal market economy. As [part of] such an ideoscape, branding is becoming central to the structuring of commercial and economic activitites in still larger parts of the world.
>
> (Askegaard 2006, p. 92)

> one may argue that brands are among the most significant ideoscapes in the globalization processes.
>
> (Askegaard 2006, p. 94)

The cultural brand perspective assumes a consumer who is very much embedded in the symbolic universes of branding:

> Branding also causes a new consumer to form, a consumer who is brand conscious in the largest sense: a consumer for whom these new symbolic universes gradually become some of the most central parts of his or her identity formation, both individually and in groups.
>
> (Askegaard 2006, p. 100)

The consumer of the cultural approach is a 'no man is an island' man. Embedded in and influenced by the surrounding culture, the cultural brand perspective assumes that it is the collective brand meaning creation that is important and relevant to the consumer: *Homo mercans* or market man (Askegaard 2006) is deeply embedded – or trapped, depending on the point of view – in consumer culture:

> Market man is forged out of the interplay between different technologies: technologies of production, which allow us to transform and manipulate things; of sign systems, which allow us to use meanings, symbols or significations; of power, which directs the conduct of individuals; and of the self, which allows us to affect our way of being so as to reach a certain state of being.
>
> (Garsten and Hasselström 2004, p. 213)

The role of the marketer implies bird perspective. Brand value is created through playing an active role in mainstream culture. The brand is subjected to social and cultural changes and thereby influenced by changes completely outside the brand manager's control. On the one hand, this means that the marketer is not the only author behind the brand meanings. On the other, a brand manager who manages to understand the most relevant cultural currents is able to write the proper 'manuscript' for the brand to benefit from pressing cultural issues of the time. In that sense, the brand gains competitive power by providing the consumer with the appropriate web of associations and the most powerful myths of its time.

The cultural perspective

The perspective of the cultural approach embeds brand consumption in a macro-level cultural context and it is linked to the tradition of cultural studies. The culture researched into in the cultural approach surrounds us all and can roughly be divided into different 'levels'; a subcultural level, a national level, and a global level. They are all valid analysis levels and concerns of the cultural brand perspective.

Viewing consumption through the cultural lens means that all aspects of consumption experiences are analysed in their respective cultural context. The approach 'borrows' methods from different scientific traditions, such as phenomenological interviews, ethnographic field studies and netnography. The macro level of analysis, however, makes the interpretation of the data different from other approaches. The following quote illustrates well how data derived from phenomenological interviews are interpreted in the cultural approach:

> Our aim was to identify the most recurrent and robust patterns of underlying cultural meanings that engendered these identified commonalities. This hermeneutic mode of interpretation is premised on the idea that a given consumer is not expressing a strictly subjective viewpoint. Instead, he or she is articulating a culturally shared system of meanings and beliefs, personalized to fit his or her specific life goals and circumstances.
>
> (Thompson *et al.* 2006, p. 55)

This is a typical example of how the researchers of the cultural approach use methodologies from different scientific traditions for data collection (in this case the phenomenological/existentialist tradition behind the relational approach) and 'elevate' their findings to a cultural level through a macro-level analysis. This will be explained in more detail in the methods and data section of this chapter.

The cultural brand perspective focuses on branding and culture, and it is characterized by having many layers and opposing views compared to the other six brand approaches in this book. Not only managerial, but also ethical, political and philosophical discussions rage in the cultural approach alongside research into what extent consumers can or cannot liberate themselves from consumer culture.

Summary

This 'cluster' of brand literature introduces the cultural brand perspective where the brand acts as a cultural artefact, broadening the focus of analysis from an individual consumer level to a macro level about the role brands play in consumer culture. The approach focuses on what brands do to culture and what culture can do to brands. Core to the cultural approach are brand icons and the countercultural anti-branding movements. Iconic brands are the ones that have managed to integrate themselves in culture more skilfully than others. At the same time, brand icons are also subjected to the greatest concerns (regarding cultural imperialism, cultural standardization and globalization). Core to the cultural approach is the idea of the marketer deliberately endowing the brand with cultural meaning and through that playing an active role in consumer culture. The brand is seen as a storied product putting shared myths relating to cultural identity projects up for consumption. The cultural approach reveals the mechanisms behind brands becoming icons. At the same time, the approach also relates to a consumer culture increasingly concerned with the branded products, pressuring for changes in the way brands behave. The consumer of this approach is a *homo mercans*, a market man woven into the intricate meaning found in cultural consumer objects. How these assumptions rub off on to theories, methods and managerial implications will be depicted in the following sections.

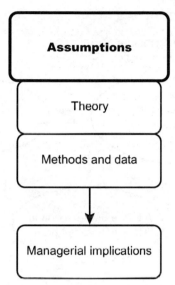

Figure 10.2 Assumptions of the cultural approach

Theoretical building blocks of the cultural approach

The cultural approach is very different from the other approaches, which implies a different structure of the theoretical building blocks section. In the other approaches, a core theme is presented alongside its supporting themes. The core theme is the main theory behind the approach and the supporting themes are notions facilitating the deeper understanding of the core theory.

The dualism and the tensions of the cultural approach are, however, reflected in the way this section is constructed. The theoretical building blocks hence consist of one supporting theme – cultural consumption – and one core theme, namely brand icons. The societal reaction to the core theme, the No Logo movement, is then reviewed followed by a viable theory (the citizen-artist brand) of how brand management can deal with the counter-reaction.

The theory on cultural branding by Douglas B. Holt (*How Brands Become Icons*) is a cornerstone in the cultural approach and serves as the core theme. Different from the majority of the publications with a cultural perspective, this theory is focused on the *management* of brands. The cultural branding model is closely related to the theory on cultural consumption formulated by Grant McCracken. Understanding the basic way of thinking about consumption in a cultural context facilitates the further reading of the theory on how brands become icons, which is why it serves as the supporting theme.

The review of these two elements could immediately seem like sufficient material to gain an understanding of brand management in cultural approach. However, in order to understand the full scope of the cultural approach, one needs to understand the other side of the ideological spectrum as well. *No Logo* by

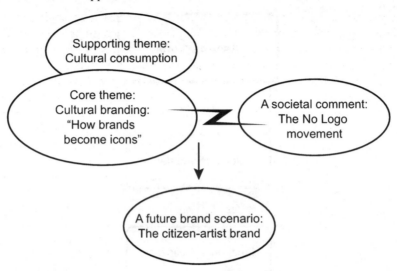

Figure 10.3 The core theme, its supporting theme (cultural consumption), the societal comment on brand icons (the No Logo movement) and the future brand scenario (the citizen-artist brand)

Naomi Klein is the most well known publication representing many of the concerns of the anti-brand movement. The anti-branding agenda is also important in the cultural approach because these mechanisms are vital to know about when aiming at iconic brand status (but also relevant for other types of brands). This is why the No Logo movement is reviewed briefly here, even though it is not a supporting theme, but rather a societal comment on brand icons.

The managerially oriented theory on how brands become icons is faced with the societal response from the No Logo movement. The tensions between the iconic brands and the anti-brand, anti-globalization movement seems contradictory at a first glance. In an analysis of these tensions, Douglas B. Holt (2002) illustrates that these opposing views might be logically connected after all and comes up with a new cultural brand construct; the citizen-artist brand. The citizen-artist brand is a viable prospect born from these cultural tensions and hence serves as a managerial guideline for how to respond to the anti-branding movement. As an interesting new theory and explanation of the tensions of the approach, this chapter would suffer from it not being mentioned, even though it does not fit the mould of a supporting/core theme presentation of key elements.

Supporting theme: cultural consumption

Canadian anthropologist Grant McCracken conceptualized a cultural perspective on consumption in the 1980s. His theories have since become central to the understanding of consumption in a cultural context. If one considers the culture definition behind this approach, it is obvious that McCracken's theory is a prerequisite for understanding the production and circulation of cultural meaning through consumption goods. It is important to notice that cultural consumption is not about the consumption of cultural objects (books, music, etc.) but is applied to all consumer goods that are regarded as equal circulators of meaning.

Pivotal in the theory of cultural consumption is the notion of culture and consumption operating as a system. This cultural consumption paradigm acknowledges that goods not only have a utilitarian character, they are also able to carry and communicate cultural meaning. The cultural meaning is mobile, flowing and always in transition. Meaning is transferred from the culturally constituted world into consumer goods and through the consumption of goods integrated into the lives of consumers. In this fashion, cultural meaning is integrated into the lives of consumers through consumption.

Cultural meaning from the culturally constituted world is incorporated into consumer goods by the advertising and fashion system. The idea is that the advertising system and the fashion system pick fragments of meaning and bestow them on products through advertising and the media. These fragments are found in the

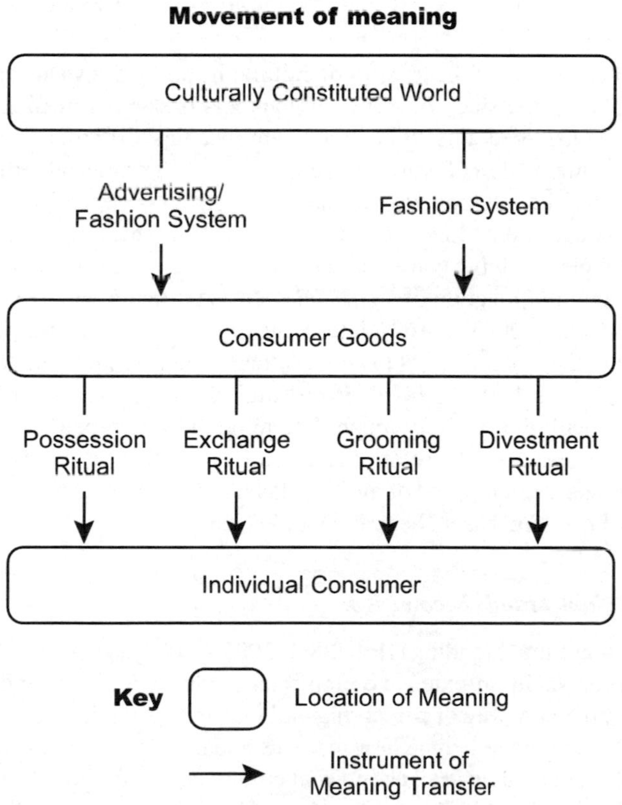

Movement of meaning

Figure 10.4 The movement of meaning; from McCracken, *Culture and Consumption* (1988), reprinted by permission of Indiana University Press

everyday life that makes up the culturally constituted world. Hence, the fashion and advertising systems function as producers of meaning. Consumer goods are hence in the cultural approach circulators of meaning recognizable to the 'enculturated' (being a member of a culture endows you with the ability to read the right kind of meaning into the goods) consumer. The consumer thereby chooses meaning adequate for his or her life by making consumption choices. If a certain consumer good delivers a meaningful take on your specific life situation you adopt this meaning through consumption of the good. This is how goods become carriers of cultural meaning besides possessing a utilitarian value. In the consumption of goods, consumers thereby also choose to consume the cultural meaning, which seems most appropriate to suit their lives:

> The consumer system supplies individuals with the cultural materials to realize their various and changing ideas of what it is to be a man or a woman, middle-aged or elderly, a parent, a citizen, or a professional. All of these cultural notions are concretized in goods, and it is through their possession and use that the individual realizes the notions in his own life.
>
> (McCracken 1988, p. 88)

This conceptualization of the transfer of cultural meaning draws heavily on semiotics. Semiotics is the study of signs and symbols in communication. Signs and symbols are considered able to communicate meaning different than the word, picture (or a composition of words, images and sound as in an advertisement, for example) itself. The interpretation of the sign systems is dependent on the interpreter and his cultural and personal background: 'The meaning of signs is arbitrary. In principle, anything could stand for anything else. It is the cultural context that frames the interpretation of signs and imbues particular signs with localized meanings' (Hackley 2003, p. 162). Intertextuality is an important aspect of semiotics; meaning that a 'text' refers to another 'text' which again refers to something else. It is obvious that the level of cultural 'literacy' and general cultural knowledge (enculturation) very much determine the interpretation of the 'text'. The marketing system is therefore the creator of a 'string of signs'; marketing communications are composed of multiple layers of meaning. The production and circulation of meaning has no beginning and no end.

Core theme: how brands become icons

The theory of cultural branding (Holt 2003, 2003b, 2004) is the core theme of the cultural approach. In an extensive empirical study of iconic brands, Holt has conceptualized a new way of perceiving and managing brands. Cultural branding is the strategic principles behind how to create and manage a brand and alter it into an icon. Cultural branding is all about what culture can do for brand value creation (figure 10.1). *How Brands Become Icons* is a thorough inquiry into the creation of the inspired and talented brand communication behind the iconic brands. The point of departure is the same as McCracken's in the sense that brands and/or products are seen as endowed with cultural meaning, but Holt's theory is more precise and demanding. He pinpoints the need for addressing certain powerful cultural issues and contradictions before one is able to create myths that are so powerful and resonant that the brand becomes iconic.

How Brands Become Icons is the first comprehensive research on branding in a cultural perspective. The theory is built from case studies of a selection of American iconic brands representing different industries, different company histories, competitive situations and consumer bases. Despite their differences, the brand icons displayed definitive commonalities that have led to their success. These success stories are the foundation of the cultural branding model, the theory of how brands become icons.

A brand icon is an identity brand' approaching the identity value of a cultural icon. An identity brand is a 'storied' brand, whose value to consumers (and, thus, its brand equity) derives primarily from identity value. Identity value is the aspect of a brand's value that derives from the brand's contributions to the self-expression of the consumer. A cultural icon is a person or thing regarded as a symbol, especially of a culture or a movement – a person, institution, and so forth – considered worthy of admiration or respect (definitions, Holt 2004, p. 11). An icon is an *exemplary* symbol. The cultural icons are exemplary symbols, resonant to a majority of people and offering the most potent and relevant solution to the cultural situation of their time. The same goes for brand icons; they have to address the most general concerns of the time in the most skilful way. In that sense, they have to perform more representative and powerful myths to mainstream culture than the identity brand.

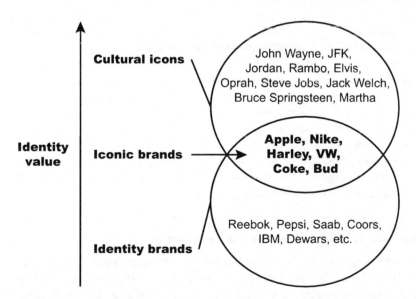

Figure 10.5 Iconic brands are brands that have become cultural icons; from Holt, *How Brands Become Icons* (2004), p. 4, reprinted by permission of Harvard Business School Press, copyright © 2004 by the Harvard Business School Publishing Corporation; all rights reserved

Reebok, Pepsi and Saab are hence considered identity brands, meaning that their use contributes significantly to their consumers' self-expression. John Wayne, J.F.K. and Bruce Springsteen are considered cultural icons serving as exemplary and powerful symbols to a majority of people. And Apple, Nike and Harley are representatives of the brand icons: the few brands approaching the identity value of the cultural icons.

Having established what a brand icon is, we now turn to the mechanisms behind the rise to iconic status. The empirical studies behind the cultural branding model establish that the rise to icon status happens mainly through advertising and can be aided by cultural industries (via product placement) and populist worlds (via viral branding):

> Identity brands must be very good at product quality, distribution, promotion, pricing, and customer service. But these attributes are simply the ante that marketers must pony up to be competitive. They aren't drivers of business success. Identity brands live or die on the quality of their communications.
>
> (Holt 2004, p. 225)

What makes the communications of the iconic brands stand out are four common denominators:

- *Target a cultural contradiction.* The iconic brands have been able to target cultural contradictions in society and perform a powerful myth to accommodate the tensions: 'Cultural branding works when the brand's stories connect powerfully with particular contradictions in American society' (Holt 2004, p. 224).
- *Act as a cultural activist.* Aspiring to the identity value of a cultural icon, radical action needs to be taken: 'Icons act as cultural leaders, as activists encouraging people to think and act differently through their stories' (Holt 2003).
- *Create original expressive culture as an artist.* Also, when it comes to aesthetics, the brand must lead the way and not just follow trends. The brand icons have managed to provide their own unique visual expression and thereby have provided consumers with something entirely new and original.
- *Develop an authentic populist voice.* A brand must be perceived as a credible representative of a 'populist epicentre' (a non-commercial place; e.g. subculture, folk culture or a social movement) which is where new non-commercial culture is being created. The brand must display a deep understanding of the point of view it represents.

Box 10.2 How Snapple became an iconic brand

In 1972 healthy fruit drink brand Snapple saw the light of day in Brooklyn. In 1993 Snapple's sales had climbed to an annual $516 million and the company was bought by Quaker Oats for $1.7 billion. The marketing strategy behind the huge financial success encompassed four steps:

- *Target a cultural contradiction* During the 1980s the United States was led by President Reagan and going through hard times in order to become a more dynamic economy. The labour market was marked by constant restructuring and downsizing. Around 1990 the labour market had become quite unbalanced, with companies and elites profiting well but also large parts of the population left with 'McJobs', sparking a current of discontent and disbelief in corporate America as well as among elected officials. Snapple managed to address this societal imbalance – or cultural contradiction – by authoring a myth about a company run by amateurs, indirectly suggesting that the 'overpaid' elites in marketing departments of other companies were not needed at all. Consuming a bottle of Snapple became a way of embracing that cultural meaning.

- *Act as a cultural activist* Before the rest of the world became truly aware of the powerful tensions in US society, Snapple acted as an instigator of the new myths regarding the company run by a bunch of playful amateurs, giving vent to deep societal frustration. Thereby, Snapple managed to comment on an important tension before most people managed to even verbalize the problems.

- *Create original expressive culture as an artist* Snapple's branding activities (new product development, advertising, design and promotion) were radically new in aesthetics, and yet unified in the expression of the brand's political voice. All these activities displayed an ironic comment on the society at the time through a credible aura of amateurism. Tennis player Ivan Lendl became a spokesperson because he was a fan, even though he mispronounced the brand name in the television ads. 'Wendy the Snapple lady' became a star of many television ads. Wendy was a clerk working at Snapple who had taken up the job of answering letters from consumers. Wendy, who was quite far from the beauty standards of advertising, become very popular as 'the real thing'. To mock the celebrity events sponsored by competing companies such as Coca-cola and Pepsi, Snapple became the sponsor of events like cherry spitting in Minnesota and yo-yo tossing in New York.

- *Develop an authentic populist voice* Snapple hired two radio hosts as endorsers of the brand. Rush Limbaugh and Howard Stern could not be more different, coming from both ends of the political spectrum, but both represented defiance against the establishment and expressed a genuine affection for Snapple. Their endorsement is one example of how Snapple gained credibility from a populist epicentre.

Source Holt (2003b)

Moving through time and cultural changes and still staying relevant is one of the great challenges of the iconic brands. The powerful myth has to be reinvented over and over again in congruence with the socio-political-economic-cultural changes: 'Iconic brands remain relevant when they adapt their myths to address the shifting contradictions that their constituents face' (Holt 2004). The cultural branding model is essentially very different from the mindshare branding model (Holt's term; in this book the consumer-based approach) as the mindshare model establishes that consistency in brand communication is what builds a strong brand. The aim of this book is the side-by-side presentation of the seven 'ideal types', not to discuss if one approach is superior to another. Emphasizing the differences between the mindshare model (the consumer-based approach) and the cultural model (this approach), however, facilitates the understanding of both approaches, which is why their most fundamental differences are depicted in table 10.1.

After having established the nature of consumption in a cultural perspective and how cultural meaning can be activated in such a powerful way that brands become icons, we will now turn to the societal, critical comment on the cultural impact of the global iconic brands.

The societal response to brand icons: the No Logo movement

In the No Logo movement branding efforts are critically analysed and linked with environmental issues, human rights and cultural degradation. The book is also a moral rebellion against the idea of corporations outsourcing production while

Table 10.1 A comparison between the mindshare branding model and the cultural branding model.

	The mindshare branding model	*The cultural branding model*
Brand communication	*Persuasion* The purpose of advertising is to influence consumer perception of the brand through rhetoric	*Myth making* Communication is the centre of consumer value. The brand is a 'storied' product and the product is merely a means to embracing the story
Brand components	*Abstract associations* The brand consists of a set of associations that is the brand's purified essence (brand DNA)	*Cultural expressions* The brand's value is found in the cultural contents of the brand's myth. The brand has a reputation for performing certain myths
Brand management	*Consistency* Brand management is about upholding consistency in communications over time	*Historical fit* – brand management is about adapting the brand's myth to cultural changes in order to remain relevant

Source Adapted from Holt (2004)

focusing on the production of images. In that sense, *No Logo* is a serious attack on the idea of branding in itself and seriously questions whether the iconic brands are selling something of real value or only empty images and promises.

Kalle Lasn is another significant voice in the anti-brand movement. Founder of Adbusters and advocating the 'uncooling', 'unswooshing' and 'demarketing' of America, Lasn's overall concern (1999) is that culture is not 'bottom-up' any more (significant cultural issues stemming from the people), but rather 'top down', reversed by big companies and global brand corporations. Thereby, culture is no longer created by the people, but by corporate America. Brands, products, fashions, celebrities, entertainments have moved from being spectacles surrounding culture to become the main constituents of culture. Human desires are manipulated through advertising; thereby an authentic life is no longer possible.

The activist agenda of Adbusters encourages 'the people' to fight 'the cool machine'. This can be done through 'culture jamming' (the distortion of commercial signs and mediums), by joining 'buy nothing days' and sticking to 'TV turnoff weeks'. Through these actions people can change the way cultural meaning is created in society.

Activist anti-brand movements also monitor corporations closely and thereby pressure for corporate social responsibility (so-called corporate watch). This pressure for more corporate social responsibility has created increasing attention in management circles for the display of corporate social responsibility.

Box 10.3 Civic responsibilities or cultural branding?

Corporations and industries that are particularly subjected to criticism seem most keen on demonstrating their corporate social responsibility. It might be iconic brands, corporations trading with Third World countries or corporations in industries that pose environmental challenges.

Starbucks release an annual CSR report available on their website. There, you can also read more about their support of African Wildlife Fund, Save the Children, and MercyCorps. The overall aim is to add to a positive development in the coffee-growing areas in South America and Africa.

As a major representative of an industry subjected to much criticism about Third World exploitation; diamond company *par excellence* DeBeers explains its social involvement in the Southern African countries. On its website you can read about the South African & DeBeers Fund directing money from the DeBeers company profits into social investment in South Africa. The company also runs an HIV/AIDS programme for their employees and their families.

At petrol company BP's website you can read about investments in sustainable energy sources for the future and download an annual sustainability report.

Source www.starbucks.com, www.debeerscompany.com, www.bp.com

A future brand scenario: the citizen-artist brand

None of the other brand approaches holds opposing views in the same manner as the cultural. The fact that the absolute champions of the branding process (the brand icons) are also subjects to a 'revolutionary' agenda aiming at their downfall is, however, important to understand. But maybe the two views are not so opposite as they first appear. Just like critical voices can comment on the impact of the iconic brands, management can benefit from an analysis of the tension between the two sides of the spectrum in the cultural branding literature.

One research article delivers an interesting take on the tensions between brand icons and the anti-brand 'No Logo' movement ('Why do brands cause trouble? A dialectical theory of consumer culture and branding', Holt 2002). It is the article that is mentioned as a key reading in the introduction to this approach. Holt's analysis provides a new logic to the opposites as he analyzes 'the emerging antibranding movement to understand tensions between the current branding paradigm and consumer culture to speculate on their future directions' (Holt 2002, p. 71).

The brand icons are the champions of the postmodern branding paradigm (the branding techniques that have proven efficient since the 1960s). The pressure and criticism they are exposed to by the anti-brand movement should, according to Holt's analysis, be seen as the beginning of a paradigm shift. The same thing happened in the 1960s, when cultural changes implied a new marketing/branding paradigm to emerge. The pressure on the champions of the postmodern branding paradigms is hence nothing more than an indication that things are about to change. Below is an illustration with a short description of the postmodern branding paradigm and the post-postmodern paradigm of Holt's (2002) analysis. Changes in consumer culture have led to changes in the marketing function, and branding techniques have changed accordingly. The move from one dominant paradigm would another has been instigated by rebellion against the dominant marketing techniques. In that sense 'Consumers are revolutionary only insofar as they assist entrepreneurial firms to tear down the old branding paradigm and create opportunities for companies that understand emerging new principles' (Holt 2002, p. 89).

If a new branding agenda is about to emerge, it is relevant to look at the major differences between the existing and the new. 'Authenticity' is central to understanding the proposed shift from the postmodern to the post-postmodern branding paradigm. In the postmodern branding paradigm postmodern, 'stealth' branding (where the profit motive is disguised behind disinterested, ironic brand communication) is perceived as being authentic. In the post-postmodern paradigm, openness about profit motives should be accompanied by an engaged citizenship. The authenticity problem of disguising profit motives behind a laid-back, ironic brand attitude is what is being revealed by the anti-brand movement.

In the post-postmodern branding paradigm the citizen-artist brands should be frank about profit motives, act as responsible citizens *and* be able to deliver original and relevant cultural material:

Table 10.2 The postmodern and the post-postmodern branding paradigm

	Postmodern branding paradigm	*Post-postmodern branding paradigm*
Time frame	1960s and onwards	Emerging (c. 2000)
Consumer culture	Seeking personal sovereignty and identity construction through brands	Cultivating self through consumption of brands
Marketing function	In constant negotiation with consumer culture	Providers of original and relevant cultural material
Branding paradigm characteristics	1 Authentic cultural resources 2 Ironic, reflexive brand persona 3 Coattailing on cultural epicenters 4 Life world emplacement 5 Stealth branding	The brand as a cultural resource in its own right + a community pillar + honest about profit motive

Source Adapted from Holt (2002).

As consumers peel away the brand veneer, they are looking for companies that act like a local merchant, as a stalwart citizen of the community. What consumers will want to touch, soon enough, is the way in which companies treat people when they are not customers. Brands will be trusted to serve as cultural source materials when their sponsors have demonstrated that they shoulder civic responsibilities as would a community pillar.

(Holt 2002, p. 88)

To reflect one final time on this somewhat different review of the theoretical building blocks of the approach: brand icons are brands capable of telling powerful myths commenting on the central cultural contradictions of the time. The basic understanding of consumption of goods as the consumption of cultural meaning facilitates the understanding of the cultural brand perspective and thereby serves as a supporting theme. How the culturally savvy brands influence mainstream culture is fiercely resisted by the anti-branding agenda. Even though it is not a supporting theme, but rather a societal comment, it is important to understand some of the challenges facing the branding champions. Evoking thoughts about the future of brand management, the future scenario of the citizen-artist brand is a central and managerially relevant comment on the societal resistance by the No Logo movement. Even though it seems contradictory at a first glance, the core elements of the cultural approach fit nicely together.

Summary

Core to the cultural approach is the theory on how brands become icons. So-called identity brands (strong on self-expressive benefits) have the potential for becoming brand icons by adapting to the cultural branding model. The cultural branding model is closely related to McCracken's classic theory about cultural

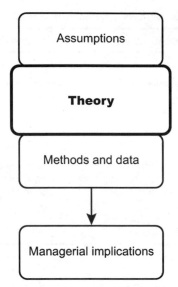

Figure 10.6 Theoretical building blocks of the cultural approach

consumption. In this view of consumption, the consumption objects are seen as cultural artefacts carrying meaning from the culturally constituted world to the consumers. Brands are regarded as cultural resources just like movies, social movements, books, magazines, etc. In this brand perspective, the tools for building iconic brands are found. Through addressing the pressing cultural contradictions as a viable cultural 'text', and being able to reinvent as changes in societal contradictions occur, the brand can approach the identity value of a cultural icon. The anti-brand movement is concerned with what branding and globalization do to culture. The encouragers of civil activism, they also raise important political questions and push for corporate social responsibility. The tensions between brand icons and the anti-brand movement can be understood as a phenomenon indicating the beginning of a new branding paradigm. In this prospect of a post-postmodern branding paradigm the brand should act as a citizen-artist, meaning being able to deliver relevant cultural material while shouldering its social and civic responsibilities. Having described the key theoretical building blocks of the cultural approach, the next section provides an overview of the methods and data used in the cultural approach.

Methods and data of the cultural approach

In order to understand the production and circulation of cultural meaning central to the cultural approach, a certain approach to data collection is required. The cultural approach displays a variety of methods and data 'borrowed' from different interpretive research traditions. What binds the studies together is that all data are interpreted in a macro perspective.

Furthermore, the basics of semiotics are important to understand if one is considering gathering knowledge about cultural consumption.

The practical methods suggested for applying the cultural branding model (how brands become icons) will be reviewed in 'Managerial implications', as they are closely intertwined with the managerial mindset of this strategic model.

Research methods and data

Understanding the production and circulation of meaning fundamental to the cultural consumption perspective requires insight into semiotic methods. When conducting semiotic marketing studies one deconstructs the meaning displayed in commercial communication. Samples of commercial communications (e.g. brand logos, television advertisements, print ads, package designs and shopping malls) are the objects of study and should be deconstructed accordingly. The objects are supposed to be made strange and unfamiliar in order to go beyond the 'taken for granted' meanings. Semiotic codes should then be decoded and the intertextual strings of signs deconstructed.

Box 10.4 Doing semiotics

Questions to ask
- What does X signify to me?
- Why does X signify this to me?
- What might X signify for others?
- Why might X signify this for others?

Sources of X
- Objects, e.g. clothes, hairstyle, make-up, logos, graphic design.
- Gesture, e.g. body types. faces, expressive gestures, postures.
- Speech, e.g. accent or dialect, use of metaphor, tone or volume of speech, use of humour.

Source Hackley (2003)

Intertextuality is an important aspect of semiotics. The commercial message (the brand in this case) is regarded as a cultural 'text' like other cultural expressions. Intertextuality is the idea of texts referring to other texts. When, for instance, a cosmetics brand signs a famous actress as their 'face', the brand becomes related to the movies the actress has starred in. These movies are linked with other cultural 'texts', such as the book behind the script, other actors, and the famous director who once won an Oscar and so on and so on.

These 'strings of signs' and 'strings of text' can be deconstructed individually or in focus groups. It is important to understand that all ends are open-ended in semiotics; meaning that there are no right or wrong answers and that the deconstruction of a 'text' will depend entirely on the enculturation of the respondent. Still, different interpretations add up to a more varied interpretation of the text.

Other methods

Other methods are used to collect knowledge of the production and circulation of cultural meaning. Cultural brand research displays a vide variety of data collection. Ethnographic, phenomenological interviews and case methods are the most important ones.

- Ethnographic studies are suitable for understanding the consumer in a cultural setting. In general, the ethnographic research tradition is aimed at under-standing man in his cultural setting and is, as such, important if one is collecting data on the cultural aspects of consumption. Conducting an ethno-graphic field study requires a high degree of immersion and no delimitations when it comes to data sources. Here, the researcher is supposed to participate in consumption practices and not delimit himself from any kind of data source. Please refer to the methods section of chapter 9 for a more full description of the ethnographic research tradition.
- Phenomenological interviews are also viable methods in the cultural approach. The approach is very much concerned with understanding the collective identity projects of consumers. Phenomenological interviews are excellent for the inquiry into individual identity projects, and through a macro-level analysis and interpretation the data from the individual inter-views can be applied to a cultural setting, shedding light on the collective identity projects of consumers. Please refer to the methods section of chapter 8 for guidelines on how to master the technique of the long, unstructured interview.
- The 'extended case method' is a discovery-oriented method of anthropo-logical descent where a relatively small sample of informants is studied closely through loosely structured, long interviews and observations in their homes and environments. The cultural approach is focused on understanding the most important cultural contradictions of the time. Investigating relevant consumer groups by means of this method might provide great insight into these contradictions. This is the research method behind the citizen-artist brand prospect.

The interpretation of the collected data is very important, because the focus of analysis is unique to the cultural approach. A 'bottom-up' interpretation of data is applied; the informants are not expected to express idiosyncratic meanings, but rather to be acting as mouthpieces of the surrounding culture: 'To study how consumer culture operates, I examine the phenomena that it structures, people's everyday consumption practices. In methodological terms, I will use microlevel data – people's stories about their consumption – to investigate macrolevel constructs' (Holt 2002, p. 73).

Box 10. 5 Doing a cultural study yourself

- Immerse yourself in the environment of research like a true ethnographer.
- Conduct long phenomenological interviews.
- Deconstruct the 'strings of signs' of commercial communication.
- Test the enculturation of relevant cultural groups by having them deconstruct the same commercial texts.
- Sample cultural knowledge of the relevant cultural context.
- Conduct extended case studies of individuals of specific interest.
- Most important: feel free to pick the most suitable methods for your research design.
- … but be sure to submit all your micro-level data to a macro-level interpretation…
- … as you bear in mind the golden rule of regarding your informants as mouthpieces of their cultural context!

Summary

The cultural approach 'borrows' methods and data from other approaches to science. Phenomenological interviews, ethnographic immersion, case methods and the semiotic decoding of commercial and cultural manifestations are all legitimate

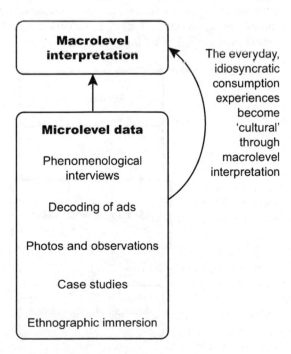

Figure 10.7 Research methods of the cultural approach

data in this approach when attempting to shed light on the cultural aspect of brands and branding. What makes the methods and data stand out compared with their use in the other approaches is the macro-level interpretation they are subjected to. The informants are not assumed to speak entirely idiosyncratic beliefs and opinions, but rather they are considered representatives of the surrounding culture.

Managerial implications

The managerial implications of the cultural approach can roughly be divided into two. A marketer can choose to implement the cultural branding model through and through in the attempt to follow in the footsteps of the iconic brands. A brand manager can also benefit from insight into this approach by becoming aware of cultural criticism and using it as an add-on to the chosen branding strategy. Finally some thoughts on the managerial implications of the citizen-artist brand, which more or less is a merger between the two.

The management of an iconic brand

The brand manager of an iconic brand – or an identity brand striving for iconic status – should get ready for a rather complicated work agenda. The brand is regarded as a medium for cultural expression and the path to icon status requires the ability to create radical cultural expressions. Supposed to act as a cultural activist quite far from the standard business school type, the brand manager is above all the composer of the brand's myth: 'As cultural activists, managers treat their brand as a medium – no different than a novel or a film – to deliver provocative creative materials that

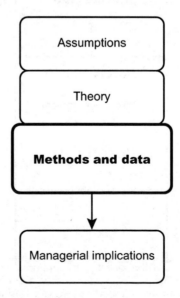

Figure 10.8 Methods and data of the cultural approach

respond to society's new cultural needs' (Holt 2004, p. 219). The activist managers should not only be able to understand the legacy of the brand as a myth creator but also be able to be a cultural trend setter by *not* exploiting what is hot and happening right now but rather be the one *defining* hot and happening.

The cultural brand management process consists of two stages: gathering and analysing cultural knowledge and composing the cultural brand strategy. The gathering of relevant cultural knowledge is required; cultural contradictions must be identified and uncovered. The identification of emerging cultural contradictions requires a thorough understanding of the cultural context, and the empathetic understanding of the identity projects of consumers is different from the gathering

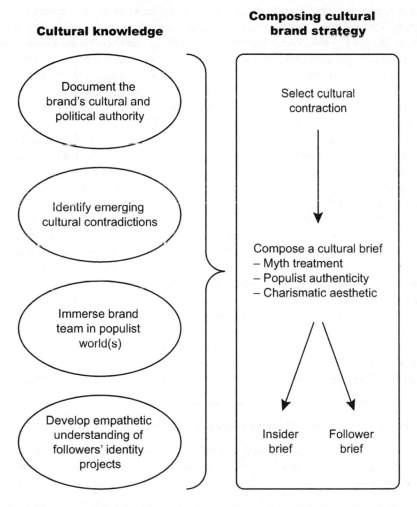

Figure 10.9 The cultural brand management process; from Holt, *How Brands Become Icons* (2004), p. 210; reprinted by permission of Harvard Business School Press, copyright © 2004 by the Harvard Business School Publishing Corporation; all rights reserved

of traditional consumer research data. A different kind of consumer knowledge is required: 'Rather than static, microscopic research that delivers a snapshot of individual consumers, genealogy is macroscopic and dialectical' (Holt 2004, p. 214).

The building of great myths requires an empathetic and deep (macro-level) understanding of the collective identity projects of the relevant consumer segment. The manager needs to deeply understand the cultural contradictions of the time and how they feed the hopes and anxieties of, for example, a generation of American urban middle-class people: 'Resonant myths spring from an understanding of people's ambitions at work, their dreams for their children, their fears of technology, their difficulties in building friendships, and so on' (Holt 2004, p. 212).

The brand manager also has to understand the reputation of the brand. In the cultural approach, the brand's reputation is considered to be the reputation for telling certain kind of stories – for competing in a certain myth market. This reputation endows the brand with a cultural and political authority, meaning that the brand has a reputation for telling stories/performing myths about a certain notion (e.g. freedom, cultural authority) aimed at certain cultural segments (political authority). In order for the brand manager to document the brand's cultural and political authority, he should look back in time to comprehend what historic activities constrain or enhance the future mythmaking ability of the brand.

Where one looks for the empathic understanding is also important. It cannot be found on the periphery of brand loyalists, it is the nucleus of brand insiders/followers that can reveal the most significant 'outlets' of the cultural contradictions. Full immersion – or preferably a 'cultural membership' – in the relevant populist worlds is therefore required.

After having identified the most relevant cultural contradiction to target, the myth has to be composed and executed in the right way. A traditional positioning statement should be substituted by a 'myth treatment' (like in the film industry) in which the brand's proposed cultural role is clarified. The execution of the brand communication should elevate itself from being a parasite on popular cultural trends; it should rather develop a 'populist authencity' on its own terms. Furthermore, the brand should communicate by means of its own charismatic aesthetics. In sum, the brand communication should adopt its own independent voice and play a proactive role in the culture of its time (eventually, re-refer to the Snapple case in box 10.2). The successful brand is the most skilful commentator and provider of relevant cultural 'text' addressing the socio-cultural tensions of the time.

Box 10. 6 The versatile brand manager of the cultural approach

Being a brand manager/cultural activist requires a distinct talent for multi-tasking. Holt proposes that the abilities of the brand manager should encompass:

- *The mindset and work methods of a genealogist.* A genealogist goes back in time in order to piece together a family tree. In much the same fashion, the brand manager is supposed to go back in time in order to understand the brand heritage and the brand's possibilities versus constraints for performing certain kinds of myths

- *A cultural historian's understanding of ideology.* National shifts in ideology are closely intertwined with cultural, political and economic changes. The brand manager who is able to understand the ideological shifts and the cultural changes they cause is skilled at targeting the most relevant tensions in society

- *A sociologist's charting of the topography of social contradictions.* Social contradictions are inevitably linked with cultural, economic and political changes. Developing an empathetic understanding of social contradictions enables the brand manager to perform powerful myths

- *The willingness and ability to take on a literary expedition into popular culture.* Managing an iconic brand is all about developing a deep cultural understanding – and being able to deliver on it as a cultural activist. Having one's ear to the ground and understanding the cultural web is therefore a prerequisite

- *The sensitivity and empathetic antennae of a writer.* Just like a writer is often able to observe life more than participate and still be the one who pinpoints the exact feelings of other people, the brand manager needs to have a sixth sense of what goes on beneath the surface of people's lives

Source Holt (2004)

The culturally aware brand manager

The insights from the cultural approach can also be used in other ways. Cultural agendas aimed at your brand can be used as inspiration or warning signs of the branding strategy losing its appeal. Therefore, Thompson *et al.* (2006) introduce the term 'Doppelgänger brand image' as a theoretical term to describe the negative autonomous brand images circulating in our culture. Where Holt views the tension between brand icons and the global brand culture in the bigger picture (in the research behind the citizen-artist brand prospect), Thompson *et al.* view the tensions in a more concrete light, presenting the 'doppelgänger brand construct'. The 'doppelgänger brand' is a brand that has been subjected to 'culture jamming' and can provide hints about the need for a change of brand strategy. Therefore, any brand manager should be very conscious of anti-brand activities and take them as warning signs of a brand strategy losing its appeal. A doppelgänger image should be seen as an early indication regarding flaws and imperfections in a brand's image and strategy;

> the analysis of a dobbelgänger image can (1) call attention to cultural contradictions that potentially undermine the perceived authenticity of a firm's emotional-branding strategy, (2) provide early signs that an emotional-branding story is beginning to lose its value as an authenticating narrative for

consumers' identity projects, and (3) offer insights into how an emotional-branding strategy can be reconfigured to fit better with changing cultural times and shifting consumer outlooks.

(Thompson *et al.* 2006, p. 51)

Box 10.7 Just another legal case or an early warning sign?

In 1999 San Francisco-based cartoonist Kieron Dwyer made comic books, t-shirts and stickers with his 'Consumer Whore' version of the Starbucks logo and sold them in the anti-Starbucks milieu. The year after, Starbucks sued him for copyright and trademark infringement. Dwyer claimed that his work was meant as a parody and as such should be protected by the US constitutional amendment of free speech. In 2000 the court decided that Dwyer was allowed to continue displaying his logo but only in extremely limited circumstances.

Sources www.illegal-art.org, www.wikipedia.org

The anti-brand No Logo movement and the pressure for corporate social responsibility (which is also an issue of non-activist consumers) are also relevant concerns of brand managers. The pressure for corporate social responsibility should not be ignored by any brand.

The citizen-artist brand manager

As explained in the section on theoretical building blocks, the seemingly contra-dictory clash between the brand icons and the anti-branding movement might indicate a shift towards a new branding paradigm. The citizen-artist brand is supposed to accommodate the new requirements of an increasingly critical consumer culture by supplying the relevant cultural material (already skilfully done by the iconic brands) *and* acting as a responsible citizen, shouldering its corporate social responsibilities. The management of this future brand scenario requires an even more versatile work agenda than the management of a brand icon; not only is the brand supposed to deliver potent cultural material but at the same time lead the way towards new dimensions in corporate citizenship.

Box 10.8 A citizen-artist brand?

When reading the following case example of PRODUCT (RED), take into consideration the whole scope of the cultural approach. Consider the nature of the brand icon, the urge for corporate social responsibility and, not least, the citizen-artist brand prospect.

In 2006 the (RED) initiative was founded by Bono, U2 and Bobby Shriver, CEO of Debt, AIDS, Trade in Africa (DATA) and first introduced to the world media at the World Economic Forum in Davos. (RED) is a new business model and could be an indicator of a new brand agenda.

The new fund-raising business model of the (RED) brand works like this. Iconic brands have the opportunity to license the (PRODUCT) RED mark and use it for specific products co-branded by (RED) and the original product brand. The corporations commit themselves to sending a fixed portion of the profits made on (RED) products directly to the Global Fund to fight AIDS in Africa (established in 2002 with the support of several world leaders, among them then UN Secretary General Kofi Annan). The sole purpose of the Global Fund is to raise funds and make grants to countries, organizations and communities that need financial help to allow them to respond to epidemics of AIDS, tuberculosis and malaria.

Iconic brands like American Express, Converse, Apple, Emporio Armani and Gap have licensed the right to create, market and sell specially designed (RED) products. Apple has designed a (RED) iPod. The Gap has, among other things, designed an entire collection of red t-shirts imprinted with words like INSPI(RED), EMPOWE(RED), WI(RED) and ADMI(RED). A bodysuit collection from BabyGap spells out words like DIAPE(RED) and ADO(RED). Gap has further committed to the cause by having more products made in Africa. If you use an American Express (RED) credit card, 1 per cent of your total spending is sent to the Global Fund. (RED) Motorola phones are available, as is a whole collection of clothing and fashion accessories by Emporio Armani. That is just to name a few of the initiatives.

These corporations commit themselves to refunding a percentage of the (RED) turnover to the Global Fund. A main point is that the consumer does not pay extra for his or her (RED) purchase – the company does. The licensing fee received by (RED) for use of the (PRODUCT) RED mark is used to manage and market the (RED) brand. By early 2008 (RED) purchases had generated more than $100 million for the Global Fund.

(RED) was created not only to raise money for, but also to create awareness of, the Global Fund and the severe issues it adresses. On 15 May (with Bono serving as guest editor) and 21 September (Giorgio Armani as guest editor) of 2006 the *Independent* went (RED). The newspaper promoted the Global Fund and 50 per cent of the day's revenue was donated to the cause. Internationally well known personalities like Tony Blair, Nelson Mandela, Bill Gates, Arnold Schwarzenegger, Condoleezza Rice and George Clooney contributed to the (RED) editions of the newspaper. An entire army of international celebrities have supported the (RED) cause by modelling the clothes and backing the projects in all kinds of ways. Check out the website below for new (RED) initiatives.

By combining the marketing power of the world's leading consumer brands with the accountability, scale and pace of Global Fund grant making, (PRODUCT) RED has created a new global brand and a new business model. Even though (RED) was created in order to raise awareness and money for the good of African women and children affected by AIDS, it is important to notice that (RED), in its own words, is not a charity. It is a commercial initiative designed to create awareness and a sustainable flow of money from the private sector into the Global Fund to fight the AIDS pandemic in Africa.

Source www.joinred.com

Box 10.9 Do's and don'ts in the cultural approach

Do	**Don't**
Acknowledge the powerful forces in consumer culture	Don't believe that the brand communication happens just between you and your customer
Use cultural feedback – also negative – to adjust your brand strategy	Don't ignore critical voices: things might spin out of control
Be open to inspiration from many different sources	Don't focus too much on spreadsheets from business school guys
Acknowledge that the brand changes over the course of time	Don't believe that the brand is made up of consistent associations
Regard your brand's reputation as a reputation for performing myths	Don't ignore political, social and ideological changes
Be a cultural activist	Don't just react to the successes of others
Be open about the profit motive of your business	Don't use stealth branding to dodge the profit motive or civic obligations

---

Summary

Marketers can benefit from cultural branding insight in different ways. The brand manager can engage fully in the cultural branding model in order to pursue the path to icon status (or learn from the best). Going down this road, the brand manager needs to adapt to an agenda of cultural activism and get ready for a rather

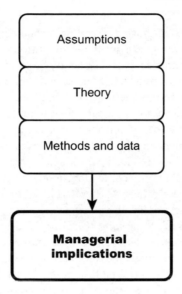

Figure 10.10 Managerial implications of the cultural approach

complicated work method. The brand manager needs to gain a deep insight into cultural issues in society and be able to use this insight to perform brand myths connecting to the most important cultural contradictions of the time.

Insights from this approach can also be used to become aware of the importance of monitoring if the brand is being subjected to criticism or even 'culture jamming'. This can be an early warning sign of a branding strategy losing its appeal or a pressure towards displaying more corporate social responsibility.

The implications of the citizen-artist brand prospect should also be taken into consideration by brand managers.

Comments from the 'founding fathers' (6)

Cultural branding

Douglas B. Holt, Saïd Business School, Oxford University

I developed the cultural branding model to explain how brand symbolism works. I'm also concerned with how brand symbolism influences other dimensions of the brand such as perceived quality, distinctive benefits, and trust (Holt 2002). Conventional theories of branding do a particularly poor job of theorizing brand symbolism (Holt 2005). So I've spent the last decade conducting research to address this gap.

Conventional brand theories have yoked brand symbolism to the dominant psychological models without considering its distinctive qualities. This is a major weakness because, outside of certain technology- and service-driven categories, where brands are built largely through reputation effects, branding's big stakes are decided increasingly by cultural symbolism.

Branding has been dominated by these psychological assumptions for nearly four decades. In this view, which I call the mindshare model, the brand is a set of valued associations in the individual consumer's mind. So branding is reduced to being actions that systematically reinforce these associations. The American ad man Rosser Reeves developed the foundational intuition for this idea in the 1950s with his idea that each brand required a Unique Selling Proposition that should be repeated over and over to install it in consumers' minds. Al Ries and Jack Trout made this idea hegemonic with the publication of a series of *Ad Age* articles that culminated in the 1980 publication of *Positioning the Battle for your Mind*. They introduced a powerful metaphor that won over the marketers worldwide: we live in a world that has far too many messages for people to process, so branding is a battle for mental real estate. The firm needs to identify a cognitive gap in the benefits and associations important to the product category and then seek to own this mental real estate through ultra-simple ultra-consistent brand communications. Beginning in the 1980s, consumer psychologists have published scores of academic articles, textbooks and management books that rely on this foundational intuition to advance a general theory of branding that paralleled what Reeves, Ries, and Trout had previously developed for practitioners. The goal of branding is to claim valued cognitive associations in a product category, and consistently communicate these associations in everything the brand does over time to sustain the brand's hold on this cognitive territory.

The mindshare model works fine for certain aspects of branding, but it is fundamentally flawed as a theory of brand symbolism. Mindshare branding – as well as its various New Age cousins such as emotional branding, brand personality, brand archetypes, relationship branding – is but one model for branding, as this book makes clear. The mindshare approach is a basic tool for the day-to-day brand management of established brands – the incremental and rote aspect of branding. When it comes to the most important, exciting and strategically crucial role of branding – using branding to build extraordinary new businesses and drive economic value – mindshare is a dead end.

To address this gap, I developed a cultural theory of branding. Cultural branding is conceived specifically to explain how branding works as an innovation engine, to drive significant new domains of customer value. To do so requires an entirely different theory of consumer motivations and desires: moving from the essentialist, static, individual-level constructs of mindshare theory to social and cultural constructs that are grounded in historical contexts. And the application of this new theory in practice demands different research techniques and different conceptions of strategy.

Cultural branding overview

To build the cultural branding model, I conducted detailed cultural histories (i.e. brand genealogies) of many iconic brands, including Budweiser, Marlboro, Volkswagen, Mountain Dew, Nike, ESPN, Jack Daniels, Coca-cola, Corona, Snapple, and Patagonia. Most of these brands are American, but I have expanded the research since then to Europe, Japan, Latin America, and also global brands.

Brand symbolism delivers customer value by providing culturally resonant stories and images that groups of consumers use to buttress their identities. The collective need for such stories arises in response to major shifts in society. Cultural theorists term stories that provide this functional role a myth. The most important and valued brand stories respond to – and often help to lead – major shifts in society and culture. My theory seeks to explain why particular branded stories and images are so valued at particular historical junctures.

Brands establish powerful durable symbolism (i.e. become iconic) when they perform powerful identity myths: simple fictions that address cultural anxieties from afar, from imaginary worlds rather than from worlds that the consumer lives in. Identity myths are useful fictions that stitch back together otherwise damaging tears in the cultural fabric of the nation. These tears are experienced by people in their everyday life as tensions or anxieties. People use myths to smooth over these collective tensions, helping them to create purpose in their lives, to cement their desired identity in place when it is under stress. Academic research has demonstrated that the extraordinary appeal of the most successful cultural products has been due to their mythic qualities—from Horatio Alger's rags-to-riches dime novels of the nineteenth century to John Wayne westerns, to Harlequin romance novels, to the action-adventure films of Willis, Schwarzenegger and Stallone. Iconic brands work the same way.

Brands become iconic when they address societal desires, not individual ones. Iconic brands perform myths (through any customer touchpoint) that symbolically resolve the identity desires and anxieties stemming from an important cultural tension. Iconic brands earn extraordinary value because they address the collective anxieties and desires of the nation (and sometimes beyond). We experience our identities – our self-understandings and aspirations – as intensely personal quests. But, when scholars examine consumer identities in the aggregate, they find that identity desires and anxieties are widely shared across a broad swathe of a nation's citizens. These similarities result because, even though they may come from different walks of life, people construct their identities in response to the same historical changes that impact the entire nation, and sometimes regions or the entire globe.

Over time, as the brand performs its myth, consumers come to perceive that the myth resides in the product. The brand becomes a symbol, a material embodiment of the myth. So as customers drink or drive or wear the product they experience a bit of the myth. This is a modern secular example of the *rituals* that anthropologists have documented in every human society. But, rather than religious myth, in modern societies the most powerful myths have to do with identities. Customers use iconic brands as symbolic salves. Through the products in which they are embedded, customers grab hold of the myth and use it in their lives to make their identity burdens a bit less burdensome. Great myths provide for their consumers little epiphanies— moments of recognition that put images and sounds and feelings on barely perceptible desires. Customers who make use of the brand's myth for their identities forge powerful emotional connections to the brand.

To understand some of the basic features of cultural branding, it is useful to contrast the cultural branding with the conventional mindshare model:

From building associations to performing myths

The mindshare model assumes that brand symbolism consists of abstract associations in the consumer's mind. Thus the purpose of advertising is to influence these associations. The communication content is treated as instrumental rhetoric. Consumers are assumed to discard this rhetorical material and only absorb (or not, depending on the success of the ad) associations to the brand.

The cultural branding model turns this view of brand communications on its head. For iconic brands like Coke and Nike and Budweiser the brand's communications are the centre of customer value. Customers buy the product primarily to experience the stories that the brand performs. The product is simply a conduit through which customers get to experience the stories that the brand tells. When consumers sip a Coke, or Corona, or Snapple, they are imbibing more than a beverage. Rather they are drinking in identity myths that have become imbued in those drinks. The brand is a *storied product:* a product that has distinctive brand markers (trade mark, design, etc.) through which customers experience identity myths. Because the mindshare model ignores the particular contents of the brand's communications, the model is unable to decipher how brand symbolism works.

From abstractions to cultural expressions

The mindshare model proposes that the brand consists of a set of abstractions. Descriptions of brands are full of abstract adjectives and nouns like security and performance and quality and ruggedness. In cultural branding, in contrast, the brand's value is located in the particulars of the brand's cultural expression: the particular cultural contents of the brand's myth and the particular expression of these contents in the communication. For Corona the brand exists on the Mexican beach and the evocative expression of the beach in its 'nothing's happening' style of advertising. For Coke in

'Teach the world to sing' the brand existed in the idea that in the hippie counterculture could be found the seeds of peace and racial harmony. For Snapple's early 1990s breakthrough '100% natural' campaign the brand was centred in loud-mouthed Wendy telling silly stories of Snapple drinkers, and in the barbed political soliloquies of Howard Stern and Rush Limbaugh. Abstracting these cultural expressions to 'relaxation' and 'friendship' and 'quirky', respectively, strips these brands of their most valuable assets.

The mindshare model abstracts away the messiness of society and history in search of the brand's purified essence. This distilled model denies the brand a role as an historical actor in society. In its insistence that brands forge a transcendental identity lodged in consumers' minds the mindshare model ignores that identity value is created and transformed in particular historical contexts. A theory of brand symbolism must detail the brand's stakes in the transformation of culture and society and the particular cultural expressions the brand uses to push for these transformations.

From transcendental consistency to historical fit

In the mindshare model the brand's associations transcend time and space. Therefore explanations of the evolution of brands boil down to whether or not the brand maintains consistency in the face of organizational and competitive pressures that push for zigging and zagging. Brand management is about stewardship: finding the brand's true 'identity' and maintaining this compass point come hell or high water.

Yet the brands I have studied succeed by moving away from their initial branding – their supposed DNA at the time – to address shifting currents in American society. In fact, all of the iconic brands that I've studied, with histories extending more than a decade, have had to make significant shifts in order to remain iconic. Brands that haven't adjusted properly – like Pepsi, Levi's, and Cadillac – have lost much of the brand equity. These reinterpretations of the brand are necessary because, for a myth to generate identity value, it must directly engage the most acute cultural tensions of the day. Coke celebrated America's triumphs against Nazi Germany in World War II but then suddenly shifted to dramatize ways to heal internal strife around war in the early 1970s and then racial divisions in the early 1980s. Corona, originally a brand that represented collegiate hedonism, later was retooled to provide a soothing antidote to the compression and anxieties of the networked free agent work that came to a head in the 1990s.

Iconic brands are built using a philosophy the opposite of that espoused by the mindshare model. The brand is an historical entity whose desirability comes from performing myths that address the most important social tensions that pulse through the nation. For iconic brands, success depends upon how well the brand's myth is modified to fit historical exigencies, not by its consistency in the face of historical change.

Much work remains to be done on cultural branding. To develop this area, the discipline of marketing must embrace theories and methods that it has for decades pushed to the margins, rather than continue to insist against all evidence that its favoured psychological assumptions are universally applicable to resolve all important branding questions.

Student questions

1   Describe the oppositional concerns of the cultural approach.
2   Explain the difference between an identity brand and a brand icon.
3   What is the consumer perspective in the cultural approach?
4   What makes the application of methods to the cultural approach stand out?
5   What does it tell you that the (RED) initiative was first presented at the World Economic Forum in Davos?
6   Describe the benefits (RED) obtain by collaborating with iconic brands.
7   Describe the benefits the iconic supporting partners (Apple, Converse, etc.) obtained by joining (RED).
8   How does (RED) tap into corporate social responsibility?
9   What would be your arguments if you were to describe (RED) as a citizen-artist brand?

References and further reading

Key readings are in **bold type**.

Alden, D. L., Steenkamp, J-B. E. M. and Batra, R. (1999) 'Brand positioning through advertising in Asia, North America, and Europe: the role of global consumer culture', *Journal of Marketing*, 63 (January): 75–87

Allen, C. T., Fournier, S. and Miller, F. (2006) 'Brands and their meaning makers', in C. P. Haugtvedt, P. M. Herr and F. R. Kardes (eds) *Handbook of Consumer Psychology*, Mahwah NJ: Lawrence Erlbaum Associates

Arnould, E. J. and Thompson, C. J. (2005) 'Consumer culture theory (CCT): twenty years of research', *Journal of Consumer Research*, 31 (March): 868–82

Askegaard, S. (2006) 'Brands as a global ideoscape', in J. E. Schroeder and M. Salzer-Morling (eds), *Brand Culture*, London: Routledge

Frank, T. (1997) *The Conquest of Cool: Business Culture, Counterculture, and the Rise of Hip Consumerism*, Chicago: University of Chicago Press

Garsten, C. and Hasselström, A. (2004) '*Homo mercans* and the fashioning of markets', in C. Garsten and M. L. de Montoya (eds), *Market Matters: Exploring Cultural Processes in the Global Marketplace*, New York: Palgrave Macmillan

Gay, P. du, Hall, S., Janes, L., Mackay, H. and Negus, K. (1997) *Doing Cultural Studies: the Story of the Sony Walkman*, London: Sage Publications

Hackley, C. (2003) *Doing Research Projects in Marketing, Management and Consumer Research*, London: Routledge

Holt, D. B. (2002) 'Why do brands cause trouble? A dialectical theory of consumer culture and branding', *Journal of Consumer Research*, 29 (June): 70–90

Holt, D. B. (2002) 'Brands and Branding', Harvard Business School Note 503–045, Cambridge MA: Harvard Business School Publishing (hbsp.com)

Holt, D. B. (2003a) 'What becomes an icon most?' *Harvard Business Review*, March: 43–9

Holt, D. B. (2003b) 'How to build an iconic brand', *Market Leader*, 21 (summer): 35–42

Holt, D. B. (2004) *How Brands become Icons: The Principles of Cultural Branding*, Boston MA: Harvard Business School Press

Holt, D. B. (2005) 'How societies desire brands: using cultural theory to explain brand symbolism', in S. Ratneshwar and D. G. Mick (eds) *Inside Consumption: Consumer Motives, Goals, and Desires*, London: Routledge

Holt, D. B. (2006) 'Jack Daniels's America: iconic brands as ideological parasites and proselytizers', *Journal of Consumer Culture*, 6 (3): 355–77

Holt, D. B., Quelch, J. and Taylor, E. (2004) 'How global brands compete', *Harvard Business Review*, 82 (September): 68–75

Kates, S. M. (2004) 'The dynamics of brand legitimacy: an interpretive study in the gay men's community', *Journal of Consumer Research*, 31 (September): 455–64

Klein, N. (2000) *No Logo*, London: Flamingo

Kozinets, R. V. (2002) 'Can consumers escape the market? Emancipatory illuminations from Burning Man', *Journal of Consumer Research*, 29 (June): 20–38

Lasn, K. (1999) *Culture Jam: The Uncooling of America*, New York: Eagle Brook

McCracken, G. (1988) *Culture and Consumption: New Approaches to the Symbolic Character of Consumer Goods and Activities*, Bloomington and Indianapolis IN: Indiana University Press

McCracken, G. (2005) *Culture and Consumption II. Markets, Meaning, and Brand Management*, Bloomington and Indianapolis IN: Indiana University Press

Mick, D. G. (1986) 'Consumer research and semiotics: exploring the morphology of signs, symbols, and significance', *Journal of Consumer Research*, 13 (September): 196–213

Schroeder, J. E. (2005) 'The artist and the brand', *European Journal of Marketing*, 39 (11–12): 1291–1305

Thompson, C. J. and Arsel, Z. (2004) 'The Starbucks brandscape and consumers' (anticorporate) experiences of glocalization', *Journal of Consumer Research*, 31 (December): 631–42

Thompson, C. J., Rindfleisch, A. and Arsel, Z. (2006) 'Emotional branding and the strategic value of the doppelganger brand image', *Journal of Marketing*, 70 (January): 50–64

Willmott, M. (2001) *Citizen Brands: Putting Society at the Heart of your Business*, Chichester: Wiley

Websites

www.adbusters.org
www.bp.com
www.corporatewatch.org.uk
www.corpwatch.org
www.debeerscompany.com
www.joinred.com
www.nologo.org
www.starbucks.com

Part III
Taxonomy

11   Taxonomy of brand management 1985–2006

Learning objectives

The purpose of this chapter is to:

- Get introduced to the Kuhn-based taxonomy of brand management 1985 – 2006
- Get an overview of the seven brand approaches
- Compare the proposed categorization of this book with other categorizations of brand management

---

After having guided you through the seven brand approaches, in this chapter we provide an overview of the different perspectives on key subjects in brand management reflected in the seven approaches to brand management. The taxonomy (figure 11.1) sums up the key learning points from the seven approach chapters. The background of this book and taxonomy is a systematic analysis of 300+ brand management research articles spanning the period of 1985–2006. The analysis has been executed in accordance with the logic of the methodology *The Dynamic Paradigm Funnel* (Bjerre, Heding and Knudtzen 2008). *The Dynamic Paradigm Funnel* is based on theory about how science evolves: the philosophy of science developed by Thomas Kuhn. The result of this extensive analysis – a new taxonomy of brand management consisting of seven different approaches – is according to that analysis what constitutes the academic discipline of brand management.

Other writers have however also proposed categorizations of different approaches to brand management and this chapter will finish off with a look at how some of these alternative categorizations of brand management can be compared with the categorization and taxonomy proposed in this book.

Taxonomy of brand management 1985–2006

In figure 11.1, the most significant traits of each approach are presented side by side. By going through the characteristics of each approach, a clear overview of the seven brand approaches is gained. It is important to notice that each approach

	The economic approach	The identity approach	The consumer-based approach
Time of origin	Before 1985	Mid-1990s	1993
Key reading	McCarthy, E. J. (1964), *Basic Marketing, a Managerial Approach,* Homeward: Richard D. Irwin, Inc. Borden, N. (1964), The Concept of the Marketing Mix, in G. Schwartz (ed.) *Science in Marketing*	Hatch, M.J. and Schultz, M. (1997) 'Relations between organizational culture, identity and Image', *European Journal of Marketing*	Keller, K. L. (1993), 'Conceptualizing, Measuring, and Managing Customer-Based Brand Equity', *Journal of Marketing*
Keywords	The economic man, transaction theory, marketing mix, the Four Ps	Corporate branding, identity, organizational culture, vision, image	Customer-based brand equity, brand image, brand associations
Brand perspective	Functional	Corporate	Cognitive construal
Consumer perspective	Economic man	Stakeholder	Computer
Scientific tradition	Positivism/empiricism	Socio-economic constructivism/interpretivism	Cognitive psychology
Methods	Scanner panel data, laboratory settings, quantitative data	Organizational culture studies and organizational values Heuristic methods, storytelling.	Cognitively based association maps, interviews, projective techniques
Managerial keyword	Control	Monologue	Programming
Supporting themes	'Traditional' marketing, the Four Ps	Organizational identity, corporate identity, image, reputation	Cognitive psychology, the information-processing consumer
Brand value creation	Marketer ↓ Consumer	Marketer ↓ Consumer	Marketer ↑ Consumer

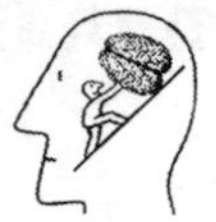

Figure 11.1 Taxonomy of brand management 1985–2006

The personality approach	The relational approach	The community approach	The cultural approach
1997	1998	2001	Around 2000
Aaker, J. L. (1997), 'Dimensions of brand personality', *Journal of Marketing Research* Plummer, J. (1985) 'How personality makes a difference', *Journal of Advertising Research*	Fournier, S. M. (1998), 'Consumers and their brands: developing relationship theory in consumer research', *Journal of Consumer Research*	Muñiz Jr, A. M. and O'Guinn, T. C. (2001), 'Brand Community', *Journal of Consumer Research*	Holt, D. B. (2002), 'Why do brands cause trouble? A dialectical theory of consumer culture and branding', *Journal of Consumer Research*
Brand personality, self, archetypes	Dyadic brand–consumer relationship, brand relationship quality	Brand communities, brandfests, the brand triad, the internet	Globalization, popular culture, brand icons, No Logo
Human	Human	Social	Cultural
Psychological	Existential being	Tribe member	*Homo mercans*
Human personality psychology	Existentialism, phenomenology	Anthropology, microperspective	Cultural studies
A mix of quantitative and qualitative methods, scaling techniques	Depth interviews, life story method	Ethnography, netnography	Macro-level analysis on microlevel data
Symbolic exchange	Friendship	Discretion	Bird perspective
Personality, consumer self, brand–self congruence	Animism, relationship theory	Community theory, subcultures of consumption	Cultural consumption, No Logo, the citizen-brand prospect

Figure 11.1 continued

is presented as an 'ideal type'. We emphasize the ideal type of each approach rather than eventual nuances and similarities, because it enables us to understand the differences between the mindsets underlying each approach. For example, the perception of the brand–consumer exchange in the identity approach has evolved over time from a perception of linear communication towards an assumed co-creation of brand value. In practice most of the approaches have evolved and often embraced new developments and accommodating critique. The differences between the approaches in practice are hence more blurred than they are as presented in the framework of this book. The most important developments and discussions are included in each approach chapter, but we have chopped a toe and squeezed a heel in order to provide our readers with as much clarity as possible. In the following, we will go through the main categorizations of the model.

The time of origin (or academic conceptualization) of each brand approach is more or less precise. Some of the approaches are born from a specific, ground-breaking article introducing a whole new brand perspective. These approaches can be dated to a specific publication. Others emerge incrementally and from the hands of several researchers, they can only be dated approximately. The seven approaches are presented in a chronological order reflecting when the approaches were conceptualized in the context of brand management. In the cases of the easy-to-date approaches, the ground-breaking articles are identified as *key readings*. In the other approaches, key readings are research articles central to and representative of the approach; written by the most important and influential researchers constituting the approach.

Key words are the main concerns of the approach. The *brand perspective* describes the overall 'take' on the brand in the given approach. We have focused not only on clarifying the different brand perspectives, but also on the different *consumer perspectives* associated with the different brand perspectives.

Each brand approach can be traced to a specific *scientific tradition*. The clarification of the respective traditions implies differences in consumer perceptions and methods and also hints towards differences in philosophical standpoints. These aspects of the proposed taxonomy might seem difficult and over the top, but in our experience it actually facilitates the understanding of the discipline to add the assumed, 'taken for granted' stuff, as it guides the overall concerns of each approach: what is investigated; which methods are presumed valid; view of man (as consumer) and so on. When it comes to *methods*, the model makes it very clear that the methods formally applied to brand management research have developed from a focus on quantitative methods to the use of a wide variety of methods, and that they are primarily qualitative in the later approaches.

At the heart of brand management is the ability to create brand value. The arrows reflect the implied perception of the *brand value creation* in the brand–consumer exchange. The managerial implications of each approach are complex, but we have tried to sum them up in seven different words. The *managerial key words* evolve from reflecting control with the process of brand value creation to key words reflecting a perception of the brand manager having to acknowledge the influence of other forces on the brand value creation. In the theoretical building blocks of each approach, we have presented core themes and supporting themes. The *supporting themes* form the backdrop of the main theory of the approach, and reflecting upon them should facilitate the understanding of each approach.

The model also contributes with an overview of how it is assumed that brand management can endow brands with value. The two first approaches (economic and identity) assumed that brand value is created in the domain of the marketer. This brand value creation shifted in the third approach (consumer-based approach), where it is a thorough understanding of the consumer that is presumed to be at the heart of superior brand value creation. In the personality approach and the relational approach, the creation of brand value is presumed to be dialogue-based and takes place in dyadic exchange between the consumer and the marketer. The community approach adds the triadic brand–consumer relationship to the assumptions of what drives brand value creation: making the arrow point in three different directions, because real brand value is assumed to be created not so much in the interaction between marketer and consumer, as was the case in the previous approaches, but in the interaction between consumers. In the last approach, the addition of macro-level culture makes the assumed brand value creation very complicated, because the marketer is assumed to be dependent on macro and consumer culture more than on the exchange with one or more consumers.

Other categorizations of brand management

Other writers have also proposed different frameworks with the attempt to pin down the elusive nature of the brand by systemizing the field into different categories. In this section, we will relate the categorization and taxonomy of this book to other categorization frameworks of brand management and reflect upon the relevance of the framework categorization of this book in comparison with the other categorizations. The analysis underlying our proposed taxonomy stems from a Kuhnian mindset and reflects Kuhn's philosophy of science and its theories on how formalized knowledge in scientific disciplines evolves. The results of the analysis and the taxonomy are hence tightly connected with the data of the approach, namely research articles. In the review of each approach, other relevant literature has been added to enable a full and accurate picture of each approach, but it is important to point out that the *identification* of the seven brand approaches is solely based on research articles. The other frameworks stem from other analyses with other backgrounds and use other denominators for categorizing brand management. It is not our intent to add confusion by these comparisons; our aim is rather to enhance clarity by pointing out the similarities between ours and other frameworks – even though they stem from different mindsets and analyses there are significant similarities in the end result. We will review the study 'Divided by a common language: diversity and deception in the world of global marketing' by Mary Goodyear (1996) that focuses on different brand roles in different markets; an identification of four brand management paradigms based on using two main discriminators on brand management literature *Brand Management Paradigms* by Louro and Cunha (2001). The final categorization of brand approaches is *How Brands Become Icons* (2004) which is a comparison of four practical branding models.

The role of brands

In 'Divided by a common language: diversity and deception in the world of global marketing' Mary Goodyear (1996) investigates the marketing and branding confusion in terms of linguistics and asks the question: how can branding be defined if one does not consider the many different roles of brands in different economies, time eras and phases of market maturation? Considering these macro-level factors, Goodyear comes up with the definitions of the roles of brands shown in table 11.1. The model reflects the different roles played by brands as markets evolve. In that sense, the Goodyear framework reflects the life cycle of a brand – how branding techniques become more sophisticated as consumers become more and more accustomed to marketing techniques.

This categorization pivots around the evolution of branding techniques (and hence, different brand roles) in the context of maturing market places. In a non-industrialized economy, the majority of goods are unbranded and the mere fact that goods are packaged may be a vehicle of consumer preferences. In low-consumerized and undersupplied countries, the primary role of the brand is to serve as a reference. The manufacturer need not apply sophisticated marketing tools to selling his goods. This brand role is more or less comparable to the economic approach.

In a more mature market, the marketer is faced with more competition and, hence, has to apply other branding techniques in order to differentiate the products. This situation requires the 'three-dimensional brands' where product quality is supported by emotive advertising, where the brand's most important role is to act as a personality. As the branding techniques relate to emotions and connotations, this role is comparable to the individualistic brand approaches of our taxonomy (the consumer-based approach, the personality approach and the relational approach).

In an even more saturated market place, the consumer becomes the main driver in the branding process; the consumer 'owns' the brand and plays an active part in endowing it with commonly held values, catapulting a few brands to iconic status (as found in the cultural approach of our taxonomy).

In Goodyear's categorization, she differs between classic branding and post-modern branding. The postmodern consumer lives in a highly literate consumer culture and is – through sophisticated brand literacy – able to see through the classic roles of brands. The highly empowered postmodern consumer will demand responsibility and identity from the corporation behind the brands; hence the two latter roles of brands apply. The brand as organization is comparable to the identity approach while the brand as policy is comparable to the CSR-related aspects of the cultural approach

Table 11.1 The roles of brands

Marketing era	Role of brands	
Classic branding	Unbranded	Commodities, packaged goods Major proportion of goods in nonindustrialized context Minor role Europe/United States Supplier has power
	Brand as reference	Brand name often name of maker Name used for identification Any advertising support focuses on rational attributes Name over time becomes guarantee of quality/consistency
	Brand as personality	Brand name may be 'stand-alone' Marketing support focuses on emotional appeal Product benefits Advertising puts brand into context
	Brand as icon	Consumer now 'owns' brand Brand taps into higher-order values of society Advertising assumes close relationship Use of symbolic brand language Often established internationally
Postmodern branding	Brand as company	Brands have complex identities Consumer assesses them all Need to focus on corporate benefits to diverse 'customers' Integrated communication strategy essential through-the-line
	Brand as policy	Company and brands aligned to social and political issues Consumers 'vote' on issues through companies Consumers now 'own' brands, companies and politics

Source Goodyear (1996), figs 2 (classic branding) and 5 (postmodern branding).

Four brand management paradigms

In *Brand Management Paradigms* (Louro and Cunha 2001), four ruling branding paradigms are identified by the use of two discriminators: the role of the consumer in the branding process (customer centrality) and whether the brand should hold a tactical or strategic position in the company (brand centrality). These two dimensions provide four 'ideal types' of approaches to brand management.

The product paradigm reflects an approach to branding where the brand is a low strategic priority and the customer is seen as a passive player in the branding process.

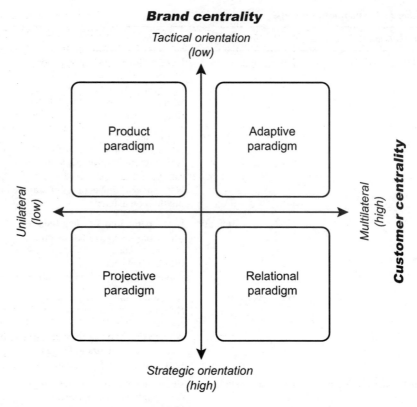

Figure 11.2 Two dimensions and four brand management paradigms; from Louro and Cunha, 'Brand management paradigms', *Journal of Marketing Management*, 17 (2001), p. 855, reproduced by permission of Westburn Publishers Ltd

If the brand strategy is perceived as central for the overall strategy of the organization, but with the same conception of the customer, Louro and Cunha label it as a projective paradigm. The third paradigm is characterized by the brand having a low strategic priority and a tactical focus supplemented by a conception of the customer as an active and primary co-creator of value, called the adaptive paradigm. The fourth and last brand paradigm in the Louro and Cunha categorization of branding is the relational paradigm. Here the brand is perceived to be key in relation to the overall strategy and consumers are assumed to be active co-creators of the brand.

The product paradigm reflects a product-centred approach to brand management. The product and its functional benefits are central to the profitability of the organization in the product paradigm. The brand holds two primary functions: the statement of legal ownership, and as a communicative tool upholding visual identification of differentiation in the marketing of the products of the company. In this brand management paradigm, brand equity is seen as something created by having the optimal marketing mix: the right price, right product, price, placement and promotion. The product paradigm is comparable to the economic approach of this book.

The projective paradigm of the Louro and Cunha categorization resembles the identity approach in our framework. It focuses on the usefulness of the brand on a strategic level as opposed to the tactical approach to branding reflected in the product paradigm. The brand is seen as a strategic entity that should be used as a template for the overall business model. Thus, the brand reflects purpose, ethics as well as core competences in an organization and vice versa. The theoretical background of the projective paradigm is the resource-based perspective. The consequence of this is that value and brand meaning are found internally. In this paradigm, competitiveness of the business is based on the organization's ability to find its own internal strengths and cultivate them with the purpose of creating a unique business culture and unique competences difficult to imitate. This idea of creating unique concepts based on sender identity is the foundation of the projective paradigm in brand management.

Where the projective paradigm stresses the internal business resources and competences as the source of brand meaning, the adaptive paradigm stresses the consumer as the source of brand meaning: 'The power of the brand resides in the minds of the consumer' (Keller 2003, p. 59). The adaptive brand management paradigm thereby resembles the consumer-based approach in the taxonomy of this book.

The relational brand management paradigm in the Louro and Cunha framework is the opposite of both the lack of review of the actions of the customers in the projective paradigm and the 'excessive' focus on the active customer in the adaptive paradigm. The relational paradigm conceptualizes brand management as a dynamic, dyadic process, in which an interaction between the creation of brand value (internally) and brand meaning (externally) on a strategic level results in a strong and relevant brand equity through an experienced meaningful relation between consumer and brand. In this paradigm, the marketer can benefit from constructing the brand as a personality because it furthers the consumer–brand relationship. This is done by implementing the acknowledgement of the consumer's active contribution to the creation of brand meaning and at the same time making brand management and brand identity the kernel of the formulation of strategy and the external business communication. In that way, both customer and brand centrality are high-ranking priorities in this paradigm. It goes without saying that this brand management paradigm covers the personality and the relational approach.

The categorization by Louro and Cunha is created through the use of other discriminators and using an entirely different way of sorting existing brand models, but the proposed brand management paradigms are indeed comparable to the taxonomy of this book. As described above, the first five approaches are covered by the four brand management paradigms, and the latter two emerged around and after the publication of *Brand Management Paradigms* in 2001.

Four branding models

In *How Brands Become Icons* (2004), Holt proposes four different branding models; cultural branding, mind-share branding, emotional branding and viral branding. Holt does not embed the four branding models in a chronological

Table 11.2 Four brand management paradigms

		The product paradigm	The projective paradigm	The adaptive paradigm	The relational paradigm
Brand–consumer exchange metaphor		Silence	Monologue	Listening	Conversation
Marketing focus		Product orientation	Brand logic	Customer orientation	Relationship
Brand Management	BRAND MANAGEMENT FOCUS	Marketing mix	Brand identity	Brand image	Relationship
	BRAND DEFINITION	Logo, legal, instrument	Identity system, company	Image, shorthand device, risk reducer, adding value, value system	Relationship, personality, evolving entity
	BRAND ROLES	Product-centred roles supporting communication, advertising and legal protection	Firm-centred roles associated with the unilateral creation and sustenance of competitive advantage through the differentiation and/or efficiency (cost leadership)	Consumer-centred roles facilitating decision-making, reducing risks inherent to product acquisition and providing emotional value	Symbolic partner coconfiguring the relational domain for firm–customer interaction
	DIMENSIONS OF BRAND MANAGEMENT	Marketing programme, brand elements as residual decisions	Organizational strategy, brand identity charter, brand elements, marketing programme	Brand image, brand elements, marketing programme	Organizational strategy, brand identity charter, brand image, brand history, brand elements, marketing programme
	PERFORMANCE METRICS	Product-based (financial perspective)	Brand-based (internal perspective)	Consumer-based (customer perspective)	Process-based (balanced scorecard)
	BRAND MANAGEMENT STRUCTURE	Functional, product/brand management, product/market	Functional, product/brand management, product/market	Functional, product/brand management, product/market	Customer management, entrepreneurial brand management
	STRATEGIC ORIENTATION	Internal	Internal	External	Internal/external
Strategy formation	STRATEGIC FOCUS	Product and positions	Resources and capabilities	Contexts and consumers	Integrations and interactions

Source Adapted from Louro and Cunha (2001), p. 857

Table 11.3 A comparison of axioms across four branding models

	Cultural branding	Mind-share branding	Emotional branding	Viral Branding
Key words	Cultural icons	DNA, brand essence, genetic code, USP benefits, onion model	Brand personality, experiential branding, brand religion, experience economy	Stealth marketing, coolhunt, meme, grass-roots, infections, seeding, contagion, buzz
Brand definition	Performer of, and container for, an identity myth	A set of abstract associations	A relationship partner	A communication unit
Branding definition	Performing myths	Owning associations	Interacting with and building relationships with customers	Spreading viruses via lead customers
Required for a successful brand	Performing a myth that addresses an acute contradiction in society	Consistent expression of associations	Deep interpersonal connection	Broad circulation of the virus
Most appropriate applications	Identity categories	Functional categories, low-involvement categories, complicated products	Services, retailers, specialty goods	New fashion, new technology
Company's role	Author	Steward: consistent expression of DNA in all activities over time	Good friend	Hidden puppet master: motivate the right consumers to advocate for the brand
Source of customer value	Buttressing identity	Simplifying decisions	Relationship with the brand	Being cool, fashionable
Consumers' role	• Personalizing the brand's myth to fit individual biography • Ritual action to experience the myth when using product	• Ensuring that benefits become salient through repetition • Perceiving benefits when buying and using product	• Interaction with the brand • Building a personal relationship	• 'Discovering' brand as their own, DIY • Word of mouth

Source Holt 2004, p. 14, reprinted with permission by Harvard Business School Press, Boston MA.

context, but focuses on presenting and comparing the most widely used (in practice) branding models. Holt labels the mind-share branding model the dominant branding model since the 1970s. In the 1990s emotional branding became a managerial priority as well, and with the rise of the internet viral branding techniques also became applied to branding practices. The cultural branding model is based on Holt's research into how brands become icons (please refer to chapter 10).

It is obvious that the cultural branding model is the equivalent of the cultural approach of our taxonomy; the mind-share branding model is comparable to the consumer-based approach; the emotional branding model sums up the personality and the relational approach; while the viral branding model resembles the community approach.

Overview

A new taxonomy of brand management is proposed in this book. It is based on an exhaustive analysis of the most influential research in brand management covering the last twenty-one years; it hence offers a research-based categorization of brand management. A comparison with other categorizations of brand management indicates that, despite different starting points, the frameworks and especially the results of the categorizations are comparable in many ways.

Table 11.4 Comparison of brand management categorizations

Categorization	This taxonomy	Goodyear (1996)	Louro and Cunha (2001)	Holt (2004)
Discriminators	A Kuhnian analysis of research papers	Macro-level analysis of market evolution	Customer centrality and strategic priority (in literature)	Widely used branding models (in literature and practice)
Comparable brand categories	The economic approach	Brands as reference	The product paradigm	
Comparable brand categories	The identity approach	Brand as company	The projective paradigm	
Comparable brand categories	The consumer-based approach	Brand as personality	The adaptive paradigm	Mind-share branding
Comparable brand categories	The personality approach	Brand as personality	The relational paradigm	Emotional branding
Comparable brand categories	The relational approach	Brand as personality	The relational paradigm	Emotional branding
Comparable brand categories	The community approach			Viral branding
Comparable brand categories	The cultural approach	Brand as icon + brand as policy		Cultural branding

It is interesting to compare our analysis with the Goodyear categorization, because the starting point of the two frameworks is so different. Goodyear's analysis provides insight into how brands play different roles as a market evolves and its consumers become more sophisticated, which is quite different from the Kuhnian approach used in this book. The proposed brand roles are, however, highly comparable to the evolution of brand management as a scientific discipline. Hence, the macro-level analysis of evolving market places is comparable to the analysis of how the academic discipline has evolved (even though the proposed evolution of brand roles does not fit the chronology of the taxonomy).

In Louro and Cunha's framework, the most influential brand management literature is categorized by two discriminators (brand centrality and customer centrality). The four brand management paradigms identified in that framework more or less cover five approaches of our taxonomy.

Holt compares axioms of the four most popular branding models. The side-by-side presentation of these models is very much comparable to the five latest approaches of the taxonomy in this book.

Concluding remarks

The proposed taxonomy of the seven approaches hence complements existing frameworks or categorizations of brand management even though it stems from a different background. The taxonomy provides much detail to enhance understanding of brand management, both when it comes to width and when it comes to depth. The fact that the taxonomy proposes seven approaches to brand management provides a very detailed insight into the subject. Furthermore, the

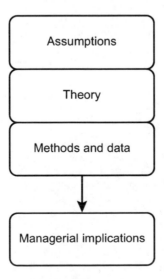

Figure 11.3 The logic of the approach chapters

chosen background of research articles and Kuhnian philosophy of science has provided the taxonomy with a detailed and logical structure based on the interconnectedness between assumptions, theories, methods and data and managerial implications. This structure provides the reader with a thorough and deep understanding of brand management as an academic discipline, and it is our hope that it is a step in the direction of understanding the elusive nature of the brand better.

References and further reading

Bjerre, M., Heding, T. and Knudtzen, C. (2008), 'Using the dynamic paradigm funnel to analyse brand management', in K. Tollin and A. Caru (eds) *Strategic Market Creation: A New Perspective on Marketing and Innovation Management,* Chichester: Wiley

Goodyear, M. (1996), 'Divided by a common language: diversity and deception in the world of global marketing', *Journal of the Market Research Society,* 38 (2): 105–23

Holt, D. B. (2004), *How Brands Become Icons: the Principles of Cultural Branding,* Boston MA: Harvard Business School Press

Louro, M. J. and Cunha, P. V. (2001), 'Brand management paradigms', *Journal of Marketing Management,* 17: 849–75

Notes

1 These diverse academic backgrounds of the scholars investigating brand identity often lead to opposing views and endless discussions of how to combine elements and what to call these elements. For the sake of clarity, this book defines the internal elements of brand identity: *corporate* **identity** as the visual and strategic aspects of brand identity and *organizational* **identity** as the behavioural and structural aspects of brand identity.
2 In the literature behind the consumer-based approach there is quite a lot of theory about brand extension. If you want to know more about the thoughts on brand extensions in the consumer-based approach, good places to turn are Keller (1993) and Aaker and Keller (1990).
3 Be aware that the exchange between the consumer and the social and cultural context is not a one-way exchange but dyadic. The more dyadic perspective on this process is elaborated in chapters 9 and 10.
4 The theory was first published as a Ph.D. dissertation in 1994.
5 Examples of how life themes, life projects, and current concerns are pivotal points in the brand relationship theory are to be found in figure 8.4.
6 Not to be confused with brands managed according to the cultural approach, which is applying cultural principles to the management of brands from all industries.
7 Holt's term, not to be confused with the identity approach of this book.

Name Index

Subject Index

Lightning Source UK Ltd.
Milton Keynes UK
UKOW03f1604220913

217637UK00002B/39/P